What Works For T... W9-AZM-475

Praise for the book ...

'For too long development practice has focused on the moderate poor and left out those who suffer from extreme and chronic deprivation. Now at last, by gathering and presenting current ideas and experience on assisting the poorest and helping them to help themselves, this book does an outstanding service. If all development professionals were to go into retreat for three days and read, reflect and debate this book, and then apply it in their work, it could touch and transform the lives and livelihoods of many tens or even hundreds of millions of those who are most deprived and excluded.

What works for the poorest is one of the most important development books of the decade – a treasury of ideas and experience.'

Professor Robert Chambers,
Institute of Development Studies at the University of Sussex, UK

'The "dollar-poor" proportion of people in the developing world halved (to 25 per cent) in 1981–2005. Of these 1.4 billion, about 400 million remain extremely and chronically poor. This book, based on field experience in Bangladesh and elsewhere, gives highly practical guidance on what we know about the ultra-poor, how to identify them, and what best advances them. There are surprising successes: integrated programmes, long written off as too hard to administer and co-ordinate, did well in several countries; "just give them the money" worked well in Vietnam; and for countries unable to afford or manage such approaches, donor funding of targeted programmes can slash ultra-poverty without harmful side-effects. The authors have listened to the poorest, recognized their diversity, and provided strong evidence that they can, and do, fend for themselves in support of programmes of disimpoverishment.

Professor Michael Lipton,
Poverty Research Unit, University of Sussex, UK

'Bangladesh's poorest citizens are the outcome of permutations of powerful forces. The team that has written this book knows more than others about how these forces may be resisted and how that resistance may be organized, resourced and supported. Everyone committed to the MDGs worldwide should know this book.'

Professor Barbara Harriss-White,
Oxford University

'Einstein once noted ruefully that efforts to combine practice and theory too often left us with a world in which "nothing is working, and no-one knows why". Happily, contemporary efforts to integrate scholarship and action in the quest to reduce global poverty are yielding a fruitful array of innovative responses whose efficacy is both demonstrated and understood. This book showcases the best of these initiatives.'

Michael Woolcock,
World Bank

What Works For The Poorest?

Poverty reduction programmes for the world's extreme poor

Edited by
David Lawson, David Hulme, Imran Matin and Karen Moore

PRACTICAL ACTION
Publishing

Practical Action Publishing Ltd
Schumacher Centre for Technology and Development
Bourton on Dunsmore, Rugby,
Warwickshire, CV23 9QZ, UK
www.practicalactionpublishing.org

© Practical Action Publishing, 2010

ISBN 978 1 85339 690 8

Since 1974, Practical Action Publishing (formerly Intermediate Technology
Publications and ITDG Publishing) has published and disseminated books and
information in support of international development work throughout the world.
Practical Action Publishing Ltd (Company Reg. No. 1159018) is the wholly owned
publishing company of Practical Action. Practical Action Publishing trades only
in support of its parent charity objectives and any profits are covenanted back to
Practical Action (Charity Reg. No. 247257, Group VAT Registration No. 880 9924 76).

Cover photo: A woman collects zinc shards from broken stones at a zinc
mine in Morocco. © Giacomo Pirozzi/Panos Pictures

Cover design by Practical Action Publishing
Indexed by Andrea Palmer
Typeset by S.J.I. Services, New Delhi
Printed by Replika Press, India

Contents

PART III: POLICIES AND PROGRAMMES FOR THE POOREST: CASE STUDIES

PART IV: MAKING IT WORK: FINDING THE MONEY AND SPREADING THE KNOWLEDGE

Figures

Tables

Boxes

Preface

This book has arisen out of collaboration between the Chronic Poverty Research Centre (CPRC), the Research and Evaluation Department of BRAC in Bangladesh (BRAC-RED), and the Brooks World Poverty Institute (BWPI) at the Institute for Development Policy and Management (IDPM), University of Manchester.

In Bangladesh, colleagues from these, and other, institutions found themselves researching, designing and monitoring programmes for the 'extreme poor', 'ultra poor' and 'poorest'. Often these were the people who could not be reached by Bangladesh's many excellent microfinance institutions. The researchers and programme managers tried to find out what practical actions could be taken to support and assist the poorest people.

Out of this common interest grew the notion of mounting an international conference for the exchange of ideas and practical approaches to improving the well-being of the extreme poor. That conference was mounted at the BRAC Centre in Dhaka 2006. More than 200 delegates from over 20 countries participated in the conference. This volume is drawn from the papers at that conference and seeks to provide a coverage that attempts a 'balance' of themes, approaches, issues and geography.

Many excellent papers were presented at the conference that we have not been able to include in this book. Most of the original papers and presentations are available on the BRAC-RED website (www.brac.net/research). Our book cannot claim to be comprehensive, but it does seek to raise awareness of the hundreds of millions of people trapped in extreme poverty and to strengthen understanding of the forms of practical action that can support their own efforts to improve their lives.

A large number of people and organizations have made the conference and book possible: without their support the conference could not have been convened nor the book written. Particular thanks to the staff of BRAC for organizing a superb conference during a general strike – a remarkable achievement. Our thanks to Fazle Hasan Abed, Founder of BRAC, and Rabeya Yasmin, Head of BRAC's Challenging the Frontiers of Poverty Reduction Programme (CFPR), for their support and contributions. We are especially grateful to Nahleen Zahra, Nasheeba Selim, Mehnaz Rabbani, Abdul Mannan Miah and Syed Suaib Ahmed, and the many other BRAC colleagues who made the conference such a relaxed but productive event. Our special thanks also to Denise Redston, Sarah Bridges, Marie Ahti and Solava Ibrahim for administrative and editorial support. Many others also provided support: to all of them our sincere thanks.

We also acknowledge the financial assistance of BWPI, CPRC, DFID, CIDA and the Aga Khan Foundation.

Last but not least, our gratitude to the many poor and very poor people who, over the years, have helped the authors and editors of this collection to further understand the nature of extreme poverty and the indomitable spirit of the world's poorest to improve their lives and achieve social justice.

David Lawson, Manchester; David Hulme, Manchester;
Imran Matin, Dhaka; and Karen Moore, Paris.

Foreword

What determines poverty reduction? If we knew the answer to that, the poor would be millionaires. Poverty, however we define it, and much rides on how we define it, has gone down in some parts of the world and gone up in others over the past half-century. How did this happen, the ups and the downs? In the development discourse, the Holy Grail seems to be finding a watertight causal connection to policy instruments that can then be wielded by benevolent philosopher kings to better the lot of the poor. But there are at least two problems. First, finding that causal connection to specific policy instruments is problematic. Second, benevolent philosopher kings, who can make things happen for the poor, are not to be found outside of Kallipolis. The kings we actually have often turn out to be neither philosophers nor benevolent.

Let us start with the first problem. The familiar discussion about economic growth and poverty does not of course reveal a tight causal connection between policy instruments and poverty reduction; it is clear that there is a correlation between the two variables but these are influenced by a multitude of factors, policy instruments among them. But it must give pause that there is a negative correlation between them, and that nobody has found a case where actual negative growth has accompanied poverty reduction. Equally, it must give pause that the correlation between economic growth and poverty reduction is not perfect, indeed far from so when poverty is defined to include deprivation in dimensions other than income. Further, which policy instruments give rise to economic growth is itself debated, and there is the further complication of how these instruments themselves affect poverty directly.

Thus while it is not clear why anybody would be against growth per se, even somebody or especially somebody whose primary objective is poverty reduction, it is perfectly legitimate to question whether this or that policy instrument will or will not lead to poverty reduction, whether directly or indirectly through the growth channel. Put another way, the debate on whether growth leads to poverty reduction or not is a non-debate, since growth is itself not a policy instrument. Much more fruitful is a debate on propositions such as the following: 'legal systems that protect private property, low taxes, low tariffs, low controls on foreign direct investment, an open capital account, lead in the medium term to higher poverty reduction'; or 'legal systems and social customs that eliminate discrimination against women and minorities, land reform, relatively high public expenditures on health and education, a system of social protection lead, in the short term and in the medium term, to greater poverty reduction'; or 'governance structures which make government transparent and accountable, higher decentralization in government, low levels of corruption in national and local government, a judiciary that is independent and courts to which all have relatively easy access, lead to higher poverty reduction in the medium term'.

Even these propositions, better though they are for debate than the sterile 'growth is good for poverty' formulation, could do with sharpening, with clearer specification of which policy instruments exactly are being discussed. After all, as is now well recognized, 'institutions' can themselves be endogenous, and a correlation between a particular institutional form and poverty reduction (or higher economic growth) cannot be taken to the bank as a causation (or cannot be taken to the World Bank as a policy recommendation). Moreover, the detail of country context and specificity is important. A cross-country correlation, even if interpreted as causation, must allow for variations around the regression line, and we must understand phenomena like the 'Bangladesh paradox', where a country with one of the worst indicators on governance and corruption nevertheless has delivered some of the best improvements in social indicators (relative to appropriate comparators) in the last two decades.

Allied to the importance of country specificity is the importance of 'poverty specificity'. Just as a country can grow with worsening poverty, national poverty can decline with increases in poverty among significant sections of the population, or at least stagnation or much lower rates of poverty reduction in these groups. This is the pattern that has been prevalent in fast-growing countries over the past two decades – rising inequality, and relative stagnation or even immiserization in 'pockets of poverty'. The determinants of poverty reduction would seem to be more complex, then, than national-level policy instruments, complex enough though that nexus is by itself.

A philosopher king might well ponder these things as he wishes that if only he could find the determinants of poverty reduction, he would reduce poverty. That poverty persists might indicate one of two things, however: either the determinants of poverty reduction are not known, or they are known but are not being put in place. Of course, it could be a combination of the two. Let us, however, now focus on the second.

Why might it be that knowledge of poverty reduction is not put to use to reduce poverty? The answer must be that application of these instruments that are known to reduce poverty would (of course) benefit the poor but would not benefit some others, indeed it may harm them. It is not in the interests of these others for these instruments to be applied, and they will work to make sure they are not applied or, if they are applied, to undermine their implementation on the ground. In fact, in the absence of far-reaching altruism, it is a reasonable assumption that individuals and groups will work to advance policies and interventions that will benefit themselves – if they benefit others, that is by and large neither here nor there to them. More to the point, individuals and groups will work to oppose policies and interventions that hurt them – the fact that they benefit others, even the poor, will cut no ice. This way of looking at things leads to a simple conclusion. The determinants of poverty reduction are policy instruments that benefit the dominant coalition of political power but which, incidentally and also, benefit poverty reduction. If a set of instruments harms the interests of the dominant coalition, it will not be implemented, even if it is known to be a determinant of poverty reduction.

I recognize of course that the above is too simple, too simplistic. For a start, the poor are themselves a group with divergent interests. Although debates on policy reform are often presented in terms of one group of the rich blocking changes that would benefit the poor, policy reform often pits the interests of one group of poor against another. And the non-poor themselves have divergent interests. Further, narrow sectional interests are not all that matters. Appeals to altruism and national solidarity work sometimes. And history shows that negative externalities from poverty through diseases and the like are a powerful motivating force among dominant interests. But the central point remains, that poverty reduction requires an alignment of the interest of the poor with the interests of the dominant coalition.

What does this line of argument mean for analysis of poverty, and for political advocacy on behalf of the poor? First, there is a lot that we do not know about the determinants of poverty reduction, even from a narrow technocratic perspective. Specifically, although we now know that specificity and context matters, we know far less about how exactly it matters, and about the detail of how different poverty reduction instruments actually work. Second, although we now know that international, national and local politics matters in determining which policies and interventions are chosen, and thus whether poverty reduction will happen or not, we know far less about the detail of what sorts of configurations of dominant interests align with the interests of the poor, and when that was not the case, how change happened which shifted the coalition in favour of the poor. Third, it means that to advocate for poverty reduction must mean not only advocacy for instruments that we know will lead to this outcome, but it also means advocating for a realignment of the dominant coalition in a way that will align it with the interests of the poor. Specifically, this means that we should advocate for empowerment of the poor so that they can indeed challenge the dominant interests, to shift alliances in a way that will make possible policies and interventions for poverty reduction.

The chapters in this volume are an excellent attempt at generating knowledge that is detailed and context specific on poverty reduction, using a full range of qualitative and quantitative methodologies from the social sciences. They take us beyond the first cut of cross-country regression analysis to examine why particular interventions work in particular settings, and when they do not, why not. The knowledge presented here is invaluable in identifying the determinants of poverty reduction. My hope is that it will also help in the more difficult task of actually changing the policies and interventions in the direction of poverty reduction, by helping those who advocate for the interest of the poor. Because, ultimately, it is the empowerment of the poorest that works for the poorest.

Ravi Kanbur is T.H. Lee Professor of World Affairs, International Professor of Applied Economics and Management and Professor of Economics at Cornell University, USA.

CHAPTER 1
What works for the poorest?

David Hulme and David Lawson

This chapter introduces the reader to the objectives of this collection, examines 'who' the poorest are, and provides an introduction to the chapters that follow. There are many books on poverty and the poor, but few have focused on the extreme poor. We seek to partially fill this gap and provide practitioners and policymakers with ideas and experiences that may provide insights and guidance. The poorest cannot afford to wait for economic growth to trickle down or good governance to emerge. They may die or have their capabilities (e.g. physical and mental health, cognitive abilities, reproductive capacity) disabled or destroyed. This is why this volume hopes to: (i) raise awareness of the problems faced by the poorest people in low and middle-income countries (the developing world); (ii) encourage policymakers and development practitioners to identify and prioritize projects, programmes and policies that will assist the poorest; (iii) provide a number of practical examples for practitioners and policymakers of 'what works for the poorest'. These may serve as 'models' for action but our preference is for them to inspire new experiments based on a mix of inspiration and the nitty-gritty routines of planning, implementing, monitoring, learning and strengthening projects and programmes in the field.

Introduction

Over the past 15 years the world has experienced an unparalleled period of economic growth, and dramatic reductions in income (and consumption) poverty. This is a cause for celebration but, at the same time, we must note that the benefits of this contemporary growth spurt have been very unevenly spread. The world's richest 150 people now own assets that have the same value as those held by the poorest 3 billion and the cumulative effects of the fuel, food and credit crises has driven 50 to 100 million people back into extreme poverty.

At the global level the benefits have been concentrated within China and India, while other regions – sub-Saharan Africa, much of South Asia, the Andean region, the states of the former Soviet Union, and the Pacific – have improved little and, in some cases, life has got harder. A group of around 50 countries, mainly in Africa, are locked in poverty traps that keep the well-being levels of their population very low (a more accurate concept might be ill-being) and ensure national economic stagnation (Collier, 2007).

At the sub-national level, it is evident that the types of broadly-based growth that generated the relatively egalitarian East Asian Miracle of the mid and late 20th century – growth with mass poverty reduction – are different from contemporary growth processes. In the Chinese and Indian 'successes', hundreds of millions of people have gained few or no benefits and large numbers remain destitute or vulnerable to destitution. Indeed, reports suggest that the lives of millions have worsened as China's 'iron rice bowl' has been broken and India's rural economy has de-agrarianized. The recently discovered continent of 'sub-Siberian Asia', a contiguous area stretching across Northern India and Bangladesh to Central and Western China, the countries of Central Asia and back around to Afghanistan, Pakistan and Nepal, has economic and social indicators much lower than the rest of Asia (Hulme, 2010).

This extreme and chronic poverty has spatial and social relational dimensions. Spatially, it is often concentrated in particular areas – for example, the *chars* in Bangladesh, the drylands of Southern Andhra Pradesh in India, mountainous and landlocked regions across Africa, and 'settlements' outside South Asia's major cities. Socially, it is concentrated within specific groups – indigenous or 'tribal' groups (in Botswana, India, Viet Nam, Uganda, Bolivia and elsewhere), ethnic and religious minorities, internally displaced people and refugees. At the micro level – the household, village or community – particularly vulnerable individuals including older people, widows, orphans, disabled people and others, are likely to find that they can barely maintain their lives and that they have minimal or no prospects for improvement. At the extreme, the poorest simply disappear, dying unregistered but easily preventable deaths.

This volume arises out of the concerns of a group of development practitioners, policymakers and researchers about the poorest, and seeks to provide some ideas and guidance about how the poorest might be assisted in their personal efforts to sustain themselves and improve their prospects. There have been significant breakthroughs in assisting the poor – from jobs in garment factories, to cash transfers, to microfinance – but there is also a growing recognition that these have rarely reached the poorest. The book's orientation is explicitly practical and policy focused. It does not seek to propound general theories about causes of extreme poverty or universal generalizations about how to tackle it. The focus is on the micro- and meso-level projects, programmes and policies that seek to improve the condition of the world's poorest people in the short and medium-term.

We realize that this leaves us open to criticism. Neoclassical macro-economists can argue that we have neglected the analysis of international trade, economic liberalization and macro-economic policies. From the opposite end of the ideological spectrum, radical political economists can argue that we fail to examine the social relations engendered by contemporary global capitalism, ranging from global financial crises to worker exploitation to violent conflicts.

We acknowledge such lacunae in this volume and refer the reader to other sources (CPRC, 2008; Collier, 2007; Greig et al., 2007) that address such 'macro' issues. In our defence, we argue that there has been a relative neglect in the literature on how to assist the poorest in operational terms. This volume seeks to partially fill this gap and provide practitioners and policymakers with ideas and experiences that may provide insights and guidance.

In this volume we seek to:

1. Raise awareness of the problems faced by the poorest people in low and middle-income countries (the developing world).
2. Encourage policymakers and development practitioners to identify projects, programmes and policies that will assist the poorest in the next few years. The poorest cannot afford to wait for growth to trickle down or good governance to emerge: they may die or have their capabilities (e.g. physical and mental health, cognitive abilities, reproductive capacity) disabled or destroyed before growth reaches them.
3. To provide a number of practical examples for development practitioners and policymakers of 'what works for the poorest'. These may serve as 'models' for action but our preference is for them to inspire new experiments based on a mix of inspiration and the nitty-gritty routines of planning, implementing, monitoring, learning and strengthening projects and programmes in the field.

We are fully aware that writing and editing papers about assisting the poorest is the easiest part of such efforts. Planning and managing these initiatives on a day-to-day basis is the critical ingredient, of which the world needs more.

Who are the poorest?

Defining and/or identifying 'the poorest' is challenging in terms of both concepts and methods. There are five main ways in which extreme poverty can be conceptualized. The most common are income or consumption-based poverty lines based on an assessment of the amount of money needed to acquire food that meets the minimum calorific needs of a human being. These are used by most economists and policymakers. This is commonly estimated to be around 2100 to 2500 calories per day for an adult, but there are many assumptions and technical issues behind such estimations. In many developing countries the extreme poverty line is defined as a percentage of the overall poverty line.

Since 1990, a global 'extreme poverty' line has been identified – the widely used US$1/day measure (which in 2008 became the US$1.25/day measure). This was computed by World Bank economists for the *World Development Report 1990*, which argued that for 1985 anyone with consumption valued at less than $1 (in purchasing power parity terms) was extremely poor.[1] The application of this yardstick to the global population in 2000 suggested that

1.2 billion people were extremely poor (Chen and Ravallion, 2004). Subsequently Chen and Ravallion (2008) have argued that a $1.25 extreme poverty line is now appropriate. This most recent application increases the estimates of the poor for 1990 and 1999 significantly (Table 1.1). It suggests that there were 1.7 billion extremely poor people in 1999 and that this had declined to around 1.4 billion by 2005. However, despite its apparent simplicity, there are big questions about the arbitrariness of the original $1/day line and about the quality of data available. A particular disadvantage of this concept is that it cannot be used in the field to practically identify the poorest people.

Large numbers of development specialists (managers, policymakers, researchers) believe that assessing poverty purely in terms of income and consumption is logically flawed and prefer the concept of 'human development'. This developed out of the work of Paul Streeten, Mahbub ul Haq and Amartya Sen and has been popularized by the United Nations *Human Development Reports*. Human development views poverty and extreme poverty as multidimensional deprivation: lack of food and income, illiteracy, inadequate access to health services and potable water and other factors. This concept has much to recommend, but unfortunately it has proved impossible for proponents of human development to specify a household or individual-level human development measure (see Hulme and McKay (2008) for a discussion). Barrientos (2003) shows how a multidimensional list might be used to identify the poor and poorest by computing deprivation measures for several dimensions (e.g. housing quality, water, food) and specifying the number of deprivations at which a household could be judged to be poor or extremely poor. However, such efforts experience great criticism because of the many assumptions that lie behind the lists, and the choice of cut-off points and the number of deprivations needed to be classed as poor or extreme poor.

A third possible means of identifying the poorest is in terms of the duration of poverty. The Chronic Poverty Research Centre (CPRC) has been spearheading such an approach (Hulme and Shepherd, 2003; CPRC, 2004). CPRC (2004, 2008) has used the $1/day measure to estimate that over 400 million people are chronically poor: that they had been in extreme poverty for 5 years or more. CPRC has encouraged the use of human development measures, but these have only been taken up to a very limited degree (Baulch and Masset, 2003; Gunter and Klasen, 2008). Interestingly Gunter and Klasen's (2008) work suggests that the correlation between chronic poverty in the income and non-income dimensions is very low, and non-income poverty is certainly more stable over time than income poverty. Calvo and Dercon (2008) have argued that analytically and practically the challenge is to identify who is likely to stay poor in the future. These are the people who policy must try to prioritize.

A particularly important component of CPRC's work has focused on the intergenerational transmission of poverty. Arguably those households in which the poverty of the parents is likely to be transferred to children – through the

Table 1.1 Counting the poorest: $1-a-day poverty estimates (1980–2005) in millions (as percentage of global population)[1]

Source	Measure	1980	1981	1984	1985	1987	1990	1993	1996	1998	1999	2001	2002	2005
WDR (1980)	Indian poverty line	780* (36)												
WDR (1990)	$370 p/a at 1985 PPP				1,116 (33)									
WDR (2000)	$1.08-a-day at 1993 PPP					1,183 (28)	1,276 (29)	1,304 (28)	1,190 (25)	1,199 (24)				
Chen and Ravallion (2004)	$1.08-a-day at 1993 PPP		1,482 (40.4)	1,277 (32.8)		1,171 (28.4)	1,219 (27.9)	1,208 (26.3)	1,097 (22.8)		1,096 (21.8)	1,089 (21.1)		
World Bank (2008)	$1.25-a-day at 2005 PPP		1,900 (52)	1,813 (47)		1,723 (42)	1,818 (42)	1,799 (39)	1,658 (34)		1,698 (34)		1,601 (34)	1,374 (25)

Sources: WDR (1980); WDR (1990); WDR (2000); Chen and Ravallion (2004); and World Bank (website 2008).
* Excluding China
[1] for a discussion of the $1-a-day poverty measure see David Hulme (2010) *Global Poverty*, Routledge, London.

blocking of their capabilities by poor nutrition, ill health, lack of education and other factors – can be regarded as among the poorest.

The fourth means of identifying the poorest is more intuitive and is an approach that is used by organizations and practitioners at the field level. It is to identify an indicator that can be easily assessed and is believed to reveal that an individual or household is experiencing extreme poverty. The most common such indicator is access to food: 'have you gone without food this year?' or 'how many meals a day do you eat?' Kabeer (this volume) found that the simple question 'what category best describes the food situation in your household over the last year: chronic food shortage, occasional food shortage, 'break-even' food supply, or food surplus?' could identify the consumption poor with great accuracy. Combinations of indicators can be used as shown by Sen and Begum (this volume). Data on housing quality, land holding and occupation can be used to rapidly identify the poorest people in Bangladesh.

The fifth approach is participatory. This includes a variety of different methods ranging from the widely-used Participatory Rural Appraisal techniques described by Robert Chambers (1994) to the more Freirian and dialogical methods (proposed by Xavier Godinot (2000) in *Participation works: Involving People in Poverty in Policy Making*). This approach has received much attention in recent years with Narayan et al. (2000) *Voices of the Poor* and Krishna's (2009) 'Stages of Progress' methodology. The BRAC Targeting the Ultra Poor (TUP) Programme analysed by Hulme and Moore (this volume) uses the classic PRA technique of wealth ranking to initially identify the poorest people in rural Bangladesh before proceeding to use more 'objective' methods.

While there is no general agreement on what approach is best for identifying the poorest there is now a well established and easily accessible set of resources describing how researchers and practitioners can go about this task.

How do the poorest survive?

The popular image of the poorest, drawn from television coverage and newspapers, is of children and desperate mothers on the edge of survival in the context of a natural disaster or a famine. Such images do indeed capture one aspect of extreme poverty, but it goes beyond gut-wrenching photographs that produce outbursts of charitable donations, responses by aid agencies, and publicity-seeking promises. Providing famine relief, emergency assistance, tents and potable water is very difficult – but it also may be one of the easiest aspects of assisting the poorest because of the responses of politicians in the face of such desperate scenes.

For the vast majority of the extreme poor, deprivation is not a sudden, intense experience. Rather, it is an enduring, day-to-day experience overshadowed by vulnerability, destitution, physical pain and easily preventable death (for oneself or one's children and close relatives) in the near future. It is grinding poverty – manually labouring for 8 to 16 hours a day to provide for the minimum food requirements of one's family, waiting for weeks for sick children to get better (or die) because basic health services are not accessible, watching other children go to school while you cannot attend because your parents cannot buy a uniform, being beaten, or worse, most days by your employer – these are the characteristics of poverty that is extreme and endures. Such 'quiet violence' (Hartmann and Boyce, 1984) rarely attracts the media or politicians.

For most of the world's poorest people survival is not based on assistance from donors, NGOs or government programmes. Instead, they survive primarily from their own efforts – casual labouring, gleaning, recycling waste, begging, gathering common property resources – and the support that is offered by relatives and neighbours. Njuma, an elderly, childless widow in Uganda provides an example. She survives from gifts of food from her neighbours and gleaning post-harvest coffee beans for $0.02 to $0.03 an hour (Box 1). Maymana and Mofizul, a widow and her disabled son, have survived by a more complex set of strategies embedded in the social relations they have in a rural area of Bangladesh (Appendix 1). Their own efforts, relatives and support from rural elites both assists and constrains them. For most of the poorest the poverty-reduction initiatives of NGOs, governments and donors are too distant to be relevant. Only a very limited set of public actions, such as immunization and emergency relief, are likely to reach the poorest with any regularity.

Box 1.1 Njuma, the gleaner

Njuma lives in a relatively remote village on the slopes of Mount Elgon in Uganda. She is a childless widow who is almost 70 years old. Her house is a small mud hut with a dilapidated grass roof. Since her husband died, around 7 or 8 years ago, she has lived alone and has been largely dependent on gifts of food from relatives and neighbours. They do not wish to see her suffer from hunger but they are also poor and vulnerable and do not see it as their role to provide beyond her minimum nutritional needs. If she gets sick she just has to wait until she gets better, as she has no access to health services. She gets no support from the government or NGOs.

Despite feeling tired, often low-spirited, and having no formal access to land or productive assets, she seeks opportunities to be economically active. Her main work is gleaning coffee from the bushes of neighbours when they have finished picking. It takes a lot of work to harvest one or two kilograms of beans from bushes that have been picked already, are poorly maintained and on steep slopes. We estimate that she earns the equivalent of US$0.02-0.03 for each hour she works. The government's economic surveys and the census would class her as poor and not working. An alternative view is that she is employed in some of the lowest paid work in the world. Gleaning is the only way she can get the money to replace her one worn dress or pay someone to patch the holes in her roof before the wet season starts. We also suspect it is of psychological importance to Njuma – she may be dependent, but she has plans of her own.

Source: Hulme in CPRC (2004: 3)

Overview and intentions of this book

Identifying the poorest

The first section of this volume considers the issue of *Creating Knowledge about the Poorest*. We open with this issue because we believe that at the present time anti-poverty policies still treat the poor as though they are a single homogeneous group who can be assisted by the same type of programme. We seek to encourage researchers and practitioners to disaggregate the poor and, in particular, pose the questions 'who are the poorest' and 'is anyone working with the poorest to improve their situation?' This raises questions regarding the methods that can be adopted in understanding issues that underpin poverty.

Chapter 2 by Serajuddin, Zaman and Narayan illustrates the use of classical income-based measures of poverty to identify the poorest people, in this case using Bangladesh as an example. It examines whether the poorest benefited from the upturn in the country's economic growth rate, and in particular focuses on the five year period between 2000 and 2005. It finds that growth in Bangladesh has been pro-poorest in terms of both income and social indicators. This is excellent news for those amongst the country's poorest people who have benefited. However, thirty-five million extremely poor Bangladeshis (a quarter of the population) are still waiting for the benefits of growth to trickle down to them. Alarmingly, extremely poor people in the western part of the country have seen little improvement in their living conditions and perhaps a spatial poverty trap is emerging.

Creating such knowledge has great policy relevance both internationally and nationally. First, it demonstrates that labour-intensive growth can be good for some of the poorest, and challenges the ideological claims of anti-globalizers who claim that growth is automatically bad for the poorest. Second, within Bangladesh it challenges policymakers to review conventional wisdom about the geographical areas that need special assistance. Historically, there has been a tendency to view the northern parts of the country, and especially the *monga* (seasonal food deficit) regions, as the poorest. This new evidence suggests that a west-east divide may be more significant than a north-south divide. This has profound policy implications for programming food aid and poverty reduction projects but further testing of this proposition is urgently needed.

The volume then moves on to provide a focus on alternative methodological approaches to analysing and understanding poverty. Lawson (chapter 3) explores whether knowledge about the poorest can be deepened by undertaking combined quantitative and qualitative research (a 'Q-squared' approach). Over the last few years there has been an increased emphasis on moving away from purely quantitative, and the more 'neoclassical' based studies of analysing poverty, to combining qualitative and quantitative research methodologies. However, much of the earlier combined methods work simply cross-references quantitative findings to separate qualitative findings (for example Barahona and Levy, 2003, for Malawi). As noted in Lawson et al. (2008), although such work is useful in its own right – for example, authors are able to assess the validity of quantitative results and provide a dynamic dimension to one-off household survey data – in the main such work operates in parallel, i.e. it does not use the same sampling frame or applied integrated methods to the same households.

Lawson's chapter explores this combined methods approach through an analysis of Uganda's nationally representative panel dataset for 1992–99 with detailed life history interviews of 95 households collected from the panel. This reveals the significance of health problems, and particularly HIV/AIDS, in explaining how households descend into and/or become trapped in poverty. It also permits a deeper understanding of the ways in which poor people use their agency to try to cope with such problems. It indicates that poor people reduce their consumption in an attempt to 'asset smooth' (i.e. retain a minimum level of productive assets) so that they can remain productive. Rich country-based analysts who fret about very poor people becoming 'welfare dependent' if social programmes provide small 'handouts' to them would do well to adopt such mixed methods so that they can appreciate how even the poorest people are constantly striving to improve their lives.

Following the combined methods approach Kabeer (chapter 4) then examines the very different evidence that emerges when different criteria are used to assess who is very poor. In Bangladesh, she finds, as have others, that the extreme poor remain so because they start off poorer than most other people and are caught in 'livelihood traps' that provide few or no opportunities for upward mobility. More interestingly, however, she finds that the extreme food poor have much lower prospects of upward mobility than the extreme income poor. This has significant implications for policy as it suggests that programmes should focus on using food poverty to identify the poorest rather than income poverty. Using this criterion is easier, more accurate, and more likely to identify those who are most likely to remain trapped in poverty.

The materials in this first section of the book by no means cover all of the possibilities about how to obtain knowledge of the poorest. However, the section does provide three distinct alternatives that raise issues regarding the methods that can be adopted in understanding issues that underpin poverty and provide alternative analyses. The section also indicates how the techniques reflect a relative transition for researchers and practitioners regarding how such work has been undertaken. There has clearly been a partial move away from single methodologically based studies of poverty, particularly within an economics and development studies disciplinary focus (see Hulme and Toye (2006) for more detailed discussions).

Targeting the poorest

The second section examines *Targeting the Poorest*. The majority of literature on targeting currently focuses only on distinguishing between the poor and the non-poor. It is important to transcend such a limited position so as to ensure the more 'difficult to reach' poor are not excluded from development policy and action. Policies that have favoured the non-poor and moderate poor have not necessarily reached or benefited those living in extreme poverty. However, the task of identifying and targeting the extreme poor is far from being straightforward.

Sen and Begum (chapter 5) relate the issues of macro-level poverty measurement to the more applied issue of how to accurately and rapidly identify very poor people so that programmes can target them. The chapter presents a methodology for identifying and targeting the poorest. In rural Bangladesh, it shows that very simple assessment criteria can be identified and used with great confidence. No single criteria is robust for rural Bangladesh but if the criteria of size of land owned, quality of housing, and main occupation of a household are combined then the poorest can be identified and targeted with great accuracy. In line with several of the chapters in the volume, the chapter also helps show the way in which collaboration between researchers and practitioners can produce practical findings that can improve programme performance at field level.

Alviar, Ayala and Handa (chapter 6) provide further evidence that targeting effectiveness is best determined by a dynamic range of factors, and conclude that combining multiple targeting approaches tends to improve performance. This chapter considers the increasingly important poverty reduction instrument of cash transfers. It describes and assesses targeting in the Kenya Cash Transfer for Orphans and Vulnerable Children (CT-OVC) as a useful example for environments with high poverty and low technical capacity, characteristic of much of sub-Saharan Africa.

A theoretical review of targeting performance and mechanisms is provided by a discussion of combined targeting systems in situations where the prevalence of poverty makes it difficult to distinguish the poorest. Such targeting methods carry high administrative costs, and can be infeasible in low capacity environments. The Kenya CT-OVC programme combines categorical targeting, proxy means testing, and community-based methods. Despite its complexity, the preliminary operational experience has been positive and to date, more than 25,000 households have been screened using this system of multiple targeting methods.

The Kenyan experience illustrates that relatively complex targeting systems can be implemented in low capacity environments, although the programme is still at pilot stage and has not yet been scaled-up. Initial unit costs have been high, but should fall within acceptable margins due to the long time horizon that participants are expected to be in the programme. The process of central verification is merited in the Kenyan context, and technology and use of a sophisticated information system has been of great assistance. However, it remains to be seen whether targeting performance will improve, and whether such complex schemes can be scaled-up in relatively low capacity circumstances.

While the evidence base is beginning to expand, there are still considerable gaps in our understanding of how to develop appropriate institutional arrangements to reach the poorest through targeted interventions in health. Standing and Kirk (chapter 7) consider institutional issues in scaling-up programmes for meeting the health related needs of the very poor. The chapter identifies the main institutional issues which confront attempts to target the poorest and develop programmes for this hard to reach part of the population. Different kinds and experiences of targeting are discussed in terms of their appropriateness to health programmes, and institutional arrangements for ensuring that programmes meet their goals. The chapter then looks at the increasing trend towards demand-side financing approaches for reaching the very poor on a significant scale.

The authors conclude by noting some important gaps in our understanding of how to manage scaling-up successfully. These include a lack of empirically grounded accounts of the development of institutional arrangements, and how barriers and capacity constraints can be overcome as programmes move to scale. It also notes that a clearer understanding of the successful factors involved in expanding such programmes is emerging but scaling-up requires continuous adaptation to local circumstances with only a few normative principles, such as informed consent, regarded as universal and non-negotiable (Simmons and Shiffman, 2006). This suggests that there is no 'one size fits all' solution to meeting the health needs of the poorest; local and national adaptations to political economy constraints and opportunities will provide the best ways forward.

Policies and programmes for the poorest

The third section of the book presents a number of case studies from around the developing and developed world of *Policies and Programmes to Assist the Poorest*.

Armando Barrientos (chapter 8) focuses on social protection and the evolution of income transfer programmes in Latin America. He closely examines the Chile Solidario Programme, introduced in 2002 and aimed at eradicating extreme poverty in the country. It explicitly seeks to reach Chile's poorest people, ensuring they obtain their rights and entitlements and achieve full participation in economic and social life. The design and scope of the programme is highly innovative. It is based on a multidimensional understanding of poverty and on the capability approach, and it focuses on removing social exclusion for the poorest households. It has a strong focus on reconnecting the extreme poor with their rights and entitlements and providing sustained support to extreme poor households.

Chile Solidario was implemented by integrating and modifying a large number of pre-existing public interventions focused on poor households. It benefited from the 'fiscal space' generated by years of sustained growth, and strong public service delivery capacity. The programme alerts policymakers to the fact that monetary transfers are not enough, by themselves, to lift poor households out of extreme or persistent poverty. These need to be accompanied by basic services – such as education, health, and childcare – and protection against contingencies that may push households back into extreme poverty. A key lesson from Chile Solidario is the need to think in terms of integrated programmes as opposed to isolated interventions. If programmes can be made to work then managers should ask 'is it possible to extend the scope of our intervention'? (Barrientos and Hulme, 2008).

Hulme and Moore (chapter 9) then consider BRAC's TUP Programme in Bangladesh, which emerged from earlier attempts to combine safety net programmes (food aid) with economic promotion schemes (microcredit, and business and technical services). The TUP programme provides poor households, usually headed by women, with a cash stipend, health services, social and business development training and an asset transfer (for example, milch cows, chicken packages or an initial stock of goods to trade) so that they can 'graduate' out of extreme poverty and join the poverty reduction programmes that BRAC and other NGOs offer, such as microfinance and micro-enterprise development.

This programme has received highly supportive evaluations and is now being transferred to several other countries (see Hashemi and Anand, this volume, for a discussion). There are many potential lessons to be drawn. In particular these relate to *(i)* the innovations associated with the transfer of a substantial set of assets to very poor households – in effect, a redistribution of assets from the taxpayers of aid donor countries to the ultra poor in Bangladesh – and *(ii)* the recruitment of village level elites to local committees to support TUP participants and other very poor people. The latter is a radical idea in terms of social engineering a more pro-poor context in rural Bangladesh.

The chapter notes that TUP is a very complex programme – only organizations, or partnerships of organizations, with high levels of analytical and management capacity are likely to be able to mount such initiatives at scale. Furthermore, TUP may not be applicable to some categories of ultra-poor people. The economically 'inactive' ultra-poor (frail older people, AIDS orphans, people in chronic ill-heath) and socially excluded or adversely incorporated people (bonded labourers, refugees, indigenous people in remote areas) will need more conventional forms of social protection (old-age provisions, humanitarian aid, 'free' health services, and child grants) and social change (reduced discrimination and changes in labour relations).

Hulme and Moore in chapter 9 provide a good example of how solutions for the poorest are becoming more innovative. As noted by Hanlon et al. (2010), poor people and poor countries are turning anti-poverty thinking on its head. Instead of armies of civil servants and aid workers telling the poor how to improve themselves, many developing countries are giving money to the poor, and discovering that they use it wisely. Not only do they eat more and send their children to school, but they also invest these tiny amounts of cash in their farm, in setting up small businesses, or in going further afield to search for work. A small guaranteed income can provide a starting point which allows the poor to transform their own lives.

This quiet revolution in developing and middle income countries has grown in popularity, especially since the late 1990s when the likes of South Africa and Mexico introduced child benefits and, more recently, Lesotho offered a non-contributory old age pensions system. Such transfers are often vital to the poorest families. For example, in the case of Lesotho it is often the families headed by older people that require vital additional payments that assist with taking care of HIV/AIDS orphans. The additional income that such transfers provides is commonly spent locally, buying food, clothing and inputs. This stimulates the local economy, as local people sell more, earn more, and buy more – the virtuous development cycle (Hanlon et al., 2010).

'Just giving cash' to very poor people forms the basis for chapter 10 in which Chaudhry considers cash transfers in Central Viet Nam. He discusses the Oxfam experiment with unconditional cash transfers in a development (non-emergency) context, and highlights some of the methodological and conceptual challenges that have arisen in the course of setting up research around this programme. He describes how recipient households used the one-off unconditional cash payment, and how the project challenged the existing ascribed roles of the poor and the non-poor in village politics. Positive outcomes from the project included a reported increase in voice and confidence amongst beneficiaries, with most beneficiaries feeling 'more confident' and reporting a sense of having 'more voice in the community'.

In the light of a growing international literature on the role of cash transfers on extreme and chronic poverty, findings reveal that more than just cash is required. Cash transfer projects provide a vehicle for change, a means to an end, rather than ends in themselves. NGOs like Oxfam can play a key role as advocates for change, and as facilitators. Often it is the conditions that are deeply embedded in existing relations of power and social control, relations which are unevenly stacked against the poor, and the lack of appropriate usage of resources. Under-utilization of female skills and gender-based inequalities is a major issue in exacerbating poverty (World Bank, 2001). The lack of understanding of such issues is a key explanatory factor in the failure of many countries to achieve sustainable economic growth, govern effectively and reduce poverty (Blackden et al., 2007).

The chapters by Bandyopadhyay, Oza and Nygaard (chapter 11), and Pillai and Sudarshan (chapter 12) consider the issues of gender, ostracized communities, and labour issues in marginalized communities. Bandyopadhyay et al. focus on the livelihoods of the 20–30,000 people of the Siddi community in Gujarat. The Siddis often accept entrenched poverty, deprivation and exclusion as a way of life. The chapter examines the changes in attitude, behaviour and confidence levels of Siddi women that can arise as a result of sensitive empowerment processes fostered by the Aga Khan Rural Support Programme (India). Developing viable livelihood options and involving Siddi women in successful micro-enterprises has been possible after gaining their confidence, nurturing and supporting them, and bringing them together through a set of well-structured community organizations. Confident in themselves and with a desire to achieve, these women are today venturing out, taking business risks and planning for their future, and the future of their children.

The case of the Siddi community emphasizes the importance of building individual and community trust and demonstrates the role of local leadership in motivating others. It also shows how community members created a structure through which they can take decisions in a transparent manner. The services provided were valued and nurtured by the local community as these services corresponded with communal aspirations and needs.

Pillai and Sudarshan's chapter focuses on the role of public works in poverty reduction, by considering the National Rural Employment Guarantee Act (NREGA) in India. Public works have a long history in India and have been particularly associated with a form of cash transfer to ameliorate distress of the poorest at times of famine. NREGA builds upon the experience of such programmes, such as Maharashtra Employment Guarantee Scheme (MEGS). It differs from them in that it is designed as a statutory obligation of the state and a right of the citizen. It also seeks to be distinguished from cash transfers by emphasizing on the one hand the link between productivity and earnings, and on the other the building up of assets that would in due course contribute to local economic development.

A significant proportion of the NREGA participating households send women to undertake public works. However conditions of work on the sites do not meet minimum standards and it is difficult to avoid the conclusion that so far the 'success' of the NREGA has been the transfer of cash rather than the empowerment of poor women. The process of implementation involves articulation of priorities by villagers, choice of works to reflect these priorities, and the creation of durable assets, in turn stimulating local development. However, until these systems become more responsive and better informed the choice of assets will continue to be determined at the convenience of local officials and will be restricted by the skills that are locally available.

Labour contracting also has a role in entrenching extreme poverty. Labour contractors can provide large numbers of workers, often at short notice, with no long-term employment obligations, reducing the costs to the supplier and allowing them to meet tight production schedules. Many workers hired by labour contractors are thus highly vulnerable to poverty due to the volatility of work, low wages, and lack of any benefits or protection. Often the critical point of exploitation is not within the work-place itself, but in related arrangements (which could involve several agents) for activities such as the movement of workers between countries, accommodation or provision of documents.

At the extreme, some workers find themselves in modern forms of 'economic slavery' that perpetuate their vulnerability to extreme poverty. Yet these workers are employed at the bottom of a highly profitable modern food chain, dominated by some of the world's largest firms. Stephanie Barrientos (chapter 13) focuses on the experiences of contract labour working in global food production in South Africa and the UK. She highlights the changing nature of employment relationships, and shows how the promotion of decent contract labour may come about.

There are significant challenges in addressing the rights and protection of contract workers. Much labour regulation is premised on the assumption of stable employer attachment, which such workers rarely have. The main regulatory channels require open employment records, but these workers are often 'invisible'. The mobility of labour contractors between employers makes it extremely difficult for labour inspectors or social auditors to monitor their employment practices. However, the positioning of such labour arrangements within wider social and institutional settings of global production networks does provide new points of leverage to promote decent work. For example, the vulnerability of supermarkets to adverse publicity has promoted the extension of voluntary codes to contract labour.

In many developing countries, governments have tried to find appropriate health financing strategies to improve health care access among the poor and very poor. Studies have shown that user fees at public health facilities have become one of the barriers to accessing health care for the poorest in many developing countries (Palmer et al., 2004). As a result, alternative strategies have been developed, such as fee exemption schemes, Health Equity Funds (HEF) and Community-Based Health Insurance (CBHI).

Chapter 14 provides a link between the programmes associated with what works for the poorest and how we might find the money for such programmes by focusing on alternative health financing strategies. In this chapter, Men and Van Pelt consider the problems facing Cambodia's urban poor in accessing health services – problems common to many rapidly urbanizing parts of the world. The authors highlight the role of Health Equity Funds by using one HEF case study programme, operating in an urban area of Cambodia, a country that has the highest out-of-pocket health expenditures in the world. First they examine the role of HEFs in meeting the health-related needs of the poorest and review evidence regarding whether the schemes have any impact on the very poor, by analysing household data combined with hospitalization data, to determine levels of hospitalization for the poor and the very poor in terms of length of stay in the hospital, cost of hospitalization, and benefits received from the HEF. This study confirms the findings of prior empirical work suggesting HEF improves access to public health care among the poor population, particularly increasing hospitalization (Noirhomme et al. 2007), and reduces out-of-pocket expenses for health care (including costs arising from transport, food and medication) for both poor and very poor people, despite one group being more disadvantaged in socio-economic terms than the other. Further evidence in this case indicates that there is no significant difference between the poor and the very poor in terms of accessing health care services. This indicates that benefits received from the HEF by these two different target groups are equally effective. This study also found evidence that to some extent the HEF schemes help to protect households from falling into indebtedness as a consequence of health care costs and reduce poverty through impacts on health care expenditures.

Finding the finance and creating the knowledge for pro-poorest policies

The concluding section of the book looks at *Making it Work: Finding the Money and Spreading the Knowledge,* commencing with Hashemi and Anand's study (chapter 15) of the international transfer of models to meet the needs of the poorest. This demonstrates that rapid progress can be made in sharing knowledge as long as those concerned focus on learning from experiences in other countries and not on replicating programmes in very different environments. The chapter raises the issues of lack of provision of financial services for the poorest within a social protection context. It argues that microfinance requires further innovation to reach down to poorer people, while safety net programmes need to link up with financial service providers to allow poor people to seek better and more sustainable livelihood opportunities.

Microfinance, providing opportunities from the top, and safety nets, providing support from below, create a framework for the poorest to move out of poverty. While some vulnerable people will always require state assistance, deliberate and careful linking of microfinance and safety nets services can offer a new hope for achieving the MDG goal of reducing poverty. The focus of their study, the Consultative Group to Assist the Poor (CGAP) graduation initiative, aims to develop new pathways of cooperation between social protection and microfinance experts. They suggest that too few microfinance specialists truly comprehend its potential to open up opportunities for the poorest. Similarly, too few social protection specialists realize how microfinance linkages can create potential for the poorest to improve their situation.

Within the microfinance institution (MFI) arena there is growing support for the view that the shift towards a commercial approach by MFIs means that microfinance will not directly target the poorest. Graduation programmes seem to be the way that MFIs will try to handle this, with the basic message being that forms of support other than market-based programmes are needed for the poorest.

Chapter 16 (by Addison) examines the resources needed to implement programmes for the poorest. It argues that these are within the capacity of middle income and economically growing low-income countries. For the very poorest countries, donor funding can cover the costs of helping the poorest without creating Dutch disease effects. Addison argues that we also need to posit the counterfactual – what are the costs, in human suffering and lower human capabilities, of not assisting the poorest?

He outlines the growth-poverty debate in the context of globalization's impact on the South's prospects for growth, namely WTO trade liberalization, rising world commodity prices, the current financial crisis and global climate change. Each of these has revenue implications. Trade liberalization will not necessarily be positive for all the world's poor, especially the chronic and extreme poor, and revenues need to be mobilized to maintain poverty reduction programmes. Trade liberalization could cut the revenue base in some countries, and global climate change could undermine efforts to increase pro-poor public spending by reducing national output.

Addison also assesses where we stand in terms of tax reform and how much progress countries have made in building the tax systems needed to meet the poverty challenges set out. Major differences remain between statutory and effective tax rates due to weak tax administration, ad hoc exemptions, and corruption. Local taxes are problematic for the poor – their share of local public spending is low – and taxing the informal sector remains difficult to justify until the net fiscal incidence (the incidence of taxes and spending taken together) is pro-poor. There remains much that we do not know about the role of revenue mobilization in poverty reduction, and this remains a fertile area for research and policy-making.

The concluding chapter of the book, by Hulme and Lawson, summarizes the main findings of this collection. It argues that we now have the methods to identify and create knowledge about the poorest. This provides a base for governments, NGOs, social activists and donors to work with the extreme poor to improve their lives and the prospects of their children. Economic growth is part of the fight against extreme poverty but committed public action is also central to eradicating extreme poverty.

Endnotes

1. For detailed discussions of the strengths and weaknesses of this measure see, Ravallion and Chen (2001), Deaton (2001) and Reddy and Pogge (2003). Particularly important is the use of the dollar as a measure adjusted to achieve 'purchasing power parity'.

Appendix 1: Maymana and Mofizul's Story

Maymana, her son Mofizul, and his wife live in a village about 30 km outside the city of Mymensingh in central Bangladesh. The area is fertile, densely populated, and relatively 'favoured' in Bangladeshi terms: it rarely experiences severe flooding, and agricultural productivity and the local economy have grown. The village is near to a main road so economic activity is fairly diversified and services are accessible. There is a high density of NGOs and microfinance institutions.

Maymana's recent life can be divided into three periods: a phase of relative security before her husband died; a descent into chronic poverty; and a period of making and securing small gains.

In the early 1990s, Maymana lived with her husband Hafeez and three children (two girls and a boy). The couple's third and eldest daughter had already been 'married off'. The household had a reasonably secure income and an asset base to fall back on in hard times: three rickshaws that Hafeez hired out on a daily basis, and an acre or so of paddy land. While vulnerable to shocks, the household probably would have been judged to be above the official poverty line. In Maymana's words, life was *bhalo* (good, alright).

Around this time, Hafeez began to get ill (possibly with throat cancer). Over time, he saw a range of medical practitioners – a 'pharmacist' in the bazaar (probably with no formal training); a government-run health centre nearby where the staff demanded bribes; a private (probably partially trained) 'doctor' in a nearby town; and a private doctor in Mymensingh. The consultations, medicine, X-rays and tests were expensive. One–by-one, Hafeez had to sell each of his rickshaws, and Maymana sold some of the little land she had inherited from her father. Eventually Hafeez was confined to his bed and Maymana was forced to take on occasional work as a maid. Weekly income plummeted, the household was dependent on rice produced from its small plot of land, and the family had to reduce its consumption and stop replacing old clothes and utensils. To Maymana's relief, they had been able to marry off her two remaining daughters – the extended family, with some involvement from Hafeez, was able to arrange the marriages, and the girls themselves contributed to their dowries through breeding single goats.

Hafeez died in 1998, pushing Maymana into despair. She had no husband, minimal income, and a sickly son with an impairment – a severely hunched back – that made physical work difficult for him. Although probably only in her late 40s, Maymana had a hearing impairment and was often tired or ill. She had two years of schooling but was illiterate. Then her father-in-law took control of the household's agricultural plot. In late 1999, despite threats and warnings, she took him to the village court. While in Bangladeshi law she almost certainly had rights to the land, the *shalish* ruled against her (as is the norm when women claim rights to land).

Without this land, she had to start borrowing, gleaning and begging for food. She and Mofizul survived based on some support from her married daughters, wider family, neighbours, and the mosque committee. Mofizul was only 12 and often sick, but he felt responsible for his mother and so looked for work and sometimes got casual employment at a local timber mill. His income helped, but at a very low daily rate it did not make a big difference. He had no education, as remains the norm for poor children with an impairment in Bangladesh.

When researchers first met Maymana in October 1999, she and Mofizul occupied a one-room mud-walled house with an old iron roof. They also had a small kitchen hut with mud walls and plastic sheeting. These two tiny buildings, and 0.09 acres of homestead land, were their only assets. They had no furniture, equipment or livestock (not even chickens) and only a few old cooking utensils. Their hut stood at the back of a number of better-constructed buildings belonging to Maymana's male paternal cousin, who had inherited the property from Maymana's father.

During the year that followed, Maymana and Mofizul patched together their livelihood from a variety of sources – casual work, gleaning, borrowing, begging and receiving charity. They survived, but were unable to acquire any significant financial, physical or natural capital. Their human capital remained low, with no new skills acquired and their health often poor. While their social networks were of great importance for survival, as discussed below, their preferred survival strategy was to work. Despite his youth, disability, ill-health and lack of education, Mofizul was determined to make a living, and as he matured, his wage rate was increased from one-sixth to one-half the adult male rate. However, due to the nature of the work, Mofizul's ill-health, and the illegality of the mill, he often couldn't find work.

Maymana tried to get work as a domestic help, but as she was aging, deaf and often unwell, no one was prepared to hire her. Whenever possible she gleaned rice from harvested fields and areas where rice is processed. When times were really hard she borrowed food and money. When desperate, she begged. Sometimes they received gifts or charity, including from the mosque committee during Eid. She once received wheat via the government's Vulnerable Groups Development Programme, but this support was discontinued due to her cousin's political connections. Despite these difficulties, she reported that 2000 had been much better than the previous year. Her son's earnings had reduced the need to beg for food, and careful management of that money allowed them to often substitute borrowing for begging.

In terms of poverty analysis, in 2000 the household had been both income and capability poor for three or four years, and this condition seemed likely to continue as all of the escape routes (regular employment, VGD card, micro-enterprise) were unlikely to become available. Following their decline into poverty, this deprivation has endured. While the history, structure and experiences of this household are specific, its poverty is by no means atypical of rural life: landless people dependent on casual labouring are a major group among Bangladesh's poor, and around 15% of households are headed by widows or abandoned wives who usually have few assets and suffer social discrimination. Nor is the poverty of this household unusually severe by Bangladeshi standards: throughout the research year they had something to eat every day, they did not suffer from a natural disaster and they had a level of physical assets (a mud hut and micro-homestead) that millions of Bangladeshi's can only dream about.

By mid-2005, Maymana and Mofizul's prospects looked better. In 2003 they had been able to build a new house of a better size, with mud-plastering and tin roof in excellent condition. A very small, thatched kitchen shed stood nearby, and the home now contained some basic furniture. Mofizul was shortly to marry a cousin. He was well socialized with his co-workers, and not treated differently by them because of his impairment. Several factors contributed to the improvement in their material and social position over these five years – Mofizul's successful entry into the adult labour market (and later the adult institution of marriage); the effective way in which they managed their finances; and Maymana's acquisition of a government old-age pension, alongside broader social support from people in their neighbourhood.

In late 2003 Mofizul started work in the brickfields and earned a full male adult rate. In 2005, the brickfield owner suggested to a researcher that he considered paying this rate for doing 'small jobs' as charity. However, while Mofizul's impairment and health do mean that he has to work a longer day head-loading bricks than other casual labourers in order to earn this wage, the brickfield owner's perception of Mofizul as a charity case actually may be limiting his wage. Nonetheless, Mofizul was able to set aside a significant portion of his earnings each day with a money-guard at the brickfield. When work at the brickfields is unavailable during the rainy season, or when he felt too unwell to work there, he was able to find casual work in shops and as a houseboy. His savings grew, and in mid-2003 Mofizul and his mother used this money, along with Maymana's first pension instalment and some cash Maymana was 'minding' for her daughter (or, possibly, her daughter was minding for Maymana), to build their new house.

Both Maymana and Mofizul had suffered illness over the past two or three years, and often felt tired, but neither had faced a serious health shock. However, Mofizul had spent a significant amount on unsuccessful consultations with doctors about his back problem and in purchasing a brace, to which friends and relatives contributed. He found the brace to be uncomfortable and tiring to wear while working, so he abandoned it. In early 2005, Mofizul was forced to spend more on the diagnosis and treatment of his younger sister, who later died, leaving behind a young daughter and son.

Source: Hulme and Moore for CPRC (2008)

References

Barahona, C. and Levy, S. (2003) 'How to generate statistics and influence policy using participatory methods: reflections on work in Malawi 1999–2002', paper presented at Q-Squared in Practice: A Conference on Experiences of Combining Qualitative and Quantitative Methods in Poverty Appraisal, University of Toronto, May 2003.

Barrientos, A. (2003) *Non-contributory Pensions and the Well-being of Older People: Evidence on Multidimensional Deprivation from Brazil and South Africa*, Mimeo, IDPM, Manchester.

Barrientos, A. and Hulme, D. (2008) *Social Protection for the Poor and Poorest*, Palgrave Macmillian, London and New York.

Baulch, B. and Masset, E. (2003) 'Do monetary and nonmonetary indicators tell the same story about chronic poverty? A study of Vietnam in the 1990s', *World Development* 31(3): 441-454.

Blackden, M., Canagarajah, S., Klasen, S., and Lawson, D. (2007) 'Gender and growth in Africa: evidence and issues', in G. Mavrotas and A. Shorrocks (eds), *Advancing Development: Core Themes in Global Development*, Palgrave Macmillan, London and New York.

Calvo, C. and Dercon, S. (2008) 'Chronic poverty and all that: the measurement of poverty over time', in T. Addison, D. Hulme, and R. Kanbur (eds) *Poverty Dynamics: Inter-disciplinary Perspectives*, Oxford University Press, Oxford.

Chambers, R. (1994) 'The origins and practice of Participatory Rural Appraisal', *World Development* 22(7): 953-970.

Chen, S. and Ravallion, M. (2004) 'How have the world's poorest fared since the early 1980s?', *World Bank Research Observer* 19(2): 141-169.

Chen, S. and Ravallion, M. (2008) 'The developing world is poorer than we thought, but no less successful in the fight against poverty', *Policy Research Working Papers Series*, WPS no. 4703. Available from: http://papers.ssrn.com/sol3/papers.cfm?abstract_id=1259575 [accessed 5 July 2009]

Collier, P. (2007) *The Bottom Billion*, Oxford University Press, Oxford.

CPRC (2004) *The Chronic Poverty Report 2004-05*, Chronic Poverty Research Centre, Manchester. Available from: http://www.chronicpoverty.org/cpra-report-0405.php [accessed 5 July 2009]

CPRC (2008) *The Chronic Poverty Report 2008-0: Escaping Poverty Traps*, Chronic Poverty Research Centre, Manchester. Available from: http://www.chronicpoverty.org/cpra-report-0809.php [accessed 5 July 2009]

Deaton, A. (2001) 'Counting the world's poor: problems and possible solutions', *World Bank Research Observer* 16 (2): 125-147.

Godinot, X. (2000) *Participation Works: Involving People in Poverty in Policy Making*, ATD Fourth World, London.

Greig, A., Hulme, D. and Turner, M. (2007) *Challenging Global Inequality*, Palgrave Macmillian, London and New York.

Gunter, I. and Klasen, S. (2008) 'Measuring chronic non-income poverty', in T. Addison, D. Hulme and R. Kanbur (eds) *Poverty Dynamics: Inter-disciplinary Perspectives*, Oxford University Press, Oxford.

Hanlon, J., Barrientos, A., and Hulme, D. (2010) *Just give money to the poor: A revolution from below that challenges our attitudes to poverty, development and aid* (forthcoming), Kumarian Press, Sterling, US.

Hartmann, B. and Boyce, J. (1984) *A Quiet Violence*, University Press Limited, Dhaka.

Hulme, D. (2010) *Global Poverty* (forthcoming), Routledge, London.

Hulme, D. and McKay, A. (2008) 'Identifying and measuring chronic poverty: beyond monetary measures', in N. Kakwani, and J. Silber (eds), *The Many Dimensions of Poverty*, Palgrave Macmillian, London and New York.

Hulme, D. and Shepherd, A. (2003) 'Conceptualising chronic poverty', *World Development* 31(3): 403-424.

Hulme, D. and Toye, J. (2006) 'The case for cross-disciplinary social science research on poverty, inequality and well-being', *Journal of Development Studies* 42 (7): 1085-1107.

Krishna, A. (2009) 'Subjective assessments, participatory methods and poverty dynamics: the stages of progress method', (forthcoming), in T. Addison, D. Hulme, and R. Kanbur, *Poverty Dynamics: Measurement and Understanding from an Interdisciplinary Perspective*, Oxford University Press, Oxford.

Lawson, D. with Hulme, D., and Muwonge, J. (2008) 'Combining quantitative and qualitative to further our understanding of poverty dynamics: some methodological considerations', *International Journal of Multiple Research Methods* 2(2): 191-204.

Narayan, D., Patel, R., Schafft, K., Rademacher, A. and Koch-Schulte, S. (2000) *Voices of the Poor: Can Anyone Hear Us?* published for the World Bank, Oxford University Press, New York.

Noirhomme, M., Meessen, B., Griffiths, F., Por, I., Jacobs, B., Thor, R., Criel, B., and Van Damme, W. (2007) 'Improving access to hospital care for the poor: comparative analysis of four health equity funds in Cambodia', *Health Policy and Planning* 22: 246-62.

Palmer, N., Mueller, D. H., Gilson, L., Mills, A., Haines, A. (2004) 'Health financing to promote access in low income setting – how much do we know?' *The Lancet* 364: 1365-70.

Ravallion, M. and Chen, S. (2001) 'How did the world's poor fare in the 1990s?' *Review of Income and Wealth* 47 (3): 283-300.

Reddy, S. and Pogge, T. (2003) 'How not to count the poor', mimeo, Columbia University, New York.

Simmons, R. and Shiffman, J. (2006) 'Scaling up health service innovations: a framework for action', in R. Simmons, P. Fajans, L. Ghiron (eds) *Scaling up health service delivery: from pilot innovations to policies and programmes*, World Health Organization, Geneva.

WDR (1980) *World Development Report 1980*, World Bank, Washington D.C.

WDR (1990) *World Development Report 1990*, World Bank, Washington D.C.

WDR (2000) *World Development Report 2000*, World Bank, Washington D.C.

World Bank (2001) *World Development Report 2000/2001: Attacking Poverty*, World Bank, Washington D.C.

About the authors

David Hulme is Professor of Development Studies at the University of Manchester and Executive Director of the Brooks World Poverty Institute and the Chronic Poverty Research Centre. His recent publications include *Poverty Dynamics: Inter-disciplinary Perspectives* (2009, Oxford University Press with T. Addison and R. Kanbur), *Social Protection for the Poor and Poorest: Risks, Needs and Rights* (2008, Palgrave with A. Barrientos), *The Challenge of Global Inequality* (2006, Palgrave with A. Greig and M. Turner), a Special Issue of the *Journal of Development Studies* (2006) on 'Cross-disciplinary Research on Poverty and Inequality' and many articles in leading journals. His research interests include rural development; poverty analysis and poverty reduction strategies; finance for the poor and sociology of development.

David Lawson is Lecturer in Development Economics and Public Policy at the Institute for Development Policy and Management and Faculty Associate of Brooks World Poverty Institute, University of Manchester. He specializes in the analysis of poverty dynamics, particularly in relation to health and gender in Africa. He has published in leading journals with his work focused on the econometric analysis of panel datasets. More recently he has been utilizing Q-Squared methodologies (quantitative and qualitative) to further understandings of poverty. Recent publications include Health and *Development* (2009, Palgrave with I. Dutta and M. McGillivray).

PART I

Creating Knowledge about the Poorest

CHAPTER 2

Pro-poorest growth: A national household survey approach

Umar Serajuddin, Hassan Zaman, Ambar Narayan

This chapter uses the case study of Bangladesh to trace the patterns of pro-poor growth and poverty reduction between the years 2000 and 2005. During this period, the national poverty head count rate dropped from 49% to 40% while the extreme poverty rate remarkably dropped from 34% to 25%. This analysis demonstrates that the growth in Bangladesh during these five years was pro-poorest. It shows how during this period the growth rate in per capita expenditures among the extreme poor population was greater than the growth rates among both the moderate poor population and the non-poor population. Even among households that remained extremely poor, various socio-economic indicators exhibited substantial improvement. A decomposition analysis shows that the rise in expenditure levels resulted more from increases in returns to household characteristics, rather than from changes in household characteristics themselves. In addition, a gradual occupational shift from the agriculture to the non-agriculture sector appears to have played a vital role in the improvement in per capita expenditures.

Introduction

In this first chapter on 'creating knowledge' about the poorest we highlight, what might be perceived to be, a relatively common micro-based approach to analysing poverty through the use of national household survey data. In this case we consider the case of Bangladesh, where beginning in the 1990s, robust economic growth was accompanied by a sharp fall in poverty. In 1991–92, about 58% of the population was poor while by 2000, about 49% were below the poverty line. In the five years that followed, poverty declined at an even quicker pace. In 2005, 40% of the population was considered poor, declining by 1.9 percentage points per year. Yet regardless of these improvements, there are still around 58 million people living in poverty. Moreover, what happened to the extreme poor? Did the growth process leave them marginalized or did their welfare increase at the same pace as other groups in society? This chapter adopts a classical approach to analysing poverty, discussing the evolving nature of extreme poverty in Bangladesh between 2000 and 2005 and assesses changes in the standard of living of the extreme poor.

This chapter is organized as follows. First, we discuss the data and methodology used in the study. Next there is an analysis of trends in extreme poverty during 2000 to 2005. Third, we describe the trends in the various socioeconomic and demographic characteristics of the extreme poor, emphasizing the changes that took place between 2000 and 2005. In the penultimate section we move on to the results from multi variate estimation exercises, presenting results of the determinants of extreme poverty, before concluding.

Data and methodology

We use two repeated cross-sections – the Bangladesh Household Income and Expenditure Survey (HIES) data from the years 2000 and 2005 – to conduct our analysis. HIES 2005 is a nationally representative survey of 10,080 households in all 64 districts across Bangladesh; HIES 2000 is also a nationally representative survey for which 7,440 households were surveyed.

In this chapter we use consumption expenditure data to measure household welfare. We choose expenditure data over income data due to conventional reasons – expenditure data is usually more precisely measured and has stronger links to permanent income (Ravallion, 1994; Deaton, 1997). We use the poverty line defined in Yoshida et al. (2007), which employs the Cost of Basic Needs (CBN) method to calculate two absolute poverty lines representing the basic needs necessary for an individual to meet a minimum living standard. A household is deemed to be below the upper poverty line if the household expenditure on food and other essential non-durable items is below the cost of a consumption bundle of food and non-food items sufficient to meet the minimum per capita nutritional requirement of 2,122 calories per day. A household is below the lower poverty line, and considered as extreme poor, if the household expenditure on food and other essential non-durable items is even lower than the cost of a food basket that meets the minimum per capita nutritional requirement. To account for regional differences in prices and consumption patterns, poverty lines were estimated for each of the 16 different geographical areas or sampling strata.[1]

In the absence of panel data we cannot make straightforward comparisons of poverty dynamics between 2000 and 2005. With our repeated cross-sectional data, we are unable to distinguish among households that moved into, moved out of, or remained in extreme poverty. While comparing extreme poor households in 2000 and 2005, we compare households in the bottom three deciles in each of these years. This is because 34% of households were below the lower poverty line in 2000 and 25% in 2005. To see how the poorest among the extreme poor households fared, we also compare households in the bottom decile.

Trends in extreme poverty 2000–2005

Data from the HIES 2000 and 2005 suggest a considerable decline in the incidence of extreme poverty, with the national rate declining from 34.3% to 25.1%. Extreme poverty declined in both rural and urban areas by almost equal proportions (24% in rural and 26% in urban areas), though rural incidence continues to be much higher than urban incidence. In the 1980s and 1990s, the pace of poverty reduction was greater in the urban areas. The rural areas began catching up toward the end of the 1990s (Sen et al., 2007).

The extreme poverty statistics, however, show substantial regional variation. As Table 2.1 shows, the incidence of extreme poverty between 2000 and 2005 fell impressively in Dhaka and Chittagong divisions (from 34.6% to 19.9% in Dhaka, and from 27.5% to 16.1% in Chittagong). Sylhet showed considerable improvement as well. In Rajshahi, extreme poverty rates declined, although the overall levels still remained very high. In Khulna, the rate remained virtually stagnant, while in Barisal, it appeared to climb slightly. (Tellingly, in Barisal, the mean real per capita expenditures of households in the bottom 3 deciles remained virtually stagnant between 2000 and 2005.)[2]

When we examine the regional distribution of the extreme poor relative to their populations, a clearer picture of regional diversity emerges. Table 2.2 shows the population distribution and the extreme poor concentration by region. Dhaka, Rajshahi and Chittagong are the most populous regions in Bangladesh, and unsurprisingly, most extreme poor households also come from these regions. To look at the distribution of the extreme poor in the different regions relative to their populations, we divided the proportion of extreme poor in each region by the proportion of population in that area. A ratio greater than one suggests that the region has proportionately more extreme poor people relative to its population.

For example, in 2000, Khulna accounted for 11.7% of the national population and 11.0% of the total extreme poor population, the ratio of extreme poor share and population share being 0.94, implying that the extreme poor

Table 2.1 Incidence of extreme poverty in Bangladesh (%): poverty head count rates using the lower poverty line

	2000			2005		
	National	Rural	Urban	National	Rural	Urban
National	34.3	37.9	19.9	25.1	28.6	14.6
Barisal	34.7	36.0	21.7	35.6	37.2	26.4
Chittagong	27.5	30.2	16.8	16.1	18.7	8.1
Dhaka	34.6	43.7	15.8	19.9	26.1	9.6
Khulna	32.2	34.0	22.8	31.6	32.7	27.8
Rajshahi	42.8	44.0	34.5	34.5	35.6	28.5
Sylhet	26.7	26.1	35.2	20.8	22.3	11.0

Source: Yoshida, Narayan and Zaman (2007)

were slightly under-represented in Khulna relative to its population. In 2005, while 11.7% of the national population belonged to Khulna, 14.8% of the national extreme poor population came from Khulna. The ratio of extreme poor and population shares rose to 1.26, implying that in five years the relative share of extreme poor had risen in Khulna. In Chittagong and Dhaka, the relative shares of extreme poor fell during this time, while in Rajshahi and Barisal, they rose (for Barisal, it rose sharply from 1.01 to 1.41).

These figures suggest that while Dhaka and Chittagong performed strongly in extreme poverty reduction, Rajshahi, Khulna and Barisal lagged, and their relative positions worsened between 2000 and 2005. The extreme poor continue to be over-represented in these three regions. Since these figures might be influenced by inter-regional migration, a dynamic only panel data can explain, we should be cautious in interpreting them. For example, the less-poor households from Barisal might be migrating to Dhaka causing the proportion of extreme poor households in Barisal to rise. However, the population shares across regions remain quite stable across the 2005 and 2000 samples, suggesting that the figures are perhaps not strongly driven by migration patterns.

Table 2.2 also includes figures of the regional distribution of the population in the bottom expenditure decile. Barisal and Khulna's share of those in the bottom decile rose sharply (in Barisal from 6.1% to 15.2%, and in Khulna from 5.6% to 14.1%).

Real per capita expenditures, provided in Table 2.3, indicate a greater than average improvement in the economic status of the bottom 3 deciles and the bottom decile between 2000 and 2005. The bottom 3 deciles of the population experienced a yearly average real per capita expenditures growth of 2.52% (total of 12.6% between 2000 and 2005), with the bottom 10% experiencing an annual growth of 2.94% (total of 14.7%). This compares with an annual increase of 2.37% for the whole population. While for the population as a

Table 2.2 Regional shares of extreme poor population relative to total population and share of bottom decile population relative to total population in Bangladesh (2000–2005)

	2000					2005				
	Population share (%)	Extreme poor share (%)	Ratio of Extreme poor/population	Bottom decile share (%)	Ratio of Bottom decile/population	Population share (%)	Extreme poor share (%)	Ratio of Extreme poor/population	Bottom decile share (%)	Ratio of Bottom decile/population
Barisal	7.1	7.1	1.01	6.1	0.87	6.4	9.1	1.41	15.2	2.37
Chittagong	20.0	16.1	0.80	17.3	0.86	19.3	12.3	0.64	10.7	0.55
Dhaka	31.4	31.6	1.01	33.9	1.08	32.2	25.5	0.79	25.1	0.78
Khulna	11.7	11.0	0.94	5.6	0.48	11.7	14.8	1.26	14.1	1.20
Rajshahi	23.4	29.2	1.25	34.5	1.47	24.0	33.0	1.37	31.0	1.29
Sylhet	6.4	5.0	0.78	2.6	0.40	6.3	5.3	0.83	4.0	0.63

Source: Yoshida, Narayan and Zaman (2007)

Table 2.3 Mean per capita monthly real expenditures in Bangladesh (in Taka)

		2000	2005	Average Annual Growth in Mean (%)
All	National	1057	1183	2.37
	Rural	963	1078	2.39
	Urban	1431	1500	0.96
Bottom 3 deciles	National	548	617	2.52
	Rural	536	603	2.50
	Urban	611	675	2.09
Bottom decile	National	432	495	2.94
	Rural	425	488	2.94
	Urban	466	520	2.32

Source: Yoshida, Narayan and Zaman (2007)

whole mean urban per capita expenditures was around 40% larger than rural expenditures in 2005, for the bottom 3 deciles the difference was only about 12% and for the bottom decile only 6.5%.

Higher than average growth *rates* for the bottom three (or the lowest) decile however does not necessarily imply that the *size* of the consumption gap between the extreme poor and the rest of the population declined. Figure 2.1 shows this distinction: while the *ratio* of high and low percentiles of per capita real consumption changed little from 2000 to 2005, the *difference* or the size of the gaps between percentiles increased. For instance, the difference between the 90th and the 10th percentiles of consumption increased from 1,284 to 1,434 Taka (at 2000 prices), even as the *ratio* between the 90th and 10th percentiles remained almost unchanged (at 3:5). This illustrates the fact that even a higher than average rate of consumption growth among the poorest may not be enough to close the gap with the non-poor, when the gaps are large to start with.

The extreme poor have significantly lower consumption variability during the course of a year than other households.[3] Figure 2.1 illustrates the per capita expenditures across different time periods for rural and urban households for 2005. The average per capita expenditures of urban households in general show a lot more variation than those of rural households, while for both rural and urban bottom 3 decile households, expenditures remain remarkably stable across the year (for mean per capita consumption of under 600 Taka, the standard deviations across time intervals is less than 20 Taka for both rural and urban samples).[4] The lack of substantial seasonal variation in per capita expenditures could have several interpretations. One possible interpretation would be that factors such as increased non-agricultural employment opportunities, migration, and government safety net programmes have helped reduce the variability of expenditures across the year.[5] Alternatively, the more likely explanation is that this stability suggests widespread chronic or 'structural' poverty where any dips beyond a certain minimum threshold would lead to serious food deficiencies.

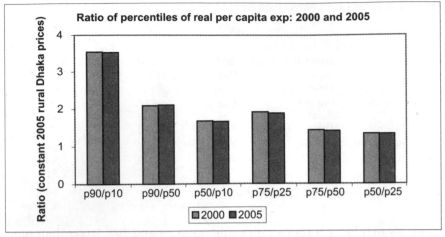

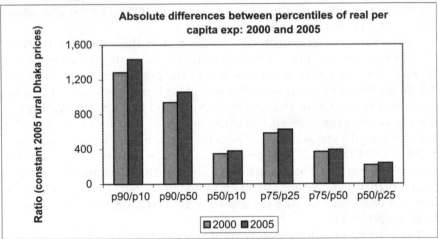

Figure 2.1 Gaps between percentiles of per capita real consumption in Bangladesh (2000 and 2005)

Evolving profiles of the extreme poor: Descriptive statistics

In this section, we analyse different characteristics of the bottom 3 deciles and bottom decile households between 2000 and 2005. We first discuss certain key welfare and asset related indicators, which provide insights into how households who are considered extremely poor by consumption standards have fared in terms of other critical dimensions of welfare over those years. We then discuss demographic, education, land, occupation, and remittance related attributes of households, as potential determinants of consumption poverty.

Household assets and demographics

We find that the higher than average per capita expenditure growth for the extreme poor households, discussed in the previous section, was matched by an overall increase in their standard of living along most dimensions. Figure 2.2 illustrates the improvements between 2000 and 2005 for extreme poor households (a larger spread/area of the hexagon indicates improvements). While these households fail to meet their daily caloric intake requirements, it is interesting that their lives appear to have improved when measured by asset ownership, electricity access, safe latrine access, literacy levels, and occupational characteristics. Even households in the bottom made substantial gains, as shown in Figure 2.2.

Table 2.4 presents summary statistics of some basic household characteristics. An important indicator of household assets, especially in rural areas is livestock ownership and the extreme poor (both bottom 3 decile and bottom decile households) appear to have increased their livestock assets values significantly more than the average households' increase. The increase appears to have come both from existing owners increasing their livestock holdings and from an increasing number of households owning livestock.

Housing conditions have also improved substantially for the extreme poor. The improvements are especially pronounced for the bottom decile households: in 2000, 11.3% had houses with corrugated iron sheets or cement walls, whereas in 2005, nearly three times as many households had corrugated iron sheets or cement walls. The increases are much greater in the rural areas than in urban areas. The bottom decile households also made significant improvements in terms of access to safe latrines and electricity connections. Based on these household indicators, the gap in living standards between the bottom

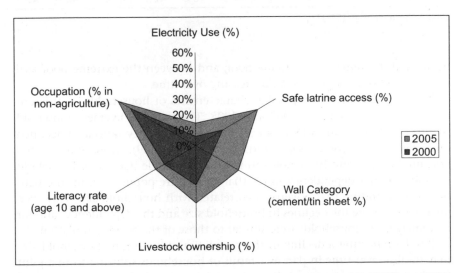

Figure 2.2 Welfare indicators of the bottom decile households in Bangladesh (2000 and 2005)

Table 2.4 Basic indicators of household assets and demographics of the Bangladeshi sample (2000–2005)

	All households		Bottom 3 deciles		Bottom decile	
	2000	2005	2000	2005	2000	2005
Assets						
Average real value of livestock (Taka)	4280	5281	2623	3919	1704	3037
Livestock ownership (%)	35.2	40.3	31.6	42.5	25.3	37.0
Wall of dwelling (% with cement/tin sheet)	37.7	55.2	17.4	33.9	11.3	31.8
Roof of dwelling (% with cement/tin sheet)	76.4	89.9	64.5	81.6	57.9	78.3
Safe latrine use (%)	52.0	69.3	29.4	50.0	20.2	46.2
Electricity connection (%)	31.2	44.2	10.0	20.2	6.1	14.7
TV ownership (%)	15.8	26.5	1.8	6.7	0.7	3.8
Phone ownership (%)	1.5	12.2	0.0	0.9	0.0	0.3
Demographics						
Household size	5.18	4.85	5.55	5.27	5.63	5.42
Dependency ratio	0.77	0.69	1.10	0.97	1.22	1.10
Number of children	2.1	1.8	2.7	2.4	2.9	2.7
Number of male adults	1.6	1.5	1.4	1.4	1.3	1.3
Number of female adults	1.5	1.5	1.5	1.5	1.5	1.5
Head female (yes)	0.09	0.10	0.09	0.08	0.12	0.10
Head married (yes)	0.90	0.90	0.91	0.91	0.88	0.89
Head widowed (yes)	0.06	0.07	0.07	0.06	0.10	0.09
Head divorced/separated (yes)	0.01	0.01	0.01	0.01	0.01	0.01
Head never married (yes)	0.03	0.02	0.01	0.02	0.01	0.02
Head non-Muslim (yes)	0.09	0.12	0.07	0.12	0.06	0.10
Age of head (years)	44.5	45.3	42.7	43.0	43.0	42.4

Source: Yoshida et al. (2007)

decile and the remaining extreme poor, and between the extreme poor and other households, appears to be decreasing over time.

Table 2.4 presents demographic characteristics of households in different expenditure groups across 2000 and 2005. The national average household size has declined from 5.18 to 4.85 and the dependency ratio also declined quite significantly for all households (from 0.77 to 0.69).[6] Households in the bottom 3 deciles and households in the bottom decile had larger household sizes and higher dependency ratios than the entire population, in line with the general finding that poverty is correlated with household size. However, on a positive note the declines in household size and the dependency ratio for extremely poor households were similar to those of the entire population.

Besides reflecting a decline in the population growth rate, household size may decline over time in part as a result of households splitting from a joint family structure to a more nuclear setup. It may also decline due to increased migration – any member who has been away for more than three months is no longer considered part of that household. A closer look at Table 2.5, however, suggests that the decline in household size is associated with a decline in the number of children in a household, rather than a decline in the number of male or female adults. Also, the decline in household size is accompanied by a decrease in the dependency ratio. Thus, the decline in household size likely represents a more fundamental demographic shift (rather than household splitting or migration), related to Bangladesh's impressive performance in lowering its population growth rate from 2.9% per year in the 1970s to 1.5% by the late 1990s. This was also a period when the total fertility rate (TFR) declined from 7 in 1975 to 3.2 in 1999/2000 (Sen et al., 2007).

Land characteristics

Land is a key determinant of household welfare in Bangladesh, particularly in rural areas. In 2005, about 45% of all rural households were landless, and landlessness among extreme poor households was even higher (almost 63%). Table 2.5 presents extreme poverty headcounts by land ownership in rural areas across 2000 and 2005. Interestingly, the incidence of extreme poverty declined for households belonging to *all* land ownership categories – including the landless (from 49.2% to 39.3%), and the functionally landless (from 42.2% to 32.7%).

The decline in extreme poverty incidence for all land ownership categories likely indicates the broad-based economic growth process in Bangladesh between 2000 and 2005, which may have translated into economic gains for even the comparatively more disadvantaged households in terms of landholdings.

In spite of this broad-based improvement, the *reduction* in percentage terms in extreme poverty was the lowest among the landless/functionally landless – the share of this group in the rural population of extreme poor increased

Table 2.5 Incidence of extreme rural poverty (%) by agricultural land ownership in Bangladesh

	2000			2005		
	Population share	Extreme poor share	Extreme poverty headcount	Population share	Extreme poor share	Extreme poverty headcount
Landless:<0.05 acres	48.02	62.33	49.2	45.8	62.98	39.3
Functionally Landless: 0.05-0.49 acres	12.96	14.45	42.2	15.92	18.19	32.7
Marginal: 0.5 to 1.49 acres	17.47	14.1	30.6	18.78	13.02	19.8
Small:1.5 to 2.5 acres	9.15	5.52	22.9	8.79	3.59	11.7
Medium & large >2.5 acres	12.39	3.61	11.0	10.71	2.22	5.9

Source: Yoshida et al. (2007)

from 77% in 2000 to 81% in 2005. Moreover, the distribution of land has changed little over time, with the result that the proportion of landless/functionally landless in the rural population has remained unchanged at around 61%. From that fact, it is evident how important land ownership is for poverty reduction.

Education

Table 2.6 shows extreme poverty incidence against the educational attainments of household heads. The distribution of household heads' educational status does not change much between 2000 and 2005, and a majority of household heads had no formal education. Among extreme poor households 77.3% of household heads were without any formal education. However, the extreme poverty incidence declined for all educational groups similar to the relationship between extreme poverty incidence and land ownership – further evidence of the broad-based improvements that took place during this period.

While the education levels of household heads might be improving relatively slowly, Bangladesh's overall education levels have been steadily increasing over the past two decades. Though a large portion of the population (just under half) still remains illiterate, literacy and school attendance rates have increased tremendously, and for a low-income country the attendance rates are high in Bangladesh. Among children aged 6 to 10 years and aged 11 to 16 years, school attendance rates in Bangladesh have achieved both rural-urban parity and gender parity (Sri Lanka is the only other country in South Asia to have achieved similar results). Even more impressive is the fact that rural-urban parity and gender parity are evident even among extreme poor households.

For individuals in extreme poor households, literacy levels are much lower than for the entire population (in 2005 literacy rates are 56.7% for all households, and only 34.8% for extreme poor households). However, what bodes well for the future is the high school attendance rates for children of age

Table 2.6 Incidence of extreme poverty (%) by educational attainment of household head in Bangladesh

	2000			2005		
	Population share	Extreme poor share	Extreme poverty headcount	Population share	Extreme poor share	Extreme poverty headcount
No Education	57.3	77.1	46.3	53.5	77.3	36.3
Below class 5	4.9	3.9	27.6	4.9	3.8	19.5
Class 5	10.5	8.1	26.5	10.6	8.1	19.3
Class 6 to 9	13.8	8.0	20.0	15.0	8.0	13.4
Higher Level	13.6	2.8	7.2	16.0	2.8	4.4

Source: Yoshida et al. (2007)

groups 6 to 10 as well as 11 to 15. By 2005, attendance rate for children of age 6 to 10 was 80% overall, and 71.3% for those belonging to extreme poor households.

Occupation

During the 1990s, the decline in poverty rates was attributed to the gradual shift in the labour force from agriculture to typically more lucrative non-agricultural employment (Mahmud, 2006; Sen et al., 2007). This change continued during 2000–2005; in 2000 approximately half of the households in the bottom 3 deciles listed agriculture as their main occupation, and this proportion declined to around 43% in 2005. Mahmud (2006) further argued that during the 1990s, within non-agricultural employment itself, there was a shift from relatively low-productivity self-employed activities to higher productivity enterprises and to non-agricultural wage employment. This phenomenon appears to have slowed during the 2000–2005 period, with non-agriculture self-employment figures remaining relatively stable or showing very modest gains.

To analyse trends between 2000 and 2005, we divide occupational categories into five broad groups: *(i)* agriculture day labour, *(ii)* agriculture self-employed (farmer), *(iii)* non-agriculture day labour, *(iv)* non-agriculture self-employed, and *(v)* non-agriculture salaried. A majority of extreme poor households (almost 60%) rely on daily labour for their sustenance. In the absence of reliable earnings data, we define a household head's main occupation as the occupation in which s/he worked the most hours. While, for the entire population, there has been a subtle shift to non-agricultural occupations, the shift is more pronounced for the bottom three decile households and is even substantial for the bottom decile households.[7]

For the bottom three expenditure deciles, the proportion of household heads with agriculture day labour as their main occupation declined from 35.8% (in 2000) to 33% (in 2005); correspondingly, the non-agriculture day labour group showed an increase from 21.2% to 25%. The agriculture self-employed group declined from 19.3% to 16.1%, while non-agriculture self-employed households increased from 16.6% to 17.1% between 2000 and 2005. Salaried employees rose from 7.2% to 8.8%. For bottom decile households, the proportion of heads with main occupation as agriculture day labour fell from 43.6% to 36.3%, while non-agriculture day labour increased sharply from 21.9% to 29.5%. This shift probably greatly contributed to their increased economic welfare, since non-agricultural returns are higher, even for daily labour.

Instead of the main occupation of the household head, if we consider the main occupation in the household (as defined by the maximum number of hours worked in an occupation by any household member),[8] the shift towards non-agriculture is more prominent. This may be because the household head is more prone to stay in the same profession over time than other members of the household. Sen and Hulme (2005) argue that the reduction in agriculture activity (especially self-employed agriculture) is to a certain extent attributable to the increased agricultural productivity that has freed up farm household labour for non-farm activities.

Table 2.7 illustrates extreme poverty headcounts by the main occupational categories of household heads, which suggest that extreme poverty fell for each occupational class.[9] Day labourers continue to suffer most strongly from extreme poverty – in 2005 extreme poverty incidence was 52.1% among agricultural day labourers and 44.5% among non-agricultural day labourers. As expected, the extreme poverty rate is lowest when the household head has salaried employment (Osmani et al. (2003) have similar findings using HIES 2000 data).

Part of the explanation of why the shift from agriculture to non-agricultural employment may have contributed to lower extreme poverty incidence lies in the fact that the mean real wage rates for non-agriculture day-labourers remained about 40% higher than those for agricultural day labourers.[10] Though real wages within agriculture and non-agricultural sectors do not appear to have changed much across 2000 and 2005, there remains substantial differences across sectors.

Female participation in the labour force is still extremely low in Bangladesh; approximately 13% of all households had a female member participating in the labour force in 2005. Interestingly, in poorer households, female labour force participation is higher. Among households in the bottom 3 deciles around 15% of the households have female participation, while for the poorest 10% of households female participation is at 18.3%. There is considerable rural-urban disparity in female participation. For example, in 2005, among the bottom 3 decile households in rural areas, 12.7% had female participation in the labour force, while for their urban counterparts, female participation was 24.5%. Among the bottom decile households, female participation in both rural areas (16.3%) and urban areas (27.3%) were higher, with similar rural-urban differences.

Table 2.7 Incidence of extreme poverty (%) by main occupation of household head in Bangladesh

Main occupation of household head	All households		Bottom 3 deciles		Bottom decile		Extreme poverty headcount	
	2000	2005	2000	2005	2000	2005	2000	2005
Agriculture day labour	20.1	18.1	35.8	33.0	43.6	36.3	63.7	52.1
Agriculture self-employed	26.4	23.8	19.3	16.1	13.8	12.0	28.2	18.1
Non-agriculture day labour	16.0	16.8	21.2	25.0	21.9	29.5	50.0	44.5
Non-agriculture self-employed	22.0	22.9	16.6	17.1	15.3	15.9	29.7	24.3
Non-agriculture salaried	15.5	18.4	7.2	8.8	5.5	6.4	22.3	15.6

Source: Yoshida et al. (2007)

The female employment patterns suggest that changing employment patterns are unlikely to have contributed substantially to the observed declines in extreme poverty during 2000–2005. Overall, there has been a movement to more lucrative and stable salaried jobs, with the per centage of women with salaried jobs rising from 35.7% to 43.3%. This shift, however, is limited to the non-poor section of the economy; among women belonging to the bottom three decile households there was a very small increase in percentage holding salaried jobs (22.5 to 24%), while for bottom decile households there was virtually no change. A large share of extreme poor women remain employed as day labourers in agricultural and non-agricultural activities, where real wage rates continue to be very low. With female daily wage rates being only half of that of males it is doubtful that this made much of a contribution to the reduction in extreme poverty.

Remittances and micro-credit

Remittances are an important and growing source of household income in Bangladesh. Figures from the Government's Bureau of Manpower, Employment and Training (BMET) indicate that from 2001 to 2006, the official receipts of total foreign remittances have more than doubled from $2 billion to $5 billion. Figures from HIES 2000 and 2005 also show substantial increases in foreign remittance receipts, although the increases captured are not as impressive as the BMET figures. For example, the mean yearly receipt of real foreign remittances (per household) went up from 4,852 Taka to 5,689 Taka, an increase of about 20% over the 5 years (including all households, whether they receive remittance or not). Moreover, foreign remittances are unlikely to have directly influenced the welfare of extreme poor households since very few of them have direct access to foreign remittances[11] (Table 2.8). However, given the limitations of cross-section data, these statistics cannot take into account extreme poor households who have received remittances and consequently moved out of extreme poverty.

Table 2.8 Domestic and foreign remittance receipts by poverty groups in Bangladesh

	All households		Bottom 3 deciles		Bottom decile	
	2000	*2005*	*2000*	*2005*	*2000*	*2005*
Households receiving domestic remittances (%)	18.9	21.1	15.1	18.4	12.8	14.5
Households receiving foreign remittances (%)	8.6	8.8	3.7	2.8	2.4	1.3
Real value of domestic remittances (taka/year)	2150.1	2151.5	799.0	900.5	548.4	594.9
Real value of foreign remittances (taka/year)	4851.9	5688.8	757.2	783.6	452.2	544.2

Source: Yoshida et al. (2007)

A much larger proportion of the extremely poor households, however, have access to domestic remittances, and this figure has increased over time (from 15.1% to 18.4% between 2000 and 2005). The mean real value of domestic remittances received per household increased from about 800 Taka to 900 Taka a year (which is about 12.5% of mean expenditures for *all* bottom 3 decile households).

The remittance story is especially important if we consider certain lagging regions. In greater Rangpur, for example, extreme poverty incidence is around 41%, much higher than the national average (25%). This is also an area where domestic remittance receipts are far lower (less than 10%) than the rest of the country (about 22%). The pattern with foreign remittances is similar i.e. the regions in the Western part of Bangladesh that have progressed least in poverty reduction also receive least remittances.

Particularly interesting from this book's perspective, and some of the forthcoming chapters focus on microfinance, is that access to micro-credit doubled between 2000 and 2005. Since we do not have household level data on micro-credit access from HIES, we use data on microfinance coverage in each thana (sub-district) and correlate this with changes in poverty in those areas. Table 2.9 shows that higher levels of extreme poverty reduction is associated with higher growth of microfinance within a thana. For example, between 2000 and 2005 extreme poverty incidence fell by 5.8 percentage points in areas that have had less than 50% growth in micro-credit coverage, while in areas where micro-credit membership more than doubled, extreme poverty fell by 14.6 percentage points.

Multivariate results

As is common with a micro-econometric approach to poverty analysis we now complement the descriptive analysis with econometric insights on potential key determinants of extreme poverty. We complete the analysis by assessing how important each of these factors are, relative to each other and *net* of the effect of other factors, using multivariate regressions. While some main

Table 2.9 Increase in microfinance membership and changes in extreme poverty incidence in Bangladesh

Increase in microfinance members	Extreme poverty incidence (%)		
	2000	2005	Change
<50%	34.3	28.5	-5.8
50%–75%	32.3	22.7	-9.6
75%–100%	36.1	27.3	-8.8
>100%	39.2	24.6	-14.6

Source: Yoshida et al. (2007)

findings from our multivariate estimations are summarized here, more detailed results with a full description of the estimation methods are available
in a separate paper (Serajuddin et al., 2007). We estimate a standard reduced
form equation of determinants of consumption expenditure for the full sample of households using a basic linear econometric specification (Ordinary
Least Squares or OLS). The dependent variable is per capita consumption expenditure adjusted for spatial price differences, while independent variables
consist of household level demographic and socio-economic variables (such as
household size and composition, land ownership, education levels of household members, occupational status of household head, remittance receipts)
and regional level controls.[12] Since our interest lies in identifying which factors are important in *determining* economic well-being, we take some care to
select independent variables that are likely to be exogenous, which is to say
less likely to be influenced *by* the current economic status of a household.[13]

Our results indicate that demographic factors such as household size and
household composition are key determinants of extreme poverty in both 2000
and 2005. We find that households with more children and a higher number
of adult females tend to be worse off, while the number of male adults in the
household has little impact on consumption expenditures. If one controls
for other factors, the education of household heads seems to have a substantial influence on household welfare. Even households with heads who have
had minimal education tend to be better off than households where the head
has no education. Receiving domestic remittances is associated with higher
expenditure levels; and foreign remittances, even though received by much
fewer households, are even more important in reducing poverty.

The straightforward correlates in Table 2.9 above indicate that increasing
microfinance coverage at the thana level is associated with lower extreme poverty incidence; and the multivariate analysis shows similar results, although
the relationship is much weaker. In rural areas, the effect of the variable representing microfinance *density* at the thana level (in 2003) on household consumption is insignificant. However, interestingly, an *increase* in microfinance
membership (between 2003 and 2005) is associated with lower incidence of
extreme poverty. What this indicates is that conditional on existing coverage
in 2003, growth in microfinance membership during 2003 and 2005 was associated with a reduction in extreme poverty levels.

More than half of the population of Bangladesh are employed as daily
wage labourers and significant differences exist between them and the other
households. However, the relatively adverse consequences of being employed
as either agricultural or non-agricultural day labour appear to have declined
between 2000 and 2005 in both rural and urban areas, indicating that returns to low-skilled jobs have increased over time.[14] This result comes through
clearly when we conduct the decomposition exercise of expenditures growth
between 2000 and 2005 for the extreme poor (using the Oaxaca and Ranson
(1994) decomposition method).

More generally, the findings from the decompositions reveal that consumption growth was spurred more by changes in 'returns' to household characteristics, such as education, occupation or demographics, than due to a change in the levels of the characteristics. In other words, the improvement in welfare, or the reduction in extreme poverty rates, is attributed more to higher returns for a given level of endowment than to changes in the endowments themselves. This is consistent with the findings of the section on descriptive statistics that suggest broad-based economic improvements occurred between 2000 and 2005, resulting in higher welfare among households with different levels of endowment.

Summary of findings

The chapter has highlighted a relatively common micro-econometric approach to analysing poverty and extreme poverty in Bangladesh. It is important to distinguish between extreme poverty and moderate poverty because of the relative severity of the conditions faced by the extreme poor. Extreme poor households are those that would not be able to meet a daily 2,122 calorie per capita intake requirement even if they spent *all* their income on food only. In 2005, the mean real per capita expenditure of extreme poor households (about a fourth of the total population of Bangladesh) remained about 40% lower than that of households who were moderately poor. The expenditure levels of households in the bottom decile, the poorest of the extreme poor, were even lower. In 2005, the average per capita expenditures of bottom decile households was about 60% lower than households that are moderately poor (this, however, was an improvement from 2000, when the bottom decile expenditures were about 80% lower).

Extreme poverty in Bangladesh has traditionally been considered as being chronic or persistent in nature, with little promise of upward mobility for the extreme poor (Sen and Hulme, 2005). Yet, the intriguing aspect of poverty reduction in Bangladesh in the past few years has been the fact that overall growth has been 'pro-poorest'. Households below the lower poverty line and even the households in the bottom decile, have experienced higher than average growth in per capita expenditures than the typical household in Bangladesh.

Moreover the poorest have experienced substantial improvements in a number of socio-economic indicators between 2000 and 2005. For example, on average, households in the bottom three deciles in 2005 had higher literacy, sanitation levels and better housing conditions compared with the bottom three deciles in 2000. The same pattern was evident for bottom decile households as well. Many of these gains were greater, in percentage terms, than for the average population.

Our poverty analysis shows that extreme poverty remains associated with having larger household size (particularly having a higher number of children or female adults), having less education and small amounts of land, and being involved in low productivity jobs, particularly manual labour, both agricultural and non-agricultural. There is also some evidence that increase in microfinance access at the thana level is associated with reductions in extreme poverty. A decomposition analysis suggests that the rise in expenditure levels resulted more from increases in *returns* to household characteristics, rather than from changes or improvements in the characteristics themselves.

A period of steady broad-based growth enabled Bangladesh to make notable reductions in extreme poverty incidence during 2000 to 2005. Yet, the country still faces daunting challenges with about a quarter of the population, or around 35 million people, still living in extreme poverty. Moreover there are significant regional differences in the reduction in extreme poverty. Hence public policy needs to retain its focus on the poor in general, and on the extreme poor in particular. First, the government should focus on creating the enabling environment for job creation in the Western regions of Bangladesh (Rajshahi, Khulna and Barisal) where gains in poverty reduction have been least. This could include greater investments in infrastructure development, encouraging migration and private investment incentives in those regions. Second, special attention must be paid to increase female participation rates in the labour market and help narrow the male-female wage rate gaps. Third, investment in social programmes such as family planning and female education need to be enhanced given the links between small household size and better education and poverty reduction. Fourth, given the narrow margins under which the extreme poor live it is essential that food security policy be strengthened so that the impact of macro and natural shocks are limited on this highly vulnerable group.

Endnotes

1. For a detailed exposition on poverty measurement using the HIES 2005 and 2000, see Yoshida et al. (2007).
2. In urban Khulna and urban Barisal the situation actually worsened with the extreme poverty rates rising in urban Khulna from 22.8% to 27.8% and in urban Barisal from 21.7% to 26.4%. The situation may have worsened in relative terms in these urban areas due to the large migration of extreme poor from rural to urban areas in these three regions. We cannot compute the extent of this phenomenon with the present data. We also must be cautious about interpreting the regional poverty estimates at the rural and urban level since our data is representative at the rural and urban level nationally, or at the regional level. Lower levels of aggregation are not wholly representative. For example, the extreme poverty figures for urban Sylhet in 2000 are not fully representative due to a very small sample size.
3. For HIES 2005, households were interviewed over 18 rounds, each round lasting 20 days. A separate set of households were interviewed at each round, but caution was maintained so as to preserve the geographical

representativeness of the sample. Paxson (1993) uses a similar dataset on Thailand for her work on consumption smoothing.

4. When we examined trends across local (Bengali) calendar months stable per capita expenditure patterns emerged as well. Also, within the same year, the extreme poverty headcount appears not to fluctuate substantially across rounds. The analysis based on HIES 2000 shows similar patterns. In both 2005 and 2000, the expenditures of moderate poor households show similar stability across time.

5. Rahman and Razzaque (1998) argue that the poor in Bangladesh have become not only vulnerable to income shocks, but even resilient to them.

6. The dependency ratio of households is calculated by dividing the number of household members below the age of 15 and above the age of 64 by the number of members aged between 15 and 64.

7. When we analysed rural and urban households separately, for rural households we saw a movement from agriculture to non-agriculture activities similar to the overall national dynamics. For urban households, however, the occupation choice patterns remain quite stable, with a marginal increase in agricultural activities.

8. In about 90% of cases the household head works the maximum number of hours within the household.

9. For example, the extreme poverty headcount for household heads whose main occupation was farming or agriculture self-employed declined from 28.2% to 18% . This decline might be partly attributable to ill-performing extremely poor farming households moving away to other occupations.

10. The annual increase in the real wage rate for agriculture day labour was about 1%, while for non-agriculture day labour, it was about 0.25%. Al-Samarrai (2006) also comes up with similar figures for the real wage rates of day labourers. Without disaggregating between agriculture and non-agriculture day labour, he calculated the average annual real wage growth rate to be 0.5% .

11. Foreign remittances, of course, would have an impact on the lives of the extreme poor to the degree that they benefit from the increased overall spending in the economy.

12. We also estimate an alternative specification, namely probit regressions of the probability of being extreme poor on a similar set of independent variables. The results from these estimations are qualitatively similar to those using the OLS specification.

13. The need to limit independent variables to those more likely to be exogenous led to an exclusion of factors like housing conditions, connection to electricity or gas, and health/education outcomes among children. While all of these factors contribute a household's overall well-being, they are more likely to be a *result* rather than a *determinant* of economic well-being.

14. Part of the increase in returns to agricultural daily wage labour, however, might be due to movement of low-productivity households away from agriculture.

References

Al-Samarrai, S. (2006) 'Changes in employment in Bangladesh, 2000–2005: The impacts on poverty and gender equity', *Background Paper for the Bangladesh Poverty Assessment*, South Asia Region, World Bank.

Deaton, A. (1997) *The Analysis of Household Surveys: A Microeconometric Approach to Development Policy*, The Johns Hopkins University Press, Baltimore.

Mahmud, W. (2006) 'Employment, incomes and poverty: prospects of pro-poor growth in Bangladesh', in S. Ahmed and W. Mahmud (eds), *Growth and Poverty: The Development Experience of Bangladesh*, University Press Limited, Dhaka.

Oaxaca, R. L. and Ranson, M. (1994) 'On discrimination and the decomposition of wage differentials', *Journal of Econometrics* 61: 2–21.

Osmani, S. R., Mahmud, W., Dagdeviern, H. and Seth, A. (2003) *The Macroeconomics of Poverty Reduction: The Case Study of Bangladesh*, Asia-Pacific Regional Program on Macroeconomics of Poverty Reduction, United Nations Development Program, Kathmandu, Nepal/Dhaka, Bangladesh.

Paxson, C. H. (1993) 'Consumption and income seasonality in Thailand', *Journal of Political Economy* 102: 437–467.

Rahman, A. and Razzaque, A. (1998) 'On reaching the hard core poor: redefining the NGO strategy', Bangladesh Institute of Development Studies, Dhaka.

Ravallion, M. (1994) *Poverty Comparisons*, Harwood Academic Press, Chur, Switzerland.

Sen, B. and Hulme, D. (2005) *Chronic Poverty in Bangladesh: Tales of Ascent, Descent, Marginality and Persistence*, Bangladesh Institute of Development Studies (BIDS)/Chronic Poverty Research Centre (CPRC)/Institute for Development Policy and Management (DPM), Dhaka/Manchester.

Sen, B., Mujeri, M. K. and Shahabuddin, Q. (2007) 'Explaining pro-poor growth in Bangladesh: puzzles, evidence, and implications', in T. Besley and L. J. Cord (eds), *Delivering on the Promise of Pro-Poor Growth: Insights and Lessons from Country Experiences*, World Bank Publications, Washington D.C.

Serajuddin, U., Zaman, H. and Narayan, A. (2007) 'Determinants of extreme poverty in Bangladesh', background paper to the Bangladesh Poverty Assessment report, World Bank, Washington D.C.

Yoshida, N., Narayan, A. and Zaman, H. (2007) '*Trends and patterns of poverty in Bangladesh in recent years*', mimeo, World Bank, Washington D.C.

About the author

Umar Serajuddin is an Economist at the Social and Economic Development Group in the Middle East and North Africa (MENA) region of the World Bank. Earlier he worked at the Poverty Reduction and Economic Management group in the South Asia region of the World Bank. His work focuses on poverty and inequality analysis, labour markets, and on monitoring and evaluation.

Ambar Narayan is a Senior Economist in the Poverty Reduction Group in the central network of the World Bank, currently working on distributional analysis and impact evaluations of Bank programmes. As an economist in the South Asia Region of the World Bank until 2008, Mr. Narayan focused on the analysis of poverty, inequality and their links with economic growth, monitoring and evaluation, and the analysis of public expenditures and safety net programmes in a number of countries. He has also been involved in analysing the impact of natural disasters and designing and implementing emergency projects of the World Bank in Sri Lanka, Pakistan and Bangladesh. Mr. Narayan has been one of the lead authors of poverty assessment reports in Bangladesh and Sri Lanka and co-authored articles for scholarly publications, including books and academic journals. He holds a PhD in Economics from Brown University, USA.

Hassan Zaman is an economist at the World Bank. After working for BRAC, Bangladesh, and completing his PhD in Economics at the University of Sussex, he joined at the World Bank headquarters in Washington, D.C. working in their budget office.

CHAPTER 3

A 'Q-Squared' approach to enhancing our understanding of the chronically poor[1]

David Lawson

In recent years there has been an increased focus on analysing poverty through 'mixed methods'. This chapter combines qualitative and quantitative ('Q-squared') methods, drawn from economics and anthropology, to deepen the understanding of extreme and chronic poverty in Uganda. It utilizes a nationally representative panel dataset and life history analysis to explore the lives of chronically poor households (who make up around a fifth of Uganda's population).

The chapter illustrates the insights that mixed methods can generate and reveals that certain key factors have played a major role in poverty dynamics in Uganda. For example, the statistical association between ill health (and in particular HIV/AIDS) and chronic poverty has commonly been highlighted at the micro-econometric level. The life histories indicated that such interconnections impact on household coping mechanisms and on preferences relating to the types of assets sold. In 'times of crisis', luxury goods, such as radios, were commonly sold first, but the willingness to sell assets was dependent on the age of household heads and the location of the household. For example, older household heads were substantially less willing than younger heads to sell any livestock – firmly believing that they were looking after these assets on behalf of future generations. There also appears to be a common experience of asset smoothing in times of distress. Particularly interesting are the chronically poor households which, when experiencing shocks, tended to reduce food consumption rather than sell assets.

By adopting a Q-squared approach this chapter shows that deeper and more policy relevant findings about the processes that cause and maintain chronic poverty can be generated than by single method approaches.

Introduction

Over the last few years there has been an increased focus on genuinely combining qualitative and quantitative ('Q-Squared') research methodologies to further our understanding of poverty, and in particular chronic and transient poverty (e.g. Barahona and Levy 2004 for Malawi, Lawson et al. 2006 for Uganda). For this research we combine the strengths of quantitative analysis and life history analysis, to further insights in to chronic poverty, using nationally representative panel data.[2]

We focus on Uganda, a country that has received much acclaim for the reduction in monetary based poverty from 56% in 1992 to 31% in 2005. These impressive poverty reduction figures have encouraged a large number of both quantitative (Appleton, 2001; Deininger and Okidi, 2003) and qualitative (Uganda Participatory Poverty Assessment Process – UPPAP) studies. However, most of these poverty studies tend to be polarized – i.e. they are purely quantitative or qualitative in their approaches. Furthermore they tend to pay little attention to the fact that chronic poverty estimates suggest that a fifth of the country is permanently poor (Lawson et al., 2006).

To deepen our understanding of chronic poverty issues we extend the typical microeconometric approach to understanding poverty by using a relatively rich series of nationally based household data that includes two-wave panel data for the period 1992/99. However, we extend the panel by visiting the same households and collect life histories with the intention being to establish what can be gained from combining research methods, and what insights we can obtain regarding some of the main issues of importance for chronic poverty.

The paper is structured as follows. The next section provides a background for combining quantitative and qualitative research by reviewing some of the recent historical developments and poverty related 'Q-Squared' empirical evidence. The following section then summarizes some of the methodological issues, e.g. tracing households that need to be considered in 'Q-Squared' work, before providing some examples of how understanding chronic poverty issues can be furthered. We conclude in the final section.

Background to combining quantitative and qualitative methods for understanding chronic poverty

As noted above, there has been a recent increase in the usage of 'Q-Squared' poverty based research methods with the debate having moved forward relatively quickly from the late 1990s/early 2000s when applied papers such as Barahona and Levy (2004) for Malawi (see Lawson et al. 2008 for a further summary of literature), focused on the use of participatory techniques and cross-referenced to separate quantitative findings. Such work was useful in its own right, for example, authors were able to assess the validity of quantitative results (Barahona and Levy, 2004) and provide a dynamic dimension to one-off household survey data (Howe and McKay, in Kanbur and Shaffer 2005: 2). However, in the main such work did not operate in parallel, i.e. it did not use the same sampling frame or applied integrated methods to the same households, although Adato et al. (2004) for South Africa provided a notable exception. They combined socio-economic survey panel data separated by a five year period, with in depth semi-structured household interviews, to explain the quantitative relationships that had been established from econometric analysis.

From a Ugandan context there has been very limited genuinely integrated poverty research. The benefits of combining quantitative and qualitative based research have long been recognized. For example, McGee (2000) provided methodological suggestions of how nationally representative quantitative household surveys could be combined with Participatory Poverty Assessment (PPA) findings. Appleton and Booth (2001) also highlighted the need to take advantage of the panel data in furthering our understanding of poverty and other issues.

Of the combined qualitative and quantitative research Lawson et al. (2006) attempted to understand the factors and processes underlying chronic and transient poverty. Combining PPA findings with two-wave panel data (1992/99) the research showed that the qualitative sources added significantly to the information available from the panel survey data alone. Despite the findings being based on different sampling frames and the interviewing of different households they found that factors such as, the lack of key physical assets, high dependency ratios and increased household size were identified by both the qualitative and quantitative approaches, as major factors influencing poverty transitions and persistence. In other instances qualitative approaches identified additional factors not so easily captured in quantitative studies – for example the impacts of excessive alcohol consumption on well-being (or more accurately ill-being) in many cases.

Perhaps a more notable attempt at genuine 'Q-Squared' research for rural Uganda, was that undertaken by Bird and Shinyekwa (2003). They built on the qualitative (participatory) and quantitative livelihoods research undertaken in three districts and undertook in-depth life history interviews with the heads of nearly 25 households in 3 villages. They found poor gender relations and excessive alcohol consumption were key factors, with the latter often financed by the sale of household assets and a major cause of domestic violence and household breakdown. Additionally, they found that the poorest had suffered recurrent and composite shocks and personal tragedies compared with the persistently non-poor who had simply managed to avoid personal disaster, allowing them to retain their assets and even continue to accumulate (Bird and Shinyekwa, 2003: 31).

More recently Ellis et al. (2006) completed a study for the three districts of Mbale, Kamuli and Mubende. A total of 266 panel households were interviewed and the information complemented with community qualitative interviews. They found reasons for downward trajectories in welfare status to be: farm sub-division, chronic illness, death of household head, livestock disease, theft, and spending money on gambling and drink.

Q-Squared research: A summary of sampling, selection and practical issues

Uganda has a series of household panel data from 1992 to 2003. All of these are based on nationally representative household surveys. We base our analysis on the richest of these – the 1992/3 Integrated Household Survey (IHS) and 1999/2000 National Household Survey (UNHS), of which 1,103 panel households can be matched with confidence.[3,4]

The analysis of monetary based poverty in this paper is based on the same approach used for the national level poverty studies (Appleton, 2001). With the poverty instrument being a monetary based measure of wellbeing.[5] It is these poverty lines that form the basis of the poverty matrix in Table 3.1, where we can see that approximately 19% of the population are chronically poor, 29.6% moved out of poverty between 1992 and 1999 and 10.3% moved into poverty. The table also indicates significant regional effects, with for example almost 40% of the Northern Region being persistently below the poverty line, compared with approximately 14% of households in the Central region.

Based on the country's accepted monetary based poverty measures, a sample of households that are chronically poor (poor in both periods), never poor, moving into poverty, and moved out of poverty were selected for further collection of quantitative and life history information.

The sampling of households to be selected for further interview was based on the proportions in the national panel, with 95 households interviewed (comprising roughly equal proportions of households, across several districts and mainly two regions – Central and East, that were persistently poor, moved into poverty, moved out of poverty and have never been poor).[6] Although the selection of households was based on the panel, and roughly equal proportions of households were collected for chronically poor, never poor, moved into poverty, moved out of poverty before the interview (in line with the aforementioned monetary definitions), it should be emphasized that due to the selection of regions this does not allow us to claim a representative

Table 3.1 Poverty incidence in Uganda by region (1992–1999)

Geographic location	Poverty Status (%)			
	Chronic Poverty	Moving Out of Poverty	Moving Into Poverty	Never In Poverty
National	18.9	29.6	10.3	40.9
Urban	10.6	23.9	6.0	59.1
Rural	20.5	30.7	11.1	37.6
Central Region	13.8	29.7	8.5	47.8
East Region	16.4	36.8	10.4	36.2
North Region	38.9	22.8	18.1	20.1
West Region	16.2	27.2	8.7	47.6

Source: Lawson, McKay and Okidi (2006)

coverage of Uganda. However, it did permit us to collect data for the 'better-off' and worse areas (and 'extreme' households), different ethnic groups and stable/unstable areas, thus allowing us to provide at least some insights that go beyond the methodological issues.[7]

The practical component of undertaking 'Q-Squared' is covered in Lawson et al. (2008). Ultimately, the adoption of life histories allowed for the opportunity to provide comparative information about households as well as recording responses to open-ended questions that arise during the course of interviews. The latter focused on critical incidents, events and factors identified by households and information that households identify as important but was not part of the questionnaire design.[8] As with Bird and Shinyekwa (2003), by talking to a person about their life, we also hoped to find out about path-determination in individuals' lives and to pinpoint key moments of choice – or the absence of choice, but with the advantage of also having robust quantitative panel data to underpin this.

Findings

In highlighting some of the results that underpin our 'Q-Squared' research we now provide a selection of timeline/life history data that was collected, all of which assisted in furthering our understanding of both the methods used in chronic poverty analysis and the 'real stories' that explain why some people experience poverty and others do not.

The first part of the process involved testing whether life histories can be used to cross check whether the commonly used monetary based poverty measures, produced an accurate assessment of chronic, and transient, poverty. This involved making an assessment of the quantitatively orientated poverty indicators. For example, if a household was defined as being monetarily poor in 1992 and/or 1999 and yet they clearly recalled possessing large numbers of assets, defined themselves as non-poor, and provided explanation as regards to why expenditure/consumption may have been erroneously low then this would then be considered an error. To exemplify this further, one household that had three males for more than a decade, had also possessed more than a dozen cows, many other livestock, a well maintained three bedroom house, and owned five acres of land. Such assets had not changed over the last

Table 3.2 Poverty triangulation matrix: Proportion of sample where Q-squared approach agrees with quantitative poverty definition

		1999	
		Poor	Non Poor
1992	Poor	75%	90%
	Non Poor	71%	94%

decade, however they had previously been defined as chronically poor simply because the consumption expenditure reflected the philosophy that "we only eat when we have to and are extremely hungry – we don't have a woman in the house" (head of household).

Although we should once again note the non-nationally representative nature of the very small sample, we can see from Table 3.2 that there appears strong indications that the consumption based expenditure measure of poverty is not perfect. For example, of the monetarily defined chronically poor, approximately 75% were deemed to be in this category when retrospectively interviewed.[9]

We now move on to consider the life history interviews. For ease of future reference all households' life history interviews were summarized. For example, Box 3.1, gives a brief illustration, of a household that was monetarily defined as chronically poor between 1992 and 1999. In addition Figure 3.1 shows the time line that was drawn by the household respondent.

The advantage of using a life history method, as opposed to solely relying on looking at simple associations of descriptive data, is that this complementary method enables us see the major events in a person's life with the

---

Box 3.1 (Abbreviated) Life history of a 'chronically poor' household

'A' was born in 1947 in this village, the oldest of 2 boys and 2 girls (1 died when young). His father bought 2 cows and these soon multiplied to 40 by 1983. They all lived on the 'evicted land' from 1959 – although they had no land title. 'A' left school and looked after the animals but when the war ended in 1986 all the cows had been stolen or had died. In 1992 the household bought 2 cows, by 1995 they had 6, and since then 4 of them died and 2 were sold when the 'old man' was sick (and died in 1996). When the father was sick the family ate 3 meals per day (as with before the event) and they didn't borrow money – at the time of the funeral none of the family, including his father owed money to anybody.

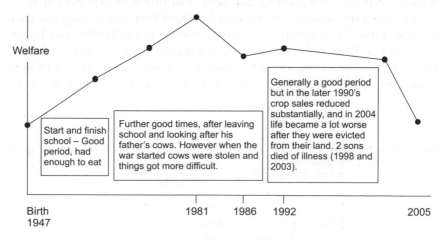

Figure 3.1 Timeline (drawn by a household respondent – example from life history interviews)

timeline diagram allowing us to clearly see the impact of such events on the interviewee's life.[10] In this case, although chronically poor, the interviewee recalls the 1992–99 period as a 'better period' in his life, than currently, although quantitative national panel data indicates that the monetary status of the household has changed little since 1992. Hence we were able to triangulate the quantitative data.

From such an example, we can already see some of the deeper understanding provided by combining methods from the same sampling frame. For example, the life history and timeline corroborate the 'bad times' suggested by the quantitative data but, the timeline also furthers our understanding of the quantitative data. For example, 2 wave panel data inform us that in 1992 and 1999 the number of cows was zero, but the life history also provides further information/reasons for changes/understanding of the processes that occurred between these two end periods, i.e. 'good times' prevailed in the mid-1990s with the number of cows/assets increasing until the death of household members.

By looking at the social, occupational factors etc., the timeline also enables us to corroborate, or negate, the quantitative welfare situation (in this case the 1992–1999 period represents a better period than currently – contradicting quantitative data that indicates the period to be similar. It is clear from Box 3.2 that even if monetarily defined as the same now as in 1992, psychologically, at least, things are worse and the family's long-term income prospects are diminished due to land insecurity.

Multi-timeline analysis

The advantage of the previous 'all in one' timeline is that in many situations you can get the interviewee to draw the line (on paper or on the ground outside the house). Such interaction helps substantially with recall/reflection. However, by disaggregating the timelines to represent, for example, an individual's economic situation, occupation, education, social and psychological conditions, migration pattern etc. this potentially reveals far more information regarding the complexity of an individual's life. Although such a method required a larger degree of time input from the interviewee we found significant rewards in further understanding the processes that underpin poverty. Box 3.2 provides a summarized version of such an approach using the social/psychological disaggregation as an example.

Although the above only summarize the overall impact of economic and social aspects over the period when combined with the education and occupation timeline information we can see that Figure 3.2 shows a downward overall trend in this chronically poor household's welfare.

In the case of this chronically poor household, there are several marked events/depressions that compound the extreme poverty status of a household. As we found for most of the chronically poor, and moving in to poverty households, social/psychological events have also had negative impact on the

---

Box 3.2 Detailed social/psychological life history (1992–99) and timeline information of a 'chronically poor' household

Economic (and Occupation) History

In 1992 the present head of household bought, with his father, 2 cows and by 1995 they had 6 cows. "I remember that my father bought a bicycle that improved our well being (+3) and the cows also (+2). During this period things were good and in 1993 we built an additional room onto his house. This put us at a good level of well being (3 or 4). However 4 cows then died and 2 were sold when the 'old man' was sick (he died in 1996).

The crops grew well during the mid-late 1990s (+1), but not since then (-1). The household size has increased from 6 (1999) to 9 (2005), this has created extra economic pressure on us (-2). In 2003, 3 goats died (-2) and in late 2003 one of my sons died after being in hospital for some time, we had to borrow 100,000 Ug Sh (30GBP) for hospital fees (-3).

In 2004 we were evicted from the land/home that we had stayed on since the 1960's, by the owner who put herdsman and cattle on the land. This resulted in a very large decline in our well-being as we had to move and I had no job (-5). Since then the man across the road from where we now live (next door to the plot of land from which the household was evicted) said we could stay on his land (increase of +1) so we now stay here. In addition I also rent 1 additional acre (increase of +1) to crop food. However, I would like to plant cash crops on this additional land but can't as the owner would charge me (at the moment I pay rent 'in kind' – by giving the landlord crops)."

From an occupational perspective several of the economic history events overlap, but as a herdsman for his father and as an agriculturist for most of his life, the household head's occupation was relatively stable until the deterioration in crop output and loss of land.

Social, psychological and cultural

"In 1996 my father was sick the family still ate 3 meals per day and we didn't borrow money – at the time of the funeral none of the family, including my father owed money to anybody. When my father died, this left a gap at the head of the family but I've tried to fill this (-1).

In 1998 and December 2003, my two sons died. The latter of these died in hospital, but we had to borrow money for hospital fees that we have still not repaid (-3). This resulted in a very large decline in well-being. Shortly after this, in 2004, we were evicted from our house and land and I moved the entire family to town (for 6 months) but I could not find a job this was a very bad time for all of us. We didn't have enough money and we could not afford to send the penultimate child to school (-4)."

Late in 2004 a former neighbour told the head that he could stay on his land so they moved to a plot of land and house that is adjacent to the old one. However, he can't tell how long he will be at this current household and plot of land, and has not asked the owner as he does not want the landlord to consider this. Therefore, although things have improved (+1, increasing overall welfare to -6), there is a feeling of great uncertainty regarding the future: "we don't know how long we have here, and things are very uncertain and I dare not ask the owner how long we can stay as this might be 'tempting fate'." He says that there have been no good events recently, other than a child having been born (+1).

Note: " " indicate quotations from the interviewee

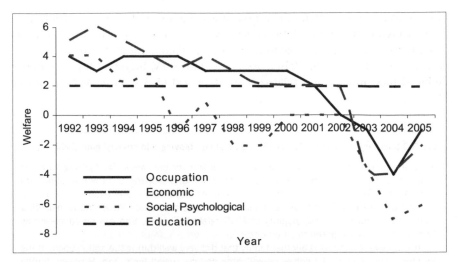

Figure 3.2 Consolidated timeline analysis for the welfare of a chronically poor household (1992–2005)

household, with a series of shocks/problems compounding each other (Bird and Shinyekwa, 2003). In this regard it was very common to see deaths from HIV/AIDS as a major propagator.

In the above case death of the father in 1996 caused a negative short term psychological and economic impact. However, this period also coincided with the loss of four cows due to disease therefore substantially depleting reserves to call upon in emergencies. Combining such events with the lower crop production that followed, this marked a period of generally lower levels of welfare – partly explaining why the poverty gap, over the period 1992–99, increased for this household.[11]

Secondly, although the occupation remains the same as in the late 1990s there is further economic and social downturn as deteriorating rainfall and crop sales reduce crop productivity and sales, combined with the death of one son. These events are then shortly followed by a third series of shocks in 2003 when assets are further reduced (death of goats through disease) and one son dies and land eviction (2004) (economic and social impacts).

Prior microeconometric work (Lawson, 2003) has found a statistical correlation between assets depletion and death/illness, the latter has been associated with chronic/deepening of poverty, at the micro level. However, rarely has causality been established. In this case we found a similar statistical association, particularly for chronically poor households and those that moved in to poverty. However, the life history findings provide far clearer clarification on the processes and reasoning why this household has been unable to escape chronic poverty.

We commonly found that the first coping mechanism for households in the extreme/chronically poor category to adopt, when faced by illness or other shocks, was to reduce their food intake. It was, for example, common for house-holds to reduce from 3 to 2 meals per day and sometimes from 2 to 1.5 meals per day (drinking tea/porridge mid-morning and cooking mid-/late afternoon). If a household had luxury based assets (i.e. radio, TV, bicycle) they commonly reduced food intake for a relatively short period (2–3 weeks), or even not at

---

Box 3.3 Summary life history (1992–99) and timeline: 'Moving into poverty' household

'A', the official household head, has been in prison for one week, for fighting with the neighbours. Her mother ('B') is too weak to crop the land properly and the household has only 'A' and her son, in reality. 'B's' other children have died – one used to run a shop at the front of the current house and two others have died since 2000. All of her other children have died (the vast majority of AIDS related disease). She has no education as "women were not supposed to sit on chairs".

It is apparent that this is another family that did very well during the coffee boom of the early/mid-1990s, until the coffee weevil came and destroyed their crop. However, during these good times it is apparent that sexual activity and the number of partners increased, and from this more children/dependants, AIDS/sickness followed, and then a depletion of assets (the radio was the first thing to be sold) to pay for medical expenses (whilst the other members of the household reduce their food intake – sometimes down to one meal per day). The children then pass over to the grandmother, or surviving uncles, upon death of the grandparent.

As we interviewed we could visibly see an unofficial support network had 'kicked in' with several people visiting and bringing things to help the old lady (e.g. firewood). Inter-estingly, this is unlikely to happen if it was just 'A' and her son – because of the respect given to elders in the community. Although 'B' says that life has got worse over the last 5 years and the official poverty line may show this (1 meal per day for 'B' and 2 for 'C'), in reality, and assuming 'A' is healthy, able to crop the land (and gets out of jail) the house-hold in all probability might be more stable now than for the last few years i.e. the death of the sick family members that were not producing any income will probably have helped reduced (monetary based) poverty levels.

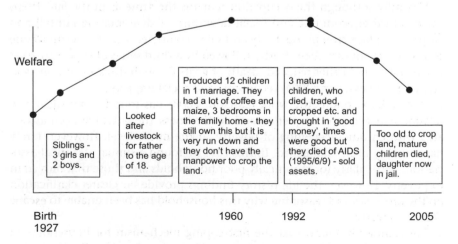

Figure 3.3 Timeline (drawn by interviewee) – 'Moving into poverty' household

all and simply disposed of the luxury asset (see Box 3.3 and Figure 3.3). Those with livestock based assets, reduced food intake for slightly longer (4–5 weeks), before selling livestock. However, if the shock and immediate cash required was extreme then all livestock would be sold, but this was very rare. Commonly, households sold, for example a cow and bought smaller divisible units, such as chickens to ensure future small-scale sales could occur in case of need.

As we have seen above the coping mechanism and processes associated with extreme poor households, and those that have moved into poverty are quite unique. Households clearly adapt to a serious shock through both human and asset capital based mechanisms. These findings were extremely typical and contrasted starkly with households that were non-poor/moved out of poverty. Demographics also played a major role in 'being able to cope'. For example, although households that moved out of poverty also experienced health shocks such as HIV/AIDS, if they had a good asset base to start with and were able to get through the expensive periods of raising kids (schooling age), benefits and human coping mechanism arise (i.e. heads are able to start sharing responsibilities). A typical example of this is shown in Box 3.4

Summary of findings

The research represents a relatively rare attempt at obtaining, qualitative poverty based, information from the same households as those in a nationally based multiple wave multiplex income and expenditure survey. Although the life history sample was too small to be nationally representative from a methodological perspective we have shown that even when using 'dated' quantitative panel data it is possible that households can be traced and that life history techniques, perhaps more than other qualitative methods, can provide relatively deep insights, especially when adopted sequentially with national representative quantitative data. When combining extended analysis, such as that from the multi-timeline diagrams with life history and quantitative data, this allows for even more understanding of the main issues that underpin poverty dynamics.

From the subject findings it is worth noting, even from our few examples, that certain key factors are likely to have played a major role in poverty dynamics in Uganda. For example, a statistical association between ill health

---

Box 3.4 'Moving out of poverty' – summary box

'A' is a teacher and excellent manager who oversees the well-being of the entire household of 10 people. She is also building assets, in terms of her daughter's education and land that she has bought. Over the longer term one can see a maternal cross generational pattern. 'E' kept the household together early on, 'A' took over 10–15 years ago, has been very heavily burdened over recent times but anticipates that her daughters will begin to share the load with her in the near future. The household is very large because of a handicapped brother, AIDS orphans and children being sent here "..whilst their parents are dying...".

(and in particular HIV/AIDS) and chronic poverty has commonly been highlighted at the microeconometric level. Furthermore, such interconnections were found to have consequences on coping mechanisms and, for example, preferences of types of assets sold. In 'times of crisis' luxury goods such as radios were commonly sold first, but the willingness to sell any assets was dependent upon the age and geographical location of the household/head (e.g. older household heads were substantially less willing to sell any livestock – firmly believing that they were looking after the assets on behalf of future generations).

There also appears to be a common experience of asset smoothing, when in times of distress. Particularly interesting are the chronically poor households that also moved into poverty. These tend to reduce food consumption at the expense of non-luxury assets for varying periods. Coping mechanisms associated with health shocks, in particular, tend to result in asset depletion but it is also common for even the extreme poor households to split larger assets into more divisible units, as a method to cope with further shocks that might occur. Hence, by combining research methods we are able to elicit more information regarding the processes that further our understanding of chronic poverty.

Endnotes

1. This research was undertaken with support from The Faculty of Humanities, General Research Support Fund, University of Manchester and ESRC's Global Poverty Research Group (GPRG) at the Universities of Manchester and Oxford (grant number M571255001). We gratefully acknowledge the assistance of James Muwonge, Anthony Matovu and Vincent Ssennono for data extraction and field interviews, and comments from anonymous referees on earlier drafts of the paper.
2. See author's webpage http://www.sed.manchester.ac.uk/idpm/staff/lawson_david.htm for links to further papers relating to the main subject findings from this research, including the methodologically based version of the research findings.
3. To ensure that the panel households were the same in both periods, a two part matching process was undertaken. The first stage matched the sex and age of the household head, allowing for an acceptable error range given uncertainty about precise ages etc. A second stage focused on those households whose head had changed over the period, for example where a household head had died and another member of the family had become the new head. See Lawson et al. (2006) for further details.
4. The meaning of quantitative analysis in this context is largely related to undertaking descriptive and econometric analysis of the household data, in the context of chronic poverty. Unless otherwise stated, qualitative in the context of this paper refers to life history analysis.
5. Monetary based poverty measure is calculated as total household consumption expenditure per adult equivalent, adjusted for variations in

prices between regions and the time period between the surveys, and the poverty line is defined with reference to minimum calorie requirements.

6. The first phase of the interviews took place between December 2005 and March 2006 and interviewed 53 households. A follow up survey took place in June 2006, which explicitly focused on households affected by ill health, with the specific focus being to examine the impact of HIV/AIDS on poverty dynamics. A total of 42 households were interviewed in this regard.

7. 'Extreme Households' refer to those that may have been extremely poor, or experienced movements from high standards of wealth into extreme poverty etc.

8. The life history interview process followed a semi structured format – an example template that was used can be viewed at http://www.chronic-poverty.org/toolbox/Lifehistories.php

9. Naturally we accept a degree of error given the recall period involved in this work.

10. The welfare indicator is based upon a person's life, as it changed over time. The initial starting point is a relative scale based on whether the person remembers/recalls being told of any health problems when born (health endowment); the degree of welfare is then judged by the interviewee and interviewer, based on the information from the interview/life history.

11. The shortfall of the welfare of this poor household from the poverty line, expressed as a proportion of the poverty line, increased from 0.67 (1992) to 0.75 (1999).

References

Adato, M., Lund, F. and Mhlongo, P. (2004) 'Methodological innovations in research on the dynamics of poverty: a mixed-method longitudinal study in Kwa-Zulu Natal, South Africa', Q-Squared in Practice Conference: A Conference on Experiences of Combining Qualitative and Quantitative Methods in Poverty Appraisal, University of Toronto.

Appleton, S. (2001) 'Education, incomes and poverty in Uganda in the 1990s', CREDIT Research Paper 01/22, University of Nottingham, Nottingham.

Appleton, S. and Booth, D. (2001) 'Combining participatory and survey-based approaches to poverty monitoring and analysis', background Paper for the Workshop held in Entebbe, Uganda, 30 May – 1 June, 2001.

Barahona, C. and Levy, S. (2004) 'How to generate statistics and influence policy using participatory methods in research: reflections on work in Malawi 1999–2002', IDS Working Paper 212, presented at Conference on Experiences of Combining Qualitative and Quantitative Methods in Poverty Appraisal, University of Toronto.

Bird, K. and Shinyekwa, I. (2003) 'Multiple shocks and downward mobility: learning from the life histories of rural Ugandans', Chronic Poverty Research Centre (CPRC) Working Paper 36, CPRC, Manchester.

Ellis, F., Ssewanyana, S., Kebede, B. and Allison, E. (2006) 'Patterns and changes in rural livelihoods in Uganda 2001–05: findings of the LADDER 2 Project', EPRC/ODG Report.

Kanbur, R. and Shaffer, P. (2005) 'Epistemology, normative theory and poverty analysis: implications for Q-Squared in practice', Q-Squared Working Paper No. 2, University of Toronto.

Lawson, D. (2003) 'Gender analysis of the Ugandan National Household Surveys (1992 – 2003)', Uganda – Revision of the Poverty Eradication Action Plan (PEAP).

Lawson, D., Hulme, D. and Muwonge, J. (2008) 'Combining quantitative and qualitative to further our understanding of poverty dynamics: some methodological considerations', *International Journal of Multiple Research Methods* 2(2): 191–204.

Lawson, D., McKay, A. and Okidi, J. (2006) 'Poverty persistence and transitions in Uganda: a combined qualitative and quantitative analysis', *Journal of Development Studies*, 42(7): 1225–1251.

McGee, R. (2000) 'Analysis of Participatory Poverty Assessment (PPA) and household survey findings on poverty trends in Uganda', Institute of Development Studies, Sussex (UK) and Department for International Development, DFID (UK).

About the author

David Lawson is Lecturer in Development Economics and Public Policy at the Institute for Development Policy and Management and Faculty Associate of Brooks World Poverty Institute, University of Manchester. He specializes in the analysis of poverty dynamics, particularly in relation to health and gender in Africa. He has consulted extensively for the World Bank, DFID and published in leading journals with his work focused on the econometric analysis of panel datasets. More recently he has been utilizing Q-Squared methodologies (quantitative and qualitative) to further understandings of poverty.

CHAPTER 4

Alternative accounts of chronic disadvantage: Income deficits versus food security

Naila Kabeer

This chapter seeks to analyse the correlates and causes of poverty in rural Bangladesh. In particular, it is interested in the chronically poor, viz. those households that began out and remained poor in the period covered by panel data for 1994 and 2001. It uses two different measures to capture chronic poverty, one based on shortfalls in income and the other on food insecurity. The analysis rests on two sets of comparisons. The first relates to differences between the chronically poor and 'the rest' of the population using the two definitions of chronic and non-chronic poverty. However, the main concern of the paper is with the second comparison which is between households classified as chronic poor by income and by food security criteria in order to establish who they were, how they differed from each other, what their situation tells us about the entrenched forms of disadvantage in Bangladesh and what our findings add to the analysis of poverty more generally.

Introduction

Defining chronic poverty

The poor, it is now widely recognized, are not a homogeneous category. The condition of poverty and the processes which give rise to it vary, not only across different contexts, but also within them. The distinction between chronic and transient poverty, like that between extreme and moderate poverty, captures some of this variation. The two variations on poverty are likely to be related: people in extreme poverty are likely to find it harder than the rest of the poor to climb out of poverty in the short or medium term. However, extreme poverty can also be a transitory phenomenon, here today and gone tomorrow.

The distinguishing feature of chronic poverty is its duration. The chronically poor may or may not be extremely poor, but they have been poor for an extended period of time. Hulme and Shepherd (2003) suggest duration of poverty for at least five years as the minimum definition of chronic poverty while recognizing that it may last for an entire lifetime and even over generations. The reason for the five year cut-off point is, in the first instance, a pragmatic one: there is often a five year gap between the data collection points when panel data is created. However, five years can be regarded as a significant period in an individual's life course and there is some evidence to suggest that people who stay poor for five years or more have a higher probability of remaining poor for the rest of their lives.

The literature on chronic poverty tells us that it generally represents the interlocking of different kinds of disadvantage – economic, social, physical, political and spatial (Chronic Poverty Research Centre, 2004). Its existence is symptomatic of the intransigence of some of these disadvantages. Like poverty itself, the causes of chronic poverty vary considerably between those regions where the majority of people are poor, and contextual factors are likely to play an important role, and those where the poor make up a minority of the population and household or individual characteristics take on greater significance.

Bangladesh is in the process of moving from the former category to the latter but at a very slow pace. Poverty went up to record levels of between 70–80% in the years following the country's war of independence in 1971 and the overwhelming majority of its population would probably have been classified as chronically poor for much of that and the subsequent decade. Since the 1990s, however, poverty has begun to decline, falling to levels of around 40% at the national level by 2000 (Sen, 2003). However, chronic poverty remains a problem, possibly accounting for a third of the rural population.

Research objectives and methodology

This chapter seeks to analyse the correlates and causes of chronic poverty in rural Bangladesh. It uses two different measures to capture chronic poverty, one based on shortfalls in income and the other on food insecurity. As Baulch and Masset (2003) report on the basis of their analysis of Viet Nam data, different measures of poverty can tell somewhat different stories about who was poor and why they were poor. We explore the extent to which this is also the case in Bangladesh and find out how different definitions and data can lead to different interpretations of who is poor and why.

The analysis in this chapter draws on survey data on the lives and livelihoods of rural households in two locations in Bangladesh, Chandina thana (Comilla district) and Modhupur thana (Tangail district). The choice of locations reflects the availability of panel data set from 1994 and 2001 on 1,184 households in two villages in each of these locations, 711 households in Chandina (60% of total sample) and 473 (40%) from Modhupur. It also draws on qualitative data collected by the author in 1998 and 2002 through open-ended interviews on the nature and causes of socio-economic change with a purposively selected group of household members and key informants in the two study locations.

The two thanas in our study represented somewhat different agro-climatic and economic contexts. Chandina was the less favourably located of the two: it was low-lying, prone to flooding, had fewer irrigation facilities, was less well-connected to the main road and to the local town of Comilla, and had higher levels of fertility and higher levels of population density. It had been largely bypassed by NGOs. With fewer local opportunities, it had a long history of seasonal out-migration to other rural localities as well as to nearby towns. More recently, international migration to the Middle East as well as some Southeast Asian countries, like Malaysia, were also on the increase. Madhupur, by contrast, did not flood as frequently, had more extensive irrigation facilities and hence more extensive cultivation of high-yielding variety rice and other crops. It has a history of in-migration although this may be on the decline. It was also better connected to main roads and to the local town of Modhupur and far better served by NGOs, most of them engaged in the provision of microfinance services. Both the study locations have experienced the declining rates of poverty documented at the national level. Poverty started out higher in the Chandina villages in 1994 but declined more rapidly than in Modhupur. As a result, while Chandina remained the poorer of the two locations by 2001, the gap between them had been reduced Toufique (2002).

This paper focuses on a particular aspect of this larger picture. It is interested in the chronically poor, viz. those households that began out and remained poor in the period covered by the panel data. Clearly, the factors which help to explain movements in and out of poverty are also likely to explain the failure to move out of poverty. However, this paper will use two different measures of chronic poverty to explore the significance of these factors. The first measure is based on income data. The surveys collected information on the household's income (including imputed income) from a variety of different sources for the 12 months preceding the survey. This was adjusted for the number of adult equivalents in the household. Minimum calorie requirements, using local rice prices, together with a 20% mark-up to allow for non-food expenditure, gave a poverty line of 4,200 Takas per person per annum in 1994. This was deflated using constant US dollars to give a poverty line income of 5,666 Takas for 2001 (Toufique and Turton, 2002). Clearly there may be disagreements about the precision of the estimation procedure, but for the purposes of this study, which is to compare trends for the same set of households over a period of time, it is consistency in measurement that matters. Our definition of the chronically income poor uses this measure and refers to all households whose annual income levels fell short of the relevant poverty line in each of the two survey years. It thus captures average levels of deprivation reported by households in the period covered by the panel data.

The second measure is based on self-reported food security. Households were asked to describe their food situation in the 12 months prior to the survey in terms of four categories: chronic food shortage, occasional food shortage, 'break-even', and food surplus. That food security had improved in the study villages was evident from the fact that the percentages of households reporting chronic food shortage had declined from 5% in 1994 to 0.2% in 2001 while the percentage reporting occasional food shortage had declined from 53% in 1994 to 11% in 2001. The vast majority of households were now in the break-even category: 67% as opposed to 37% in 1994. Finally, 22% reported food surplus compared to 13% in 1994. Our definition of chronic food poverty is based on these estimates and refers to all households that reported either chronic or occasional food shortage in both 1994 and 2001. Inasmuch as the measure captures those households who reported some period of food shortage in the reference years, it can be seen as capturing fluctuations in consumption flows and hence household vulnerability.

Table 4.1 reports on the distribution of chronic income poverty and chronic food poverty in our sample: 138 households, or 12% of our total sample, were classified as chronically poor by income criteria while 111 households, or 9% of the sample, were classified as chronically poor by food criteria. Table 4.2 examines the distribution of chronically poor households by location. Since a larger number of households in our sample come from Chandina thana, and it is in any case, the poorer of the two locations, it is not surprising that it accounts for a higher percentage of both the chronically income poor as well as the chronically food poor than Modhupur. However, differences in incidence of chronic food poverty between the two locations were far smaller than differences in the incidence of chronic income poverty.[1]

Table 4.3 examines the relationship between chronic income poverty and chronic food poverty. It shows that only 38 households in the total sample (3%) were classified as chronically poor by both income and food criteria. It is evident that our two measures of chronic poverty capture manifestations of household disadvantage in the study population that are only partly overlapping. It is therefore likely that the characteristics and causes of chronic

Table 4.1 Distribution of chronic income and food poverty in rural Bangladesh

	No. of households		No. of households
Chronically income poor	138 (12%)	Chronically food poor	111 (9%)
Non-income poor	1046 (88%)	Non-food poor	1073 (91%)
Total	1184 (100%)	Total	1184 (100%)

Table 4.2 Distribution of chronically poor by location in rural Bangladesh

	Chronically income poor (n=138) (%)	Non income poor (n=1046) (%)	Chronically food poor (n=111) (%)	Non food poor (n=1073) (%)
Modhupur thana	28	42	47	39
Biprabari	5	6	2	6
Teki	23	36	45	33
Chandina thana	72	59	53	61
Hossainpur	30	30	19	31
Darora	42	29	34	30

Table 4.3 Relationship between chronic income poverty and chronic food poverty in rural Bangladesh

	Chronically food poor	Others	Total
Chronically income poor	38 (27.5%)	100 (72.5%)	138 (100%)
Others	73 (7%)	973 (93%)	1046 (100%)
Total	111 (9.4%)	1073 (90.6%)	1184 (100%)

poverty will vary between these two categories of households. Nevertheless, both categories of chronically poor households can be taken as broadly representative of the section of the population in our study locations who have been bypassed – or excluded – by the opportunities generated in recent decades through the combined operation of market forces, state policies and NGO interventions that were found to have led to economic growth in the two locations (Kabeer, 2004).

In this paper, we will be focusing on these two categories of chronically poor households in greater detail. The analysis will rest on two sets of comparisons. The first relates to differences between the chronically poor and 'the rest' of the population using our two definitions of chronic and non-chronic poverty. However, our main concern in this paper will be on the second comparison between chronic income and chronically food poor households in order to establish who they were, how they differed from each other, what their situation tells us about the entrenched forms of disadvantage in Bangladesh and what our findings add to the analysis of poverty more generally.

Dimensions of chronic poverty: needs, resources and livelihoods

Comparing chronic poverty by income and food criteria: basic needs deficits

We begin our analysis by comparing the extent to which different categories of households met, or had the capacity to meet, their basic needs for food, water, clothing, shelter and sanitation in the two survey years (Table 4.4). Not surprisingly, chronically poor households were less well placed to meet most of their basic needs than the rest of the population, regardless of the criteria of poverty used. We therefore focus our discussion on differences between the two categories of chronic poverty. The first point to note is that, while food insecurity went down considerably among the chronically income poor, income poverty did not change a great deal among the food poor. Clearly, by definition, chronically food poor households continued to experience food shortages.

On most other indicators, the chronically income poor generally started out, and ended with, a higher capacity to meet their needs than the chronically food poor. For instance, 25% of the chronically income poor drank water from their own tube wells in 1994 compared to 16% of the chronically food poor. In 2001, the percentages had risen to 30% and 24% respectively.

In 1994, 75% of the chronically income poor had some security of shelter through the possession of homestead land compared to 70% of food poor. In 2001, the percentages had risen to 86% and 76%. Some 2% of both categories of chronically poor households had homes made of durable wall materials in 1994. By 2001, it had risen to 16% among the chronically income poor but only 6% among the chronically food poor.

The findings on the clothing indicator are only interesting in what they reveal about the overall decline in poverty in Bangladesh. Earlier qualitative research had suggested that inadequacy of clothing was a telling indicator of poverty in rural Bangladesh (see, for instance, Kabeer, 1989). This was measured in our survey by whether or not all adults in the household had at least two items of clothing. It is clear from the responses that by 1994, this was no longer a relevant measure of poverty: over 95% of all households in all categories reported at least two items of clothing and by 2001, it had risen to nearly 100%. In summary, therefore, Table 4.4 tells us that while our measures of chronic poverty based on food and income both capture durable forms of disadvantage among the survey households, the differences between the two groups in their capacity to meet minimum basic needs suggests that the chronically food poor were systematically less well placed to meet their basic needs than the chronically income poor.

Table 4.4 Basic needs indicators for the chronic income poor and the chronic food poor in Bangladeshi sample (1994 and 2001)

	Chronically income poor (%) (1994)	Chronically income poor (%) (2001)	Other hhs (%) (1994)	Other hhs (%) (2001)	Chronically food poor (%) (1994)	Chronically food poor (%) (2001)	Other hhs (%) (1994)	Other hhs (%) (2001)
Food deficit	88	30	53	8	100	100	–	–
Below poverty line	100	100	–	–	59	59	27	20
Drinking water: own tube well	25	30	45	56	16.2	24	46	56
Drinking water: others' tubewell	72	70	52	44	76.6	74.8	52.3	43.8
Drinking water: other sources	4	–	2	1	7.2	0.9	22	0.6
2 items clothing per adult	97	99	98	99	97	99	98	99
Own homestead land	75	86	75	86	70.3	75.7	75.1	86.7
Durable wall materials	2	16	16	40	1.8	6.3	15.9	40.4
Durable roof materials	49	87	69	95	45.9	82	69.1	95
Open latrine	74	64	45	35	71	64	46	35
Latrine: semi-pucca/pucca	8	16	24	46	5	16	24	46

Comparing chronic poverty by income and food criteria: resource deficits

We turn next to a comparison in the productive resources available to the two categories of chronically poor households which may help to explain these differences in their ability to meet their basic needs. We start out with an examination of their human resource base. As Lipton pointed out in his study of extreme poverty, 'the economic circumstances of people in very poor households are largely defined by food and work' (1983: 4). Information on household size and composition provides preliminary information on the balance between these imperatives.

Table 4.5 allows us to compare the likely ratio of 'mouths' to 'hands' in different categories of households in our sample. It suggests that chronically food poor households were smaller in size and had fewer children over time compared to the chronically income poor. Their main disadvantage lay in their size and composition of their adult membership. While all other categories of households reported a rise in the number of prime age male household members (though the rise was very small among the chronically income poor), chronically food poor households reported a major decline. This meant while chronically income poor households reported 1.30 prime age males in 1994 and 1.34 in 2001, the food poor households reported a decline from 1.47 to 0.84. A similar, though less marked, pattern obtained in relation to adult females. Both categories of chronically poor households reported a decline in the number of prime age females while other households reported a considerable increase. However the decline was far more marked among the chronically food poor.

The data on female headship provide some explanation for these changes. We find that the incidence of female-headed households went up for all categories of households over the study period, but the increase was much larger among chronically poor households and particularly marked among the chronically food poor. Thus it went up from 6% to 12% among the chronically income poor and from 13% to 31% among the chronically food poor. Indeed, 23% of the chronically food poor did not have *any* adult male members by the end of the study period compared to just 6% of the chronically income poor. There has, in other words, been a discernible 'feminization' of chronic poverty, particularly chronic food poverty, over the period covered by our study villages. This explains the shifts in the gender composition of households noted above. The increasing incidence of female headship among the chronically poor also explains why the education levels of household head declined for these groups over time while it rose for the rest of the population.

The table also provides information on male and female activity rates. In general, it shows that both chronic food and chronic income deficits experienced a decline in numbers of economically active men and a rise in economically active women over time. In other words, we might argue that the failure of poor households to move out of poverty over time was partly related to the feminization of their labour force. In Bangladesh, there is generally an

Table 4.5 Human resources by household category in Bangladeshi sample (1994 and 2001)

	Chronically income poor (1994)	Chronically income poor (2001)	Non-poor (1994)	Non-poor (2001)	Chronically food poor (1994)	Chronically food poor (2001)	Non-food poor (1994)	Non-food poor (2001)
Household size	5.8	5.8	5.4	5.6	4.7	4.6	5.5	5.8
Children 0-14	2.2	2.8	2.4	2.3	2.6	2.1	2.4	2.4
Prime age males 15–54	1.30	1.34	1.33	1.56	1.47	0.84	1.32	1.60
Prime age females 15–54	1.24	1.22	1.31	1.37	1.37	1.09	1.29	1.38
Older males 55+	0.22	0.21	0.23	0.23	0.32	0.25	0.22	0.22
Older females 55+	0.20	0.19	0.20	0.18	0.22	0.27	0.19	0.18
Age of hh head	43	48	42	47	47	51	42	47
% Female headship	6	12	3	8	13	31	3	6
% hh with no adult males	5	6	2	4	6	23	2	2
Economically active males 15–54	1.28	1.02	1.30	1.23	1.36	0.65	1.29	1.26
Economically active females 15–54	0.09	0.27	0.16	0.16	0.15	0.48	0.16	0.15
No. of ill/disabled	0.72	0.25	0.44	0.14	0.53	0.32	0.47	0.13
Yrs schooling of hh head	0.97	0.90	2.6	2.7	2.3	0.44	2.58	2.70
Spouse's education	0.78	1.1	1.1	1.0	1.1	0.5	1.0	1.5
Yrs schooling children 5–9	0.5	0.9	0.7	1.0	0.9	0.8	0.6	1.0
Yrs schooling children 10–14	1.8	3.5	2.1	4.1	2.30	3.03	2.07	4.80

association between household poverty and female economic activity since it is generally women from poorer households who take up paid work. However, this pattern is only evident among the chronically food poor in our table, with the difference particularly marked for 2001.

Comparing chronic poverty by income and food criteria: livelihood activities

The resource deficits of poor households serve to constrain the range of strategies that they are able to utilize in order to meet their basic needs. As economies become more monetized, their livelihood strategies have to become more market oriented. Table 4.6 reports on these activities and numbers of members involved per household in different categories. First of all, it shows a decline in numbers engaged in own cultivation for all categories of households from somewhat similar numbers in 1994. The decline is particularly marked among the chronically food poor. The decline in own cultivation is partly offset by a small rise in tenancy cultivation in all categories of households but once again, the rise is smallest among the chronically food poor. Thus we can speculate that one reason why the chronically food poor suffered greater food shortages than the chronically income poor was that they were less involved in own and tenancy cultivation, owned and operated less land and had less access to irrigation in both survey years.

Both chronically poor groups reported a far greater rise in wage labour than other categories of households but in different types of wage labour. The chronically income poor were more likely to be involved in field-based wage labour followed by non-agricultural wage labour, both activities largely dominated by men. The feminization of chronic food poverty, on the other hand, is evident in the growing prominence of bari-based wage labour among these households. There was also an increase in begging and gleaning: this is also an activity that was dominated by women in our study locations.

The chronically income poor also demonstrated somewhat greater geographical mobility over time than the chronically food poor, in that they were more likely to undertake both rural to rural migration as well as rural to urban migration. The lower involvement of the chronically food poor in own cultivation probably explains why they obtained a higher percentage of their incomes from off farm sources than the chronically income poor. The final row of the table reports on monthly per capita income by category of household. As we might expect, chronically poor households by both criteria started out and ended up with lower levels of per capita than the rest of the population. However, in a departure from the general pattern established by the table, it tells us that chronically food poor started out and ended with higher per capita income than the chronically income poor. Per capita income is thus the only criteria by which food poor households do better than income poor households in both the survey years. However, the differences between the two groups are not large, and they diminish over time because of higher rates of growth in per capita income among the income poor.

We also find that poor households in Bangladesh have been found to cope with shortfalls in earnings by relying on produce from homestead and common property resources, such as the roadside, forests, unclaimed land and water bodies and so on (Kabeer, 1989). For example, 'minor foods' were widely utilized as a means of supplementing the household diet in 1994: over 90% of households in all categories drew on such reserves at some stage in the year, many reporting regular weekly consumption. The chronically income poor were more likely to rely on such foods to cope with seasonality: 36% compared to 29% of the chronically food poor. The food poor on the other hand resorted to such food on a more regular monthly basis: 14% compared to 17%.

Table 4.6 Livelihood activities by household category in Bangladeshi sample (1994 and 2001)

	Chronically income poor (1994)	Chronically income poor (2001)	Non-income poor (1994)	Non-income poor (2001)	Chronically food poor (1994)	Chronically food poor (2001)	Other hhs (1994)	Other hhs (2001)
Own cultivation	1.5	0.35	1.7	0.67	1.7	0.15	1.7	0.67
Tenancy cultivation	0.12	0.33	0.11	0.40	0.08	0.16	0.11	0.42
Field-based wage labour	0.30	0.91	0.36	0.37	0.36	0.64	0.36	0.41
Bari-based wage labour	0.05	0.18	0.06	0.06	0.08	0.38	0.06	0.05
Formal service	0.09	0.14	0.05	0.13	0.07	0.07	0.06	0.14
Non-agriculture wage labour	0.19	0.47	0.24	0.36	0.36	0.32	0.36	0.38
Business /trade	0.23	0.09	0.26	0.28	0.21	0.14	0.26	0.27
Other	0.14	0.22	0.17	0.24	0.17	0.37	0.17	0.22
Begging	0.02	0.12	0.03	0.04	0.02	0.26	0.03	0.03
Rural migration	0.12	0.18	0.12	0.11	0.19	0.13	0.12	0.11
Urban migration	0.16	0.28	0.16	0.21	0.17	0.20	0.16	0.22
International migration	0.11	0	0.08	0.16	0.14	0.02	0.08	0.15
Adjusted per capita income	2910	4357	7898	10580	4170	5359	7642	10320
% non-agricultural income	37	49	53	63	50	68	51	61

Risk, vulnerability and the durability of poverty

Table 4.7 reports on the different forms of crisis experienced by households in the five years prior to each of the two survey years, providing important insights into the processes by which poverty is reproduced over time. The table suggests that most households experienced some form of crisis in the 5 years preceding the 1994 survey. As a result, the incidence of crisis did not vary a great deal by category of household: 97% of the chronically food poor, 96% of the chronically income poor and around 92% of other households reported some form of crisis in 1994. The incidence of crisis had declined across all categories of households in the 5 years preceding 2001 but at a markedly different rate so that marked differences were evident between the chronically poor and the rest of the population. The chronically food poor emerged as the most vulnerable, with 87% reporting some form of crisis compared to 70% of the chronically income poor. The estimates for rest of the population was around 65%.

An examination of the types of crisis reported most frequently by these households suggests that illness and accident were overwhelmingly the most frequently reported by all categories of households, with the highest frequency among the chronically poor. Next in frequency was death of a family member followed by marriage-related costs, including dowry payments. While the incidence of illness/accidents/deaths had declined over time, they continued to be reported more frequently by the chronically poor, with the chronically poor reporting a higher incidence of illness and accidents and the chronically food poor reporting a higher incidence of deaths.

It would appear that as far as the incidence of crisis is concerned, it is frequency rather than type of crisis that distinguished the chronically poor from the rest of the population. It would also appear that illness/accident/deaths are the primary form of crisis experienced by households and that they occurred with greater frequency among the chronically poor. It is worth thinking through the implications of these findings for the processes which reproduce poverty over time, given what we know about the chronically poor in our study population.

First of all, as we saw, the poor rely on their own unskilled physical labour to a greater extent than other sections of the population. Any form of illness or disability that undermines the physical capacity of even one of these members seriously undermines the households' earning capacity. However, the poor are also more likely to be vulnerable to ill-health/accident/death because of the conditions in which they live and work. Hunger and malnutrition, lack of clean drinking water, poor sanitary conditions and the toll that hard physical labour takes on the body all predispose the poor to certain categories of illness: diarrhoea, dysentery, gastric ulcers, fever, exhaustion. In addition, they are more likely than others to work in hazardous occupations.

Secondly, the poor have fewer resources to fall back on to meet the lump-sum demands often associated with medical treatment. They must either sell what meagre assets they have or borrow at usurious rates of interest, becoming more impoverished than ever as a result. Thirdly, the poor were found to be disadvantaged in their access to health care provision. For example, despite the fact that the chronically poor reported higher incidence of illness episodes as well as more ill/disabled members than other households, the chronically food poor were least likely to seek any form of treatment: 13% did not seek any form of medical treatment in 2001 compared to around 1–2% of the rest of the population. It also suggests that among those that did go for treatment, the chronically food poor were more likely than the rest of the population to go to so-called 'traditional' practitioners. These practice various dubious and usually ineffective, forms of treatment ('jhar-phuk'), but cost less than other alternatives.

For all groups of households, in both the survey years, private provision was the most widely utilized category of service provision, far more so than government provision. This is likely to reflect a number of different factors, such as private provision covering a wider and more heterogeneous range of practitioners than state provision, greater recourse to the private sector may also be explained by the fact that government provision tends to be both

Table 4.7 Insights into processes by which poverty is reproduced: Crisis events in the 5 preceding years (1994 and 2001)

	Income poor (%) (1994)	Income poor (%) (2001)	Non-poor (%) (1994)	Non-poor (%) (2001)	Food poor (%) (1994)	Food poor (%) (2001)	Non-poor (%) (1994)	Non-poor (%) (2001)
Crisis in previous 5 years	96%	70%	98%	65%	97%	87%	92%	64%
Illness-related	67%	44%	62%	26%	69%	39%	61%	27%
Death in family	9%	4%	10%	6%	12%	11%	9%	6%
Marital instability	1%	1%	1%	2%	2%	6%	1%	2%
Marriage-related costs/dowry	6%	6%	4%	8%	5%	6%	4%	8%
Loss of livestock	4%	0	2%	1%	2%	0	2%	1%
International migration/cheated by brokers	1%	0	5%	9%	2%	4%	4%	8%
Disputes (legal, shalish and others)	–	1%	1%	3%	0	2%	4%	3%
Theft/fire	2%	0	1%	1%	2%	0	1%	
Business loss/crop failure	0	0	2%	2%	1%	0	2%	2%
Loan repayment	1%	1%	0	2%	1%	2%	0	2%
Old person living alone/unemployment	0	1%	–	1%	0	5%	-1	–
General/other	4%	9%	3%	4%	5%	8%	3%	4%

physically more distant (and generally urban-biased) but also known to entail various illicit and unpredictable costs (Killingsworth, 2002).

Our findings on the incidence of crisis also feeds into the processes of chronic poverty through their implications for household headship. The much higher incidence of female-headed households among the chronically poor in both survey years suggests that the illness/accidents/deaths reported are likely to have affected their primary male breadwinner, particularly given that so many of them did not have any adult males in their membership. The high percentage of female-headed households among the chronically poor, and particularly among the chronically food poor, suggest that the absence of male provision and protection does indeed create, or heighten, household vulnerability to chronic poverty. Their vulnerability to long-term poverty is exacerbated by the fact that chronically poor female-headed households were also likely to lack any adult male members.

Predicting chronic income and food poverty: A multivariate analysis

In this section, we use multivariate statistical techniques to ascertain which of these factors were significantly associated with the two forms of chronic poverty in the two survey years. Given that we are using dichotomous variables as our dependent variables, we use logistic regression analysis to carry out our estimation. The explanatory variables consist of different measures of the household resources and activities discussed in preceding sections which were found to contribute significantly to the explanatory power of the equations. A description of the explanatory variables is provided along with the results in Table 4.8. For each of the survey years, we estimated the likelihood of being classified as chronically poor by income criteria and the likelihood of being classified as chronically poor by food criteria. The first set of results reported relate to chronic income poverty in 1994 and 2001 while the second set relate to chronic food poverty.

The findings for chronic income poverty suggest that the education and health status of family members and ownership of livestock were the key resources distinguishing the chronically income poor from other households in both years. The significance of some of the other variables fluctuates between the two years. Thus, dependency burden of children becomes significant over time as a factor differentiating the chronically income poor from the rest of the population while land-related variables become less significant. Livelihood activities also take on increasing significance over time: households with members in agricultural wage labour in the fields (a primarily male activity) in 2001 are likely to be from the chronically income poor group while those with members in business and trade, in various off-farm agricultural activities as well as in rural migration are less likely to be from this group. The experience of a crisis in the previous five years is more likely to differentiate chronically income poor households from the rest in 1994 than in 2001.

As we might expect, some of the variables predicting the likelihood of chronic food poverty overlap with those predicting chronic income poverty. Thus education (of household head, but not of the spouse) and health status of members prove important in both years while the dependency burden of children takes on greater significance. However, unlike the case with income poverty, female headship is significant in both years in differentiating the chronically food poor from the rest. Access to irrigation (but not land ownership) and experience of crisis in the five years preceding the survey also proves significant in both years in differentiating chronically food poor households from the rest.

The feminization of chronic food poverty signalled by the growing incidence – and statistical significance – of female-headed households within this group is also evident in the 'feminization of its workforce' as indicted by the increased significance of female-dominated activities, such as bari-based agricultural labour, begging and gleaning in predicting the likelihood of chronic food poverty. Access to irrigated land and to NGO loans both reduce the likelihood of chronic food poverty in later years as does involvement in international migration and certain off-farm activities. Finally, the geographical location of the household appears to have little bearing on the distribution of chronic food poverty, once these other factors have been taken into account.

Table 4.8 Logistic regression estimates of likelihood of chronic income and food poverty in Bangladeshi sample (1994 and 2001)

	Coefficients for income poverty				Coefficients for food poverty			
	1994		2001		1994		2001	
	B	Sig	B	Sig.	B	Sig	B	Sig
INTERCEPT	2.138	0.000	2.437	0.000	2.756	0.000	2.287	0.000
Children	0.078	0.262	-0.338	0.000	-0.056	0.441	-0.217	0.018
Adults	0.048	0.593	-0.086	0.376	-0.185	0.032	0.156	0.227
Female head	-0.331	0.447	-0.149	0.687	-1.201	0.002	-0.907	0.011
Ill/disabled member	-0.547	0.000	-0.813	0.001	-0.349	0.035	-1.169	0.000
Head's education	0.151	0.000	0.114	0.020	0.179	0.001	0.238	0.002
Spouse's education	0.107	0.038	0.113	0.116	-0.004	0.944	0.013	0.881
Cultivable land owned	0.004	0.110	0.005	0.249	0.004	0.162	0.011	0.157
Irrigated land operated	0.007	0.036	0.004	0.397	0.017	0.001	0.015	0.094
No. of cattle	0.234	0.055	0.334	0.017	0.231	0.124	0.106	0.586
No. of loans	-0.029	0.284	0.025	0.445	0.063	0.201	0.121	0.012
Own cultivation	0.071	0.465	0.246	0.210	0.117	0.243	0.109	0.734
Tenancy cultivation	-0.234	0.453	0.189	0.444	0.454	0.245	0.456	0.188
Field-based wage labour	0.396	0.124	-0.806	0.000	0.405	0.151	-0.119	0.607
Bari-based wage labour	0.168	0.688	-0.156	0.576	-0.482	0.217	-1.261	0.000
Business/trade	0.175	0.475	10.240	0.000	0.406	0.146	0.375	0.294
Formal service	-0.806	0.029	-0.467	0.162	-0.122	0.776	-0.123	0.794
Other non-ag. work	0.238	0.404	0.453	0.114	0.294	0.334	-0.500	0.103
Non-ag. wage labour	0.007	0.973	0.504	0.060	0.126	0.600	0.672	0.038
Begging	0.464	0.494	-0.166	0.549	0.129	0.842	-0.911	0.001
Rural migrant	-0.078	0.802	10.244	0.000	-0.319	0.266	-0.008	0.985
Urban migrant	-0.163	0.478	-0.041	0.858	0.346	0.191	0.437	0.181
International migrant	-0.542	0.128	180.829	0.994	-0.040	0.913	10.696	0.049
Crisis in past 5 years	-0.727	0.106	0.160	0.480	-1.169	0.060	-0.902	0.006
Comilla	-0.556	0.027	-0.540	0.039	0.318	0.233	0.180	0.548

Explanation of variables for Table 4.8:

Children: Number of members aged 0–14
Adults: Number of members aged 15+
Female head: Dummy variable for female headed households
Ill/disabled: Number of ill/disabled members

Head's education: Education level of household head (in years)
Spouse's education: Education level of head's wife (in years)
Cultivable land owned: Size of own cultivable land holding (in decimals of acres)
Irrigated land operated: Size of operated land under irrigation (in decimals of acres)
No. of cattle: Number of cattle owned
No. of loans: Number of loans ever-taken
Own cultivation: Number of members engaged in own cultivation
Tenancy cultivation: Number of members engaged in tenancy cultivation/fishing
Field-based wage labour: Number of members engaged in wage labour in field
Bari-based wage labour: Number of members engaged in wage labour within bari
Business/trade: Number of members engaged in business and trade
Formal service: Number of members engaged in formal service in government, NGO or private firm
Other non-ag. work: Number of members engaged in 'other' forms of non-agricultural activity
Non-ag. wage labour: Number of members engaged in non-agricultural wage labour (coolie, rickshaw pulling)
Begging: Number of members engaged in begging and gleaning
Rural migrant: Number of members engaged in rural migration
Urban migrant: Number of members engaged in urban migration
International migrant: Number of members engaged in international migration
Crisis in past 5 years: Dummy variable for whether or not household experienced crisis in previous 5 years
Comilla: Dummy variable for thana location

Summary

What do the different measures of chronic poverty tell us about deprivation and vulnerability in Bangladesh?

This paper set out to explore the assets, human resources, livelihood activities and capacity to meet basic needs among the chronically poor in Bangladesh. The findings tell us that chronically poor households in our study villages failed to move out of poverty during the period under study because they started out poorer than other households and were more likely to be constrained by illness, disability, age, gender, and by lack of education and assets from either taking up higher-value activities locally or migrating in search of new livelihoods. Their members were mainly to be found in 'livelihood traps', activities which did not require skills, capital or other assets, were consequently easy to enter, but which carried correspondingly low returns and little scope for future mobility to better paid jobs.

What is of greater interest in this study is the finding that different measures of poverty gave us somewhat differing accounts of the chronically poor. While the chronically poor were less able to meet their basic needs, had fewer human and material resources and were more likely to be found in livelihood traps than the rest of the population, regardless of whether we defined chronic poverty in income or food terms, there was little actual overlap in the households making up the two categories. It was evident that the measures were capturing somewhat different forms of disadvantage within the study population. Lipton's observation (1983) that poverty does not always decline in a continuous fashion below the poverty line appears to be relevant here. He noted evidence of discontinuities in the relationship between household income and its characteristics and behaviour. These discontinuities, which took the form of 'reversals' and 'intensifications', did not necessarily occur at the poverty line but often at lower levels of income, serving to distinguish the moderate from the extreme poor.

We found greater evidence of these discontinuities when the focus was on food poverty than on income poverty. The chronically income poor were, in other words, similar in most ways to the rest of the population, only poorer: they had less land, less access to technology, fewer livestock, fewer prime age males and females, lower levels of education among adult members, higher numbers of ill and disabled and so on. By contrast, there were a number of marked discontinuities between the chronically food poor and the rest of the population, which mainly related to the gender composition of their households. While all other categories of households, including the chronically income poor, reported constant or considerably higher numbers of prime age male household members over time, the chronically food poor were characterized by declining numbers. As a result, they ended up with markedly fewer males in this age group than any other category. While all other categories reported constant or somewhat higher numbers of prime age females, the chronically food poor reported a decline and hence ended up with fewer females in this age group than any other category.

In addition, the percentages of female household heads and households with no adult males remained constant or increased in other categories of households but both increased dramatically among the chronically food poor. Moreover, while all households reported declines in numbers of ill and disabled members, the declines were lowest among the food poor. There were a number of other differences between the chronically food poor and other households but they followed from their gender differences e.g. considerably lower levels of education of their households heads, their lower levels of involvement in cultivation and their higher levels of dependence on bari-based labour, begging, gleaning and food gathered from ecological reserves.

As we have suggested one possible explanation for the different accounts of chronic poverty provided by these two measures is that they are capturing different dimensions of disadvantage, with the income measure providing a better measure of average levels of deprivation in the two survey years and the food measure capturing fluctuations in income/consumption flows and hence household vulnerability. This explanation is partly supported by the higher levels of crisis reported by the food poor, crises which partly explain the discontinuities we have pointed to. However, there is another more simple explanation. Our study suggests that chronically food-poor households were poorer than chronically income-poor households by almost every measure of disadvantage *with the exception* of per capita income. Given the complexities involved in recalling household income over the period of a year, as was attempted in both surveys, and the simplicity of recalling whether a household experienced any food shortage during the same time period, it may be that the food insecurity is simply a better proxy for poverty in the context of Bangladesh than income poverty. This in turn suggests that we may be better off finding appropriate and easy to collect indicators of poverty than engaging in the expensive and complex exercise of estimating household income.

Endnotes

1. Most of the food poverty in Modhupur appeared to be concentrated in one village (Teki).

References

Baulch, B. and Masset, E. (2003) 'Do monetary and non-monetary indicators tell the same story about chronic poverty? A study of Vietnam in the 1990s' *World Development* 31(3): 441–453.

Chronic Poverty Research Centre (2004) *The Chronic Poverty Report 2004–05*, Chronic Poverty Research Centre, Manchester.

Hulme, D. and Shepherd, A. (2003) 'Conceptualizing chronic poverty', *World Development* 31(3): 403–423.

Kabeer, N. (1989) 'Monitoring poverty as if gender mattered: a methodology for rural Bangladesh', IDS Discussion Paper No. 255. Institute of Development Studies, Brighton, UK.

Kabeer, N. (2004) 'Snakes, ladders and traps: changing lives and livelihoods in rural Bangladesh (1994–2001)', *CPRC Working Paper 50*, published in association with IDS. Available from: http://www.chronicpoverty.org/pdfs/50Kabeer.pdf [Accessed 21 July 2009]

Killingsworth, J. R. (2002) 'Official, unofficial, and informal fees for health care', *Third Health Sector Development Technical Advisory Group*, WHO, Geneva. Available from: http://www.eldis.org/fulltext/corruption1.pdf [accessed 21 July 2009]

Lipton, M. (1983) 'Poverty, undernutrition, and hunger', *World Bank Staff Working Paper No. 597*, Washington, D.C.

Sen, B. (2003) 'Drivers of escape and descent: changing household fortunes in rural Bangladesh', *World Development* 31(3): 513–534.

Toufique, K. Z. (2002) *Sustainable rural livelihoods in Bangladesh*, IDS Research Report 45. Institute of Development Studies, Brighton, UK.

Toufique, K. Z. and Turton, C. (2002) *Hands Not Land: How livelihoods are changing in rural Bangladesh*, Department for International Development (DFID), UK.

About the author

Naila Kabeer is Professorial Fellow at the Institute of Development Studies, Sussex. Her main research focus is on poverty, gender and social exclusion and their implications for social policy, social protection strategies, citizenship and labour rights. Her most recent publications are *Mainstreaming Gender and Social Protection in the Informal Economy* (for the Commonwealth Secretariat) and *Inclusive Citizenship: Meanings and Expressions* (Zed).

PART II

Targeting the Poorest

CHAPTER 5

Identifying and targeting the extreme poor: A methodology for rural Bangladesh[1]

Binayak Sen and Sharifa Begum

This chapter argues that the extreme poor warrant specific analytical and policy focus. The task of identifying and targeting the extreme poor, however, is not easy. This is why the chapter attempts to identify the extreme poor in rural Bangladesh by devising sensitive targeting indicators that are effective in minimizing leakage to the non-poor while ensuring broad coverage of the target group. The targeting ability and representativeness of a number of indicators are examined. The analysis shows that three criteria meet these two conditions of targeting: land ownership, housing and occupation. The chapter therefore concludes that since no single indicator contains sufficient information, it is better to combine those which are most informative. Regional targeting and household-based indicators are also recommended for the design of extreme-poor oriented programmes. However, if the process of administering is left to the bureaucratic discretion of programme managers, it is unlikely that better identification will have an effect on the extreme poor. This risk can be minimized through consultation with communities and NGOs, and facilitated by effective local government. Information exchange with likeminded programmes can also contribute to the development of more socially equitable and inclusive pro-poor policies.

Introduction

The poor are not a homogeneous group and sharp divisions exist among them by sex, region, occupation, land ownership, housing, education, access to infrastructure and even clothing. Recognizing extreme poverty as a specific area of analytical focus, distinct from the general concern about poverty and deprivation, is extremely important – with the number of people living in extreme chronic poverty simply too large to ignore. The moot question is therefore how to make the poorest and most vulnerable visible in the arena of public policy. How do we devise indicators that can identify the extreme poor with relative ease, while at the same time ensuring substantial coverage of extreme poverty?

The majority of literature on targeting focuses only on distinguishing between the poor and the non-poor. It is important to transcend such a limited position so as to ensure the more 'difficult to reach' poor are not excluded from development action and policy. Policies that have favoured the non-poor and moderate poor have not necessarily reached or benefited those living in extreme poverty. However, the task of identifying and targeting the extreme poor is far from straightforward. This chapter will attempt to present a methodology for identifying and targeting the poorest of the poor. For this we use rural Bangladesh as our case study, chosen because of the extensive poverty analysis that has been undertaken and we look at how this can be extended so that effective policies can be implemented to facilitate poverty alleviation. The outline of the chapter is as follows. In the next section we highlight why focusing on 'the poorest' is of importance. The following section forms a background for the targeting analysis with a contextual perspective of 'the poorest'. We then provide a detailed discussion of the types of instruments used for poverty targeting/identification. In the final two sections of the chapter we consider some of the practical, or 'processing', issues associated with targeting before summarizing.

Why focus on 'the poorest'

The concern for the poorest is not just an issue of social justice or of moral judgement (although separation of ethics from economics was inconceivable in the days of classical political economy). Recent advances in development theory suggest that improvements in distribution are also instrumentally important in achieving higher economic growth, a faster rate of poverty reduction and higher social capital. A pro-poor distribution policy does not advocate income transfer, it strives to transform the poor from passive recipients of aid into active agents of high-quality growth. 'Distribution' implies distributing physical capital (recall land reform in the countries of the East Asian miracle, for instance) as well as human capital (broad-based access to education, health and nutrition). However, promoting pro-poor growth as a strategy for reducing poverty can only be effective if it also addresses inequalities, as the higher the level of initial inequality the lower the future growth rate (Sen, 2001).

Despite numerous NGO outreach initiatives in Bangladesh, the extreme poor have not benefited from social development programmes as they have usually targeted the poor by implementing the same techniques used to deliver microfinance schemes. It has been recognized that such programmes are known actually to exclude the poorest of the poor (Matin, 2002). Excluding the extreme poor from these initiatives means that the physically disabled and elderly who fall into this category are particularly discounted. Just as women were ignored as constituents of development until the 1970s, the disabled and elderly remain neglected in development research and action today (Matin and Hulme, 2003). Evidence from BRAC's Income Generation for Vulnerable Group Development (IGVGD) programme indicates that such beneficiaries are not successful in obtaining VGD support cards although the programme specifically aims to reach the extreme poor (ibid). Targeting the poorest of the poor should therefore identify those experiencing severe deprivation, including the disabled and elderly, so that the systematic exclusion of these groups can be rectified through appropriate initiatives and policies.

The poorest: Early images and current status

The gap between the poor and the poorest has long been a source of policy concern. As early as 1840, the French economist Antoine Buret wrote about the need for constructing the 'tableau of poverty' along with the physiocratic 'tableau of wealth'. Firmin Marbeau, who wrote one of the earlier treaties on pauperism in 19th-century France, was particularly concerned about the state of the poorest, saying that 'in a well-governed State, poverty must not degenerate into indigence. It is in the interests of the rich as much as of the poor that this should be so' (cited in Procacci, 1991: 19).

Writing about livelihood conditions in Faridpur, Bangladesh in 1910, J. C. Jack noted that the population seemed to be divided into four categories: in comfort, below comfort (but above hardship), above indigence and indigence. The first category roughly corresponds to the contemporary equivalent of 'non-poor' (those staying above the poverty line), this proportion stood at 49% in 1910. The other three categories capture successive gradations of poverty, the matched proportions being 28%, 18%, and 5%, respectively. Jack observed that these distinctions were robust to various socio-economic criteria and not derived under income/expenditure-based measures alone. His methodological position, stated over 85 years ago, is worth quoting in full because of its contemporary relevance:

> For easy comprehension ... four classes were adopted, representing varying material conditions between comfort and actual want, to one of which each family was allocated. The classification was not made upon figures of income or expenditure, but always upon an inspection of the family and the family circumstances in its own homestead. Only such families as were well housed, well-fed, well-clothed according to the evidence of the eye were permitted to be classified as living in comfort. By such a safeguard it was intended that the method of enquiry should be thoroughly practical, avoiding anything academic or mechanical, but ensuring accuracy by concomitant statistical investigation. (Jack, 1916: 8)

Although only recently recognized in poverty literature, Jack noted the difference between income poverty and other poverty dimensions. The gap between those living in extreme poverty and those who are not, is often difficult to quantify in the income dimension given the very nature of the former. Jack noted that while on the average the statistical 'figures of income probably represent correctly the facts' (1916: 81), the income of the indigent families is 'often so precarious and so largely made up of charity as to be impossible of exact calculation' (ibid). Here qualitative impressions may be more useful. The imagery of poverty as reflected in literature, is often instructive in deepening understanding about poverty. Images also help to cross-check statistics and can help form an idea about who belongs to the poorest groups.

Jack's study noted considerable differentiation among the poor. Some of the latter displayed 'poverty only in the quality of their houses and their clothes' (Jack, 1916: 66), while for others it was a clear case of undernourishment. In addition to this was the heterogeneity in occupation, which deserves attention in the subsequent examination of indicators. In Jack's study, the emphasis on the gender dimension to poverty and vulnerability also stand out:

> With few exceptions, those families which will be found in chronic need in any Eastern Bengal village will on enquiry prove to be either widows left with a family of young children or old people who are past work and who have no relatives to support them. (ibid.)

Many of the currently in vogue concepts of poverty, some of which will be discussed in this chapter, can be traced back to earlier thinking on poverty in Bengal and can assist in the development of relevant indicators for poverty monitoring and policy choices.

Differentiation statistics

Poverty trends have shown little change since Jack wrote his book. According to his estimates, 51% of the rural population in Eastern Bengal (Faridpur) lived in absolute poverty in 1910. The matched figure for 1994, obtained from a 62 village survey undertaken by the Analysis of Poverty Trends (APT) Project of the Bangladesh Institute of Development Studies (BIDS), is estimated to be 52%. The lowest two categories in Jack's classification correspond to the category of extreme poverty ('above indigence' and 'indigence') and represented 22.3% of the rural population in 1910. In 1994, the matched figure was 22.5%. Despite the difficulties in making comparisons over such a long period, the extent of poverty is strikingly similar.

The existence of extreme poverty defined in the dimension of income/ expenditure, has traditionally been verified through three major measurement approaches: using information on calorie consumption ('direct' method); using data on income/expenditure ('indirect' method) – of the type outlined in Serajuddin (this volume); and directly asking households to self-classify themselves into poor/extreme poor/non-poor categories ('participatory' or 'subjective' method). These approaches often give contradictory trends across time or space and opinions vary as to which one should be used,[2] however, all three approaches point to the large magnitude of extreme poverty.

Data for the 1995/6 Household Expenditure Survey (HES) produces poverty estimates by the *direct calorie intake* method. Following this approach, one may identify several layers among the poor. The Bangladesh Bureau of Statistics (BBS), for instance, considers two extreme poverty lines: one corresponds to 1,805 calories per day per person (i.e. about 85% of the absolute poverty line of 2,122 calories per day per person); the other line corresponds to 1,600 calories per day per person (i.e. about 75% of the absolute poverty line). Despite the arbitrariness involved in ascertaining the two extreme poverty lines, it relays an alarming message.

The proportion of the population failing to meet the 1,805 calorie norm in rural areas in 1995/6 was as high as 24% while the matched figure for urban areas is higher at 27%. Even if one takes 1,600 calories per day per person as the cut-off mark for the severest poverty, the proportion of the rural population living below that line would be 14%, and 15% for urban areas. The weight of extreme deprivation in aggregate poverty is high. Thus, as a proportion of the total rural poor in 1995/96, the rural extreme poor population was as high as 52%; again, rather strikingly, the corresponding weight for urban areas is even higher (57%). Although targeting extreme poverty in urban areas is an important concern for development policy and analysis, the focus in this chapter is on rural extreme poverty (60%). The same trend emerges when one considers income/expenditure survey data. A BIDS survey of 62 villages provides an estimate of rural income poverty.[3] It reveals that about 52% of the rural population lived in absolute poverty in 1994. This population is divided into two distinct groups: moderate poor (29%) and extreme poor (23%). In other words, in 1994 about 44% of the poor fell into the category of the extreme poor.

This wide gap between the poor and the poorest is also confirmed by subjective data. According to the self-categorization of the BIDS survey respondents, in 1994 the proportion of rural households who lived in 'chronic deficit' throughout the year was 19% (equivalent to the category of the 'extreme poor'), while households facing 'occasional deficit' stood at 32%. These two groups constitute the 'poor' category, comprising 51% of the sample.

Chronic and transitory extreme poverty

Panel data generated for many countries reveal considerable movement in and out of poverty (see for example, Lawson for Uganda – this volume), particularly between extreme and moderate poverty. Bangladesh is no exception, as indicated by the 62 village panel data. Examining project data regarding movement in and out of poverty, three important aspects emerge. First, 42% of the households classified as extreme poor in 1987/88 (a bad agricultural year with crop output affected by severe flood) persisted in extreme poverty during 1989/90 (a good agricultural year in terms of bumper crop harvest). They constituted 10% of rural households in 1989/90, and represent the *chronically* extreme poor, with little chance to ever escape from extreme poverty.

Second, about a third of the households who were termed 'moderate poor' during the first survey slipped into extreme poverty by the second survey. Such slippage is often viewed as being 'stochastic' or temporary in nature because of the association with fluctuations in crop output under rain-fed agriculture, but this may not be true in other cases. The slippage may turn out to be of a long-term nature, as in the event of the sudden death of a principal earning member or some unanticipated crisis involving damage of bullock power, ownership disputes, high social ceremony expenditures (raising dowry for a daughter's marriage) or frequently, health hazard-related risks. Such events can impose substantial coping costs not only on the poor, but also on the vulnerable non-poor.[4]

Third, the panel data indicates considerable presence of transitory extreme poverty, showing that 28% of the extreme poor graduated to moderate poverty and another 30% were actually able to cross, at least for a given period, over the poverty line. This is an antidote to the pessimism often articulated in the development policy discourse regarding the alleged inability of 'development' to reach out to people living in extreme poverty. But, again, the movement in and out of extreme poverty should be calibrated by the fact that such movement itself may have been measured in narrow terms i.e. current income (which is susceptible to annual fluctuation in the agrarian economy context). Had more durable indicators of permanent income been used, the observed fluctuation would have probably been much less.

The movement in and out of extreme poverty should not discount the principal issue advanced at the beginning of this chapter, specifically, that 'development' must begin with the poorest. It is therefore important to differentiate between the 'moderate poor' and those who are 'hardcore poor'. The latter should be accorded priority in development initiatives as they experience numerous deprivations, the severity of poverty experienced is deeper and they tend to endure poverty over an extended period of time (Matin and Hulme, 2003). The extreme poor therefore require specific policy focus based on these severe and multiple deprivations. Materialistic measurements of poverty are insufficient in effectively targeting those who are deprived in a number of capabilities such as healthcare, education, human rights and land (Hulme and Shepherd, 2003). Identifying the extreme poor necessitates a shift away from the income/consumption measurement of chronic poverty to a more holistic view, recognizing the absence of multiple capabilities (Matin and Hulme, 2003). Because the extreme poor experience poverty at more severe levels than the moderate poor, they require diversification in their coping strategies which is particularly difficult when they have low initial asset positions and multiple subsistence pressures (Sen, 2003). Policies should recognize these varied dimensions of poverty while incorporating measures to enhance voice, promote empowerment and raise the institutional capability of the poor and socially disadvantaged groups (ibid).

Targeting and identifying the poor

Principles underlying indicator choice

Before proceeding to a discussion about the indicators and their estimates for rural Bangladesh, the methodology relating to the choice of indicators will be examined. Some basic principles of targeting which merit consideration in devising indicators will first be discussed.

The indicator should aim at capturing broad *group* characteristics (group poverty) rather than focusing on *individual* targeting (Lipton, 1996). Poverty analysis does not allow for the selection of individuals for programme benefits. If the latter approach is used, as in the case of some anti-poverty programmes such as India's Integrated Rural Development Programme (IRDP) or Sri Lanka's Janasaviya, it gives incentives to provide incorrect information which causes a much higher proportion of leakage. More importantly, individual targeting stimulates changes in behaviour which tends to reduce labour income in order to achieve programme benefits (Besley and Kanbur, 1993). Such problems become even more difficult when it comes to distinguishing between extreme poor and moderate poor. But *if* one can establish that households with particular characteristics are likely to be poor, then anti-poverty projects can target these groups (indicator targeting), or identify commodities or types of employment they are likely to select (self-targeting). Self-selection is a targeting mechanism which has generally been used in Bangladesh to select recipients for microfinance schemes. The structure of self-selection is designed to discourage participation of the non-poor by offering small, short-term loans and requiring beneficiaries to attend regular group meetings (Marr, 1999).

Cost-effectiveness is another reason why group targeting may be preferred to individual targeting. Steering project benefits towards individuals would require prohibitively costly nation-wide surveys over and above the problem of under-reporting income/consumption. In short, the central principle is to identify groups that have a high probability of being poor so that projects, programmes and policies may cost-effectively target them.

Note that the concept of 'group targeting' includes not only household parameters, but also the characteristics of the geographic region in which the poor are located. The concept is sensitive to seasonal variation whereby particular periods display high distress intensity. Provided that such zones of distress are known, targeting regionally under imperfect information is best practice, especially from the vantage point of targeting the severely poor. Studies also show that errors of spatial targeting are much less than those made in individual targeting. The problem is that knowledge about the variation in poverty rates across space in Bangladesh is still too limited to be a firm guide in practice, despite some attempts to study this matter (GoB, 1991; Ravallion and Wodon, 1997). Even when the spatial poverty maps are available they typically remain restricted at the upazilla (sub-district) level. This is because poverty estimates predicted at the local levels below upazilla are vulnerable to large standard errors.[5] However, indirect evidence such as agricultural wage rate for unskilled labour suggests that there is considerable variation across villages within an upazila or a union (GoB, 1991). The suggested approach in this chapter combines insights derived from household characteristics based poverty profiles as well as analyses of the regional (and seasonal) dimensions to poverty.

The indicator(s) for targeting should not only be effective in *minimizing leakage* to the non-poor, but also in ensuring *broad coverage* of the target group. The first aspect, which focuses on the *targeting ability* (i.e. how sensitive is the given indicator in identifying the target group?), may be viewed as the necessary condition in order to be selected as a targeting indicator. The second aspect, focusing on the *representativeness* issue (i.e. how effective is the indicator in reaching the maximum numbers of the target group?), may be termed as the sufficient condition. Certain indicators may satisfy the first principle but fail to meet the second criteria, making it too restrictive. The reverse example is also true. Some of these examples are discussed below with actual poverty data.

Identifying the poorest and most vulnerable

In identifying the poorest and most vulnerable we firstly examine the predictability of extreme poverty incidence, i.e. we investigate the *targeting ability* and *representativeness* of an initial set of indicators. We sub-divide the discussion of this by considering a series of hypotheses that raise interesting questions for discussion. After giving due attention to practical considerations of easy implementation, the preferred choice of core indicators will be determined. We take evidence from the previously mentioned Analysis of Poverty Trends (APT) project. The method of investigation proceeds as follows:

'*Some indicators are expressive of extreme poverty, but remain restrictive to only a small part of it*': Indicators such as the possession of minimum clothes, access to 'safe' drinking water and sanitation fall under this category. These indicators meet the first criteria of targeting ability, but not the second criteria as they cover only a small part of the target population. For example, 57% of the rural population without a minimum of two items of clothing are considered extreme poor compared with 24% for those who have such access. But the indicator covers only 4% of the total population and 8% of the total extreme poor. Access to drinking water varies by poverty status as the incidence of extreme poverty is higher for those who do not have access to tube-well water compared with the category that do have such access (34% vs. 26%). Again, the indicator is very limited in scope, addressing only 4% of rural inhabitants.

The relative merit of sanitation as a poverty-sensitive indicator is better on this score. A considerably higher percentage of children under 10 years old who use open space fall under the category of 'extreme poor'. The incidence of extreme poverty is 35% in this case compared with only 10% recorded for the sanitary/slab category. Users of open space constitute as high as 79% of the extreme poor. Nevertheless, the indicator has obvious disadvantages as the use of sanitary facilities is not just a question of income status, but also one of the attitudes influencing the non-poor. The latter explains why only 22% of rural households use the sanitary facility even though the share of non-poor is roughly 50%. In short, targeting by this indicator will result in considerable leakage to the non-poor and moderate poor.

Numbers, however, should not be the ultimate criteria for inclusion on the list of core indicators. Some indicators may be limited in coverage but may speak of additional dimensions of vulnerability, such as gender, caste and ethnicity. Female-headed households, for example, display a much higher incidence of extreme poverty compared to male-headed households (37% vs. 22%). However, the overall percentage of such households is quite low at only 5%, barring the widespread application of this indicator (Table 5.1). However, the number should not detract our attention from the substantive point of the gendered perspective relating to poverty and vulnerability.

'*Some indicators are analytically relevant as determinants of poverty, but less sensitive to the state of extreme poverty*': Indicators such as literacy and land tenure fall under this category. While there is no denying that levels of educational attainment matter in determining long-term poverty, the first criteria of targeting ability is not satisfied. Estimates of poverty in rural areas based on the education of the household head indicate that the incidence of extreme poverty for those who are illiterate is 32%, yet for those experiencing moderate poverty, 34% are illiterate. Similar estimates reveal that this indicator is insufficient in predicting the incidence of poverty in this category, possibly due to the high levels of adult illiteracy in general. The same applies to targeting ability by tenancy status, although the variation among tenure groups is slightly less pronounced. The incidence of extreme poverty among non-cultivators is 38.5% compared to 34% of those experiencing moderate poverty. These two indicators can therefore be disregarded for the purpose of identifying the poorest.[6]

'*Some indicators capture the poorest successfully, albeit, allowing for some leakage*': Three indicators in this category stand out prominently: land ownership, housing and occupation (Table 5.2). In the past, identifying functionally landless households (those owning up to 0.5 acres) has been used as a method for targeting the poor, particularly in the context of microcredit. Indeed, the functionally landless category contains 71% of the rural households in extreme poverty. However, not all households within this land-size group can be termed as extreme poor as 57% of moderate poor households also belong to this category (Table 5.2) and there are also non-poor households in the smaller land-size groups (Ravallion and Sen, 1994). In short, land alone will not suffice for the targeting purpose.

Housing is another indicator which strongly expresses extreme poverty. The incidence of those experiencing extreme poverty who reside in the lowest two categories on the housing scale together account for 44% (Table 5.2).

Table 5.1 Estimates of rural poverty by gender status of household heads in Bangladesh

Gender status	% of households in the category	Incidence of poverty	
		Extreme	Moderate
Female-headed	5	37.3	62.7
Male-headed	95	21.8	78.2

Table 5.2 Rural poverty estimates by land ownership, housing categories and occupation in Bangladesh, 1994

Categories	% of households in category	Incidence of Poverty		% of poor households	
		Extreme	Moderate	Extreme	Moderate
Landownership (acres)					
<.50	48.6	38.3	33.3	71.0	57.2
.50 – 1.49	21.4	23.1	31.7	18.8	23.9
1.50 – 2.49	12.2	14.3	23.0	6.7	9.9
2.50 – 4.99	11.4	5.3	17.3	2.3	7.0
5.00+	6.3	4.8	8.4	1.1	1.9
Housing category					
Jhupri	1.6	63.6	27.3	4.1	1.6
1 room thatch	23.5	44.0	33.7	39.4	28.0
1+ room thatch	13.1	34.1	35.8	17.1	16.7
Tin made house	54.3	17.6	25.5	36.5	48.9
Pucca house	7.5	10.5	18.9	2.9	4.8
Major Occupation					
Cultivator	41.6	20.6	24.4	33.2	39.5
Agricultural wage labour	18.5	46.7	40.2	37.3	22.8
Non-agricultural wage labour	2.7	24.3	34.6	2.6	2.2
Rural industry, informal service, etc.	7.0	26.5	38.5	7.3	6.2
Trade	10.4	9.3	29.6	4.0	12.4
Transport	4.5	22.3	34.0	4.9	5.1
Construction	1.8	36.5	34.6	2.6	3.0
Salaried service	9.5	4.7	14.7	2.0	4.8
Others	5.8	27.6	19.7	6.1	4.0

Source: Compiled from Rahman et al. (1996)

However, this indicator is not without problems as approximately 37% of extremely poor households live in tin-made structures.[7]

Using occupation as an indicator also has potential for identifying the extreme poor. Estimates reveal that the percentage of people living in extreme poverty is highest in the case of agricultural wage labourers. According to a BIDS survey, 47% of these labourers fall under the 'extreme poor' category (Table 5.2). This observation is also vindicated by the HES data generated by the BBS. According to the latter source which uses consumption data, the incidence of absolute poverty (extreme and moderate taken together) in the agricultural labour group was 71% in 1991/92. This can be compared with the 87% combined figure derived under the BIDS survey using income data for 1994. In terms of overall poverty ranking in 1991/92, agricultural labourers are followed by fishermen and non-agricultural labourers, having a headcount index in excess of 50%. On the other end of the spectrum, the lowest poverty is reported by the formal sector service holders (14%), owner farmers (24%) and tenant farmers (37%). Rural petty traders and industrial owners/workers occupy an intermediate position. The poverty ranking, particularly for the highest and lowest poverty groups, varies little with the change in the survey year, implying the stability of this indicator.

The BIDS survey for 1994 also broadly indicates the same poverty rank-ing by occupation. Targeting by occupation also meets the requirement of representativeness. The group of agricultural labourers not only displays the highest probability of being in poverty, it also contains 37% of the extreme poor. As such, the group constitutes about a fifth of the total rural households (Table 5.2).

'Since no single indicator contains sufficient information, it is better to combine those that are the most effective': The preceding discussion shows that the poor-est on the land scale reside in the functionally landless category, the poorest on the housing scale are located in the jhupri (squatter-type housing con-structed from natural and 'recycled' materials such as leaves, gunny sacks, plastic sheeting and old bits of timber) and one-room thatch categories, and the poorest on the occupation scale relate to the category of agricultural wage labour. It seems, therefore, reasonable to combine information contained in the land, housing and occupation indicators (Tables 5.3–5.5). The objective is to find the common set that is present in the poorest category on all three scales as this will help to identify the poorest of the poor.

For example, consider the combination of housing and occupation. This can be analysed from various angles. Approximately 60% of the total agri-cultural wage labour households in the BIDS sample reside in the two lowest housing categories (Table 5.3). The incidence of extreme poverty among agri-cultural labourers dwelling in the various housing categories consistently de-clines with housing status as one proceeds from jhupri to pucca/tully housing (made out of permanent durable materials such as brick and tile) (Table 5.3). Clearly, the error of targeting can be further minimized by combining hous-ing and occupation. This is not only an issue of locating the extreme poor in quantitative terms, but also one of identifying the most vulnerable. There are differences in poverty levels even within the agricultural wage labour. Thus, 75% of agricultural labourers living in jhupri are extreme poor compared

Table 5.3 Incidence of poverty among agricultural labour households by housing category in Bangladesh

Housing Categories	% of agricultural labourer households	% of agricultural labourer households in each housing category	Incidence of poverty among agricultural labourers (%)	
			Extreme	Moderate
Jhupri	5.0	54.5	75.0	25.0
1 room thatch	54.3	42.7	54.0	35.0
1+ room thatch	15.2	21.4	51.4	43.2
Tin house	24.7	8.4	50.0	31.7
Pucca/tully house	0.8	4.4	–	100.0
TOTAL (Average)	100.0	(18.5)	(46.7)	(40.2)

to 51–54% observed for the two thatch categories. Such gradations within wage labourers can only be captured by simultaneously applying housing and occupation-based indicators.

Combining land ownership and housing can also assist in identifying the extreme poor. Microcredit programmes in Bangladesh mainly follow the criteria of land ownership, defined as owning up to 0.5 acres of land ('functionally landless'). Observations conclude that there is considerable variation in poverty even within this land-size group, a feature ignored by many of the microcredit programmes. As a result, these programmes may become restricted to the richer sections among the poor.[8] Data presented in Table 5.4 illustrates this possibility. The poorest among the functionally landless live at the bottom end of the housing scale with the lowest two housing categories containing about 40% of these households and 52% of the total extreme poor.

Similar results can be derived when information on land ownership and occupation is considered together (Table 5.5). For the functionally landless households, variation in the incidence of extreme poverty measured on the occupation scale is considerable. As before, the wage labour households stand out as the most poverty-stricken category. While there is little difference in the extreme poverty rate between cultivator and wage labour households,

Table 5.4 Poverty estimates by housing and land ownership in Bangladesh

Type of Housing	% of Poor Households		% of Landownership (acres)				
	Extreme	Moderate	<.50	.50 - 1.49	1.50 - 2.49	2.50 - 4.99	5.00 +
Jhupri	5.7	2.3	3.0	0.3	–	–	–
1 room thatch	46.1	37.6	37.0	16.7	8.1	8.0	2.4
1 + room thatch	15.1	18.3	14.6	14.6	11.2	10.7	6.0
Tin house	31.0	36.2	41.0	63.7	72.0	65.3	72.3
Pucca house	–	1.4	1.2	1.4	6.8	12.7	17.0
Tully house	2.0	4.2	3.1	3.2	1.9	3.3	2.3
TOTAL	100.0	100.0	100.0 (48.6)	100.0 (21.4)	100.0 (12.2)	100.0 (11.4)	100.0 (6.3)

Table 5.5 Incidence of extreme poverty (%) by occupation – controlling for landholding size – in Bangladeshi sample (1989–1990)

Occupation	Landholding size (acres)			
	Less than 0.50	0.5 - 2.49	2.5 – 4.99	5.00 and above
Cultivator	54.1	18.9	7.5	3.0
Wage labour	57.9	39.9	–	–
Traders	25.6	13.6	12.2	14.6
Service	35.8	20.5	17.1	16.4
Others	49.5	25.5	21.8	4.3

Source: Hossain (1995)

those who could manage to adopt trade and services are substantially better off (26–36% vs. 54–58%).

The information presented in Tables 5.3–5.5 show that there would be considerable targeting gains if one combines the poorest categories as per the three key indicators. The prospective poorest clientele in rural areas would therefore be agricultural labourers residing in jhupri or single structure thatch owning up to 0.5 acres of land.

Favouring land, housing and occupation as the set of three indicators should not create the impression that other characteristics such as region, do not matter. Indeed, the emphasis should be to prioritize the poorest areas first and then apply household level core indicators. By solely analysing infrastructure indicators, for example, considerable differences in poverty rates are noticeable. Examining areas 'with a road and electricity' and 'without a road and without electricity', data indicates that the incidence of extreme poverty is 25% in underdeveloped settings (the latter) compared with 18% in the developed setting (the former).

The 1991 Task Force Report on poverty alleviation attempted to take a closer look at this issue by actually identifying 100 of the most economically depressed upazilas (sub-districts). The Task Force mainly considered the following factors: *(i)* land area per person; *(ii)* proportion of land under broadcast aus and deep water aman[9] varieties of paddy as a measure of low productivity; *(iii)* proportion of irrigated area as a measure of the capacity to adopt modern agricultural technology; *(iv)* the proportion of functionally landless households; and *(v)* the proportion of the population engaged in non-farming activities. Similar exercises have been undertaken by the World Food Programme (WFP) using a distress zone map to implement food-assisted programmes throughout the country. Very recently, the Bangladesh Bureau of Statistics has produced an updated poverty map of Bangladesh presenting poverty estimates at the upazilla level (BBS, 2009).

If regional targeting was combined with household-based indicator targeting both in design and implementation, further gains in fine tuning extreme poor orientated programmes could be achieved.

Process issues

Avoiding the risk of bureaucratic targeting

The implementation of core indicators is an important process issue and has implications for targeting and its effectiveness. For example, the most effective set of indicators may have little impact on the status of the extreme poor if the process of administering is left to the bureaucratic discretion of the programme managers. This is particularly true in the case of indicator targeting through means-testing as opposed to indicator targeting via self-selection. The risks of leakage thus cannot be avoided in the case of bureaucratic targeting, as evidenced by the experience of Food-for-Education (BIDS, 1997). Such risks can only be minimized through local consultation with communities and NGOs, a task that can be institutionally facilitated by the presence of effective local government. The need for building and/or coalescing grassroots level initiatives outside the domain of public government, however, can create a demand-driven, receiving mechanism 'from below' and also act as a pressure mechanism on the quality of local governance (Sen, 2001). Not only should the risk of bureaucratic targeting be avoided but it is also important to minimize the risks of leakage and infiltration of the non-target group.

Existing local government machinery is far short from the task of 'managing development' at the grassroots level, and despite attempts to reinvigorate the concerns for local government,[10] the actual devolution of power to lower tiers of government is seriously restricted. Indeed if anything, the official discourse on local government is disproportionately focused on electoral issues such as appropriate methods used for voting or the gender composition of the members, rather than with the taxing, spending and jurisdictional power of the local bodies. It is therefore unlikely that local government will soon become an efficient organ of power, co-ordinating and managing development at the grassroots level, at least in the short to medium term.[11] In the absence of such effective overseeing machinery in place, it is difficult to see how the risks of bureaucratic targeting and leakage can be avoided. Even if we arrive at a consensus on the targeting indicators along the lines suggested in this chapter, the question of finding an alternative solution to inefficiencies at local levels remain.

Exchanging targeting information with locally successful self-targeted programmes

One suggestion is to detect the extreme poor who participate in programmes which are self-targeted to the needs of the poorest. A number of evaluations have indicated that programmes such as Food-for-Work (FFW) and Vulnerable Group Development (VGD) successfully target some of the poorest groups. Data reveals that the lowest expenditure households in rural areas have an overwhelming presence in the programmes, with 72% of FFW and 92% of VGD participants representing the extreme poor (Sen and Begum, 1998). Between the two programmes, VGD beneficiaries stand out as the most disadvantaged in terms of poverty ranking. A major reason for the success of VGD targeting may lie in their use of 'self-targeting'. As previously mentioned, this targeting method allows people to select themselves as beneficiaries based on programme characteristics such as inferior quality wheat, hard manual labour occupations, social stigma and gender criteria such as being an 'abandoned' female-headed household.

Although hard data is yet to be compiled on the extent to which FFW and VGD successfully reach the extreme poor, it appears that 5–10% of rural households have already been brought under their ambit. Other important facets of these programmes are their country-wide coverage and a system of monitoring which, although not without deficiencies, is able to provide important buffers to the extreme poor in times of severe economic stress. Targeting a substantial number of poor households may be an opportune entry point into the arena of pro-poor policy interventions for the poor living in rural areas. A mechanism which facilitates information exchange between FFW, VGD and policymakers may bring about favourable public policy and ensure broad-based participation of the poor in poverty alleviation programmes. Collaborating with programmes that have been successful in reaching the poorest can reduce costs and the likelihood of repeating mistakes while promoting mutuality between policymakers and the programmes. Such exchange can result in more socially equitable and inclusive pro-poor policies and analyses so that the extreme poor are not denied access to poverty alleviation interventions.

Conclusion

This chapter is premised on the emerging evidence that the poor are not a homogeneous group and that sharp divisions exist among the poor by sex, region, occupation, land ownership, housing, education, access to infrastructure and even clothing. It argues that the poorest warrant specific analytical and policy focus as policies targeted to the non-poor and moderate poor may not necessarily reach or favour the extreme poor. The task of targeting the extreme poor is evidently complex as no single factor acts as a good proxy for extreme poverty. As the majority of literature on targeting focuses only on distinguishing between the poor and the non-poor, acknowledging the extreme poor as a distinct target group with specific characteristics is important to prevent their exclusion from development action and policy.

The objective of this chapter has been to devise extreme-poor sensitive indicators by emphasizing broad group characteristics rather than individual targeting. It suggests that the indicators for targeting should not only be effective in minimizing leakage to the non-poor but also ensure broad coverage of the target group. The first aspect of this principle focuses on the sensitivity of the given indicator in identifying the target group, referred to as the *targeting ability*. The second aspect focuses on the *representativeness* issue, examining the effectiveness of the indicator in reaching the maximum numbers of the target group. Having analysed a number of possible indicators it is evident that some will meet the first criteria but fail to meet the second, and vice versa.

After examining the suitability of various indicators, three criteria met the above two conditions of targeting, these were: land ownership, housing and occupation. Considered individually, however, each allows for some leakage which can be avoided if these criteria are combined to identify the poorest of the poor. A particular conclusion derived in this chapter relates to the intuitive observation that since no single indicator, however efficient, contains sufficient information, it is better to combine those that are most informative. Following this approach, the chapter suggests that the poorest of the poor in rural Bangladesh are likely be agricultural labourers residing in jhupri or single structure thatch dwellings, owning 0.5 acres of land or less. These indicators also meet the criteria of visibility: they are easy to capture. Combining such indicators contrasts with traditional targeting approaches which mainly use gender and/or land holdings to identify the poorest.

While household level core indicators favour the set of three indicators, this should not create the impression that other characteristics such as region do not matter. The emphasis should be to prioritize the poorest areas first and then apply household-based indicators. However, even the most effective set of indicators can have little effect on the status of the extreme poor if the process of administering is left to the bureaucratic discretion of the programme managers. This risk can be minimized through local consultation with communities and NGOs, a task which can be institutionally facilitated by the presence of effective local government. Given the relative absence of the latter, an 'intermediate' solution is advocated for the short to medium term. FFW and VGD have successful track records of reaching the poorest, possibly due to their country-wide coverage, a system of monitoring which provides buffers in times of severe economic stress and the use of the self-selection approach. Promoting a mechanism of information exchange between FFW, VGD and policymakers could help facilitate more socially equitable and inclusive pro-poor policies so that the extreme poor are not denied access to poverty alleviation interventions.

Endnotes

1. This chapter is based on an earlier paper (Sen and Begum, 1998) prepared for the World Health Organization. Although there is more recent data available – i.e. Analysis of Poverty Trends surveys (2001 and 2004) and Household Expenditure Survey (2000 and 2005) – the general methodological approach remains valid.
2. There is a growing body of literature on the issue. For a Bangladesh-specific survey, see Ravallion and Sen (1996).
3. Unless otherwise mentioned, the rural estimates of indicators presented in this chapter relate to the 62 village data generated by the APT Project of BIDS collected in 1987, 1989/90 and 1994.
4. This issue is discussed in detail in Rahman (1995) and Sen (1996).
5. The recently updated poverty map for 2005 is no exception to this where local poverty estimates are generated at the level of upazilla only for statistical reasons as mentioned above (see BBS, 2009).
6. For detail on statistics presented, refer to Sen and Begum (1998).
7. It is possible that tin obtained through relief under various disaster mitigating and housing projects contributed to this anomalous outcome.
8. Hossain (1988) found that only 14% of Grameen households belonged to the agricultural wage labour category, although the targeting criteria of 0.5 acres was strictly followed.
9. 'Aus' and 'aman' are the two types of rice paddy grown in Bangladesh. The term 'broadcast' refers to the method of cultivation while 'deep

water' refers to the level of water in the field where the particular type of rice paddy is cultivated.
10. See Bill on *Gram Sarkar* (Village Government), 2003.
11. This remains a valid observation, even in the very recent political context following a local government election held in January 2009, since the broader institutional issues required for functioning upazila governance remains far from settled as yet.

References

Bangladesh Bureau of Statistics (BBS) (2009) *Updating Poverty Maps of Bangladesh: Key Findings*.

Bangladesh Institute of Development Studies (BIDS) (1997) *Enhancing accessibility to and retention in primary education for the rural poor in Bangladesh*, BIDS (Mimeo), Dhaka.

Besley, T. and Kanbur, R. (1993) 'The principles of targeting', in M. Lipton and J. Van der Gaag (eds), *Including the poor: proceeding of a symposium organized by the World Bank and International Food Policy Research Institute*, WB/IFPRI, Washington, D.C.

Government of Bangladesh (GoB) (1991) 'Task force report on poverty alleviation', *Report of the Task Forces on Bangladesh development strategies for the 1990s*. Vol. 1. University Press Ltd, Dhaka.

Hossain, M. (1988) 'Nature and impact of the Grameen Bank in Bangladesh', IFPRI Research Report.

Hossain, M. (1995) 'Socioeconomic characteristics of the poor', in H. Z. Rahman and M. Hossain (eds), *Rethinking Rural Poverty,. Bangladesh as a Case Study*, Sage Publications, New Delhi.

Hulme, D. and Shepherd, A. (2003) 'Conceptualizing chronic poverty', *World Development* 31(3): 403–423.

Jack, J. C. (1916) *The Economic Life of a Bengal District*, Oxford University Press (reprint 1975), London.

Lipton, M. (1996) 'Defining and measuring poverty: conceptual issues', background paper for Human Development Report 1997, UNDP (Mimeo), New York.

Marr, A. (1999) 'The poor and their money: what have we learned?', *ODI Poverty Briefing*, ODI, London.

Matin, I. (2002) 'Targeted development programmes for the extreme poor: experiences from BRAC experiments', *CPRC Working Paper* No 20, CRPC, Manchester.

Matin, I. and Hulme, D. (2003) 'Programs for the poorest: learning from the IGVGD program in Bangladesh', *World Development* 31(3): 647–665.

Procacci, G. (1991) 'Social economy and the government of poverty', in G. Burchell, C. Gordon and P. Miller (eds), *The Foucault effect: Studies in Governmentality*, Harvester Wheatsheaf, London.

Rahman, H. Z. (1995) 'Crisis and insecurity: the other face of poverty', in H. Z. Rahman and M. Hossain (eds), *Rethinking Rural Poverty: Bangladesh as a Case Study*, Sage Publications, New Delhi.

Rahman, H. Z., Hossain, M., and Sen, S. (eds) (1996) *1987–94: Dynamics of Rural Poverty in Bangladesh,* BIDS (Mimeo), Dhaka.

Ravallion, M. and Sen, B. (1994) 'Impacts on rural poverty of land-based targeting: further results for Bangladesh', *World Development* 22(6): 823–838.

Ravallion, M. and Sen, B. (1996) 'When method matters: monitoring poverty in Bangladesh', *Economic Development and Cultural Change* 44(4): 761–792.

Ravallion, M. and Wodon, Q. (1997) 'What are a poor farmer's prospects in rural non-farm sector', Policy Research Department, World Bank (Mimeo), Washington D.C.

Sen, B. (1996) 'Movement in and out of poverty: a tentative explanation', in H. Z. Rahman, M. Hossain and B. Sen (eds) *1987–94: Dynamics of Rural Poverty in Bangladesh,* BIDS (Mimeo), Dhaka.

Sen, B. (2001) 'Chronic poverty and development policy in Bangladesh: overview study', draft circulated at Chancellors Conference Centre, University of Manchester 7–9 February 2001.

Sen, B. (2003) 'Drivers of escape and descent: changing household fortunes in rural Bangladesh', *World Development* 31(3): 513–534.

Sen, B. and Begum, S. (1998) 'Methodology for identifying the poorest at local level', World Health Organization and Bangladesh Institute of Development Studies, Dhaka.

World Food Programme (WFP) (2004) *Local Estimation of Poverty and Malnutrition in Bangladesh*, WFP and BBS, Dhaka.

About the authors

Binayak Sen is currently at the World Bank and previously worked at the Bangladesh Institute of Development Studies (BIDS). He has a broad research interest in Bangladesh development issues and, since 2005, also worked on the problems of lagging regions and labour market issues in India, Sri Lanka, and Pakistan. His recent works include: *Chronic Poverty in Bangladesh: Tales of Ascent, Descent, Marginality and Persistence?* (with David Hulme, 2006) – a collaborative initiative between CPRC, University of Manchester, and BIDS; and several chapter contributions to a recent study of *Moving out of Poverty: The Promise of Empowerment and Democracy in India* (edited by Deepa Narayan, 2009) – a co-publication of Palgrave Macmillan and World Bank.

Sharifa Begum is currently working as Senior Research Fellow in the Population Studies Division, Bangladesh Institute of Development Studies, and is also the Chief of the Population Studies Division. Her current research interests include fertility and its determinants, ageing and elderly, morbidity, reproductive health, family planning, women's issues, and poverty and its interface with demographic phenomena. She received her MA in economics from the University of Dhaka, MSc in Medical Demography from London School of Hygiene and Tropical Medicine and PhD in Population Studies from the International Institute for Population Sciences, Bombay, India.

CHAPTER 6

Testing combined targeting systems for cash transfer programmes: The case of the CT-OVC programme in Kenya

Carlos Alviar, Francisco Ayala and Sudhanshu Handa

Cash transfer (CT) programmes have gained increasing importance within poverty reduction strategies in recent years but national governments and donors have queried how well targeted such programmes are. This chapter describes and assesses targeting instruments in the Kenya Cash Transfer for Orphans and Vulnerable Children (CT-OVC) – an example of a CT in the 'high poverty and low technical capacity' environments characteristic of sub-Saharan Africa.

The chapter starts with a theoretical review of targeting performance and mechanisms. This is followed by a discussion of combined targeting systems in contexts where high levels of poverty make it difficult to identify the poorest. The Kenya CT-OVC programme combines categorical, proxy means test, and community methods of targeting. Evidence from the CT-OVC indicates that targeting effectiveness is determined by a dynamic range of factors and suggests that combining multiple targeting approaches tends to improve performance. Despite its complexity, the initial operational experience has been positive and has covered 25,000 households. The chapter identifies a number of major challenges including: information constraints, operational costs and community acceptance, and sustainability. It remains to be seen whether these relatively complex targeting mechanisms can be scaled-up in low capacity environments. Variations of the model are planned for similar programmes in Tanzania and Bangladesh.

Introduction

Cash transfer (CT) programmes represent a new wave of anti-poverty programmes in developing countries. Emanating from Latin America and the Caribbean and now taking root in many parts of the developing world, these CT programmes (usually but not always conditional on recipient behavioural obligations) use a variety of targeting mechanisms to ensure that programme resources reach the poorest and most vulnerable. Indeed the political acceptance of these programmes is thought to be due in part to their ability to reach the poorest in a transparent and cost-effective manner. In theory, targeting also increases the poverty impact of a programme when there is a tight poverty-alleviation budget. For these reasons, in recent years, targeting is seen by some to be an essential factor in the design of social protection programmes, both to maintain political support and to ensure that scarce resources reach the poorest and most vulnerable.

As noted in Sen and Begum's chapter (this volume) which considered the linkages between standard poverty measures and targeting, good targeting is hard to do. Grosh (1997) reviews the lessons and experiences with various targeting methods used in developing countries. She begins by stating that 'targeting can work' most of the time, and especially when dealing with the selection of beneficiary households from the poorest two quintiles. Nevertheless, she reminds us that 'it doesn't always' work and cases do exist where a random selection of beneficiaries would have allotted a greater share of programme resources to the poor than did the targeting system. Furthermore, we must not underestimate the importance of implementation and project design as key factors affecting the dynamics of any poverty reduction scheme. For example, Grosh goes on to cite country income levels as well as the degree to which governments are 'held accountable for their actions, and the degree of inequality' (1997: 24) as determinants of improved targeting performance. These dynamic relationships need to be understood when deciding on the type and number of targeting systems to be used. But to what extent do they improve the effectiveness with which we implement targeting systems? The answer is not much because there are pre-existing conditions that we cannot affect, but they do provide us with the possibility of predicting how successful targeting systems might be in a given situation.

More important to this chapter and the productive contribution to the literature on targeting systems are the determinants of targeting performance which are controllable by programme officials and project managers. Coady et al. (2004) review the targeting effectiveness of programmes from around the world, and conclude that there is no magic bullet to ensuring targeting success; that is to say, no one approach seems to dominate another, implying that success depends as much on administrative capacity and operational efficiency as it does on the actual instrument used. However one conclusion from their analysis is that multiple targeting methods tend to work better than single mechanisms, a result which is important for this chapter.

The purpose of this chapter is to present and assess the targeting instrument used in the Kenya Cash Transfer for Orphans and Vulnerable Children (CT-OVC). This experience is useful for a number of reasons. First, as mentioned earlier, CTs are expanding rapidly throughout the developing world, and are seen as an important response to chronic poverty, food insecurity, and under-investment in human capital. This is the case even in the very poorest regions such as sub-Saharan Africa (SSA) where per capita incomes are below US$1,000 and sometimes half that figure. Among the very poorest countries, targeting is necessary, at least in the short and medium term, due to limited state resources and high levels of poverty (often over 40%). In these countries, the policy discussion has focused on social protection for the poorest 10–15% of the population, so it is important to document an example of a situation where only a tiny proportion of the poor are targeted for programme benefits. Second, in situations of high poverty and low technical capacity as in much of SSA, a key question is the type of targeting instrument that can work in practice, and the associated administrative costs implied by such systems. Finally, the CT-OVC programme in Kenya is a useful case study because it involves multiple targeting instruments, which is unique in the SSA context, and can thus provide useful lessons for other new and upcoming programmes in the region.

Why target?

The socio-political arena historically has included two main schools of thought, or principle techniques, when it comes to the topic of beneficiary selection for social protection programmes: universal selection and targeting. Over the past two decades the tendency to rely on universal selection has been gradually replaced by targeting to select beneficiaries for social protection programmes in developed countries as much as in underdeveloped countries (Mkandawire, 2006). Fiscal restrictions and budgetary constraints forced officials to improve the effectiveness of their targeting methods in order to identify those households that were truly poor. Implementing social programmes around the truly poor and vulnerable population proved to be the only way to effectively deliver the significant reductions in poverty that had been promised (Castañeda et al., 2005).

The principle benefit that targeting provides is reflected in the cost-effectiveness of a programme; that is to say that for any given cost, the poor will receive more benefits, or, said another way, that in order to provide any fixed level of benefits a programme's budget can be reduced (Grosh, 1994). Targeting a certain quantity and quality of benefits to the most needed will in turn reflect a bigger change or impact in their welfare than it would have in better off beneficiaries. Though, one of the major problems facing the targeting of public programmes is the difficulty in acquiring reliable information from the possible beneficiaries of the programme. This is especially true with poverty reduction programmes, where the eligibility criteria for a programme can depend directly on the answers to questions concerning the income and consumer spending of the potential beneficiaries (Valdivia and Dammert, 2001), creating an incentive for applicants to be dishonest. For this reason, and in consideration of the budgetary constraints to government spending, CT programmes have been forced to continually improve their methods and introduce various mechanisms with the goal of correctly identifying the target population.

Targeting performance and alternative targeting instruments

Targeting performance

Targeting in social programmes can be analysed within the framework of three distinct criteria: *(i)* Targeting effectiveness (related to inclusion and exclusion errors); *(ii)* Targeting efficiency (related to its administrative costs); and *(iii)* Targeting transparency. Targeting effectiveness refers, on one hand, to minimizing the probability of committing a type I error or type II error. A type I error, or an error of exclusion, refers to the case where individuals are excluded from the programme when they should really be included. Type II error, or error of inclusion, occurs when individuals are included in the programme when they should really be excluded because they do not meet the selected criteria. The efficiency of the targeting system is related to the administrative costs of the implementation and execution of the designed system and is normally compared to the benefits provided by the programme to the beneficiaries. The quantity and quality of the benefits provided, the frequency with which they are issued and the period of exposure to the programme are integrated into the analysis. Transparency refers to the entire process of beneficiary selection, and includes elements such as a system of checks and balances, the degree to which the procedures, rules, and processes are clear and acceptable to the stakeholders, the provision of information, and avenues for recourse and appeals.

Four basic procedures help to determine the consistency or reliability of targeting systems in the quest for performance improvement. First, the maximization of the coverage of the poor can be determined by means of sampling techniques where the total population of impoverished households is compared to the portion of sampled households that are covered by the particular programme (this captures exclusion errors). The minimization of leakage to the non-poor is done by means of indicators which measure the portion of beneficiaries who fall within the poorest quintile (it covers the inclusion errors). Cost-effectiveness is achieved by reducing the overall administrative cost of employing the targeting scheme, such as costs of interviewing, the number of ineligible households interviewed, the complexity of the questionnaire, and the frequency of actualizations and recertification; these costs are typically related to the number of individuals screened. Finally, transparency is shown in the processes of information gathering, the management of information systems, the evaluation of household eligibility and the mechanisms for monitoring and control. It also refers to the quantity and quality of the information received by the communities, the beneficiaries and other stakeholders.

Targeting mechanisms

Targeting mechanisms can generally be divided into three broad categories: individual/household assessment, categorical targeting, and self-selection.

The first of these is based on an evaluation and verification of each and every individual or household that can be eligible for a programme. The second is based on specific characteristics or categories, such as households with children under 5, or individuals over age 60, or all households in a specific geographical area. The third and final mechanism allows anyone to participate, but the programme is designed in such a way as to discourage or encourage particular groups to participate. For example, a universal school feeding programme only reaches households with children who attend school, while a public employment scheme with a low wage would only attract able-bodied individuals who cannot find employment at a higher wage.

Individual or household assessment

Individual/household assessment is a targeting mechanism of direct evaluation and verification of each of the eligible households for the programme. The eligibility of the potential beneficiaries depends directly on the decisions taken by the programme officials (administrators, managers, etc.). The evaluation of households or individuals may include the verification of income, the application of a survey in order to gather information on the applicant, and/or the calculation of a score for each applicant. Since comprehensive verification and evaluation of each applicant is required, this approach is both attractive for CT programmes but also entails the highest administrative costs. There are four ways of undertaking individual assessments: verified means test, simple means test, proxy means test, and community based targeting.

The *verified means test* is a system that determines eligibility for poverty alleviation programmes by carrying out a rigorous evaluation of the potential beneficiary's income and assets by verification of the household through requiring the presentation of documents related to the applicants' payroll, taxes, property, etc., all of which facilitate the recollection and processing of transparent and credible results. Verified means tests are applied more frequently in developed countries that can generally rely on formal information gathering and complete documentation of income, consumption, and well being. The efficacy of this type of targeting is derived directly from the fact that information can be gathered in a reliable way from existing sources and so reduces the administrative cost.

Unlike the verified means test, the *simple means test* is a system that does not undertake an independent verification of incomes of the potential beneficiaries. Generally, home visits are performed in order to verify through a qualitative analysis the levels at which the potential beneficiaries appear to live. By means of the home visits, the information presented by the beneficiary on the application is compared with the qualitative observations of the programme officials during the visit. This type of targeting system can be used for direct cash transfers as well as in-kind benefits or pay extension programmes. The disadvantage of this mechanism is that the beneficiaries could have sufficient incentives to underestimate incomes, provoking failures in the targeting system that can cause inclusion errors, or the provision of benefits to house-holds that are not be eligible for the programme.

The *proxy means test* (PMT) involves the easy recollection of individual char-acteristics (easily observed and difficult to manipulate) or household charac-teristics that are related to levels of well-being or income. It is based around a point system which is calculated for each household, and which finally de-termines the given household's eligibility for the programme through the ap-plication of econometric regression models and the calculation of principal components. In recent years, it has been successfully and frequently applied in underdeveloped countries because of the highly informal labour markets present in these countries that prevent the collection of reliable information on income. In addition, the recent application of this targeting mechanism has shown strong positive results in terms of cost-efficiency and transparency (Castañeda et al., 2005). One of the advantages of this mechanism is that, to a certain extent, it guarantees horizontal equity by assuring that potential bene-ficiaries receive equal treatment even when evaluated by different programme officials. On the other hand, costs may be higher due to the high levels of administration, personal literacy, and advanced information systems required during the different stages of the implementation process of this mechanism. Other advantages of the PMT are that it avoids disincentive for revealing the work status or the true earnings of applicants. The results under this targeting mechanism can almost match the comprehensiveness of a verified means test, and tend to be more precise than a simple means test, due to the use of mul-tiple variables which tend to capture long term or chronic poverty, as opposed to a single income measure which can fluctuate and may not be representative of long term well-being at any given point in time.

Community-based targeting is a mechanism in which determined agents of the community are put in charge of evaluating the eligibility of potential programme beneficiaries. The advantage of the community based targeting is the fact that community members often have better information about the poor or vulnerable members of the community – their resources, needs, and circumstances – than outside organizations, who have to acquire it through information gathering activities. What is more, the activities of collecting, organizing, and verifying information are costly and can drive up general ad-ministrative costs of a social programme if undertaken by outside targeting mechanisms. In the end, community based targeting avoids some costs of other targeting mechanisms because it takes advantage of the existing knowl-edge of community members, which can ultimately be as good as or even better than information collected by outsiders.

Community-based targeting also has significant benefits which are not di-rectly related to cost savings. In order for central governing agents to truly re-turn power to the local communities, they must do more than simply transfer resources. They must also begin the process of transferring the responsibilities that come with the proper selection of beneficiaries and the creation of eligibil-ity criteria that is equitable, just, and which can also identify the poorest and most vulnerable groups within the local population. In order for this transfer of responsibility to take place, members of the community must undertake the following activities: identification of the transfer destination (i.e. the beneficiary); monitoring the distribution of benefits; and potentially be involved in some parts of the process of benefits distribution. Community actors or agents can be derived from a number of pre-existing groups and community organizations like religious groups, NGOs, local government officials, community leaders, local personalities, among others. Community-based targeting is seen to be more transparent as it involves the perception and participation of the communities, creating ownership and empowering its members.

The disadvantage of the system of community based targeting results from the fact that it is relatively unscientific and can easily be manipulated. Therefore, this mechanism has the possibility of creating conflicts and divisions within the community at the moment of the selection of programme beneficiaries if there is disagreement among community leaders or the impression of prejudice, nepotism, or favouritism of any kind. This suggests that community based targeting would be best suited for communities that are very united, clearly defined by regions, or socio-demographic groups, which may be the case in many rural areas in SSA. It also suggests that this mechanism may be less appropriate for urban and other densely populated areas with high mobility and no clear community structure. With higher heterogenic communities, more checks and balances are required.

Categorical targeting

As mentioned previously, categorical targeting of potential beneficiaries involves the application of eligibility criteria which are based on specific characteristics. Those applicants who possess the predetermined characteristics would then fall within the category of programme beneficiaries. This category could be determined by the age of the beneficiary, sex, or geographic region, to name but a few. Generally speaking, though, categorical targeting relies on one of two mechanisms: geographic targeting or demographic targeting.

Geographic targeting requires knowledge of the general geographic distribution of the poorest and most vulnerable groups in a specific area. The mechanism always functions best when focused in areas with a high percentage of the population living in poverty or with desired characteristics. If this is not the case, and the programme was to be applied in areas where a large portion of the population is among the non-poor, there would be a much higher probability for errors of inclusion, which will ultimately provoke inefficient targeting results. The advantages of this mechanism are that it can be very efficient, with low levels of exclusion errors, and administrative costs. A serious disadvantage is that levels of migration could increase in the area of programme coverage and that the resulting relocation of households would reduce the effectiveness of the programme. Experience with geographic targeting from various countries suggests that it is best utilized in combination with other targeting mechanisms that can ensure that the programme resources are being effectively and efficiently distributed to the poorest and most vulnerable households in the area of impact.

The basic tools needed to carry out geographic targeting are poverty maps, geographic information and social indicators, infrastructure coverage indicators and geographic maps of basic needs (Castañeda et al., 2005). A recurrent problem related to this type of targeting is that the required information is not always available or with the pertinent levels of aggregation for the different regions of the developing countries. Results from several different studies have demonstrated that the leakage and under coverage rates for programmes diminish when the size of the geographic area is smaller rather than larger (Grosh, 1994).

The second type of categorical targeting is demographic targeting based on age, sex or household structure. Demographic targeting is based on the selection of groups who are easily defined by a particular characteristic that is clearly correlated with poverty or vulnerability. In addition, if these characteristics can be easily verified, then this mechanism will incur low costs of administration. Similar to geographic targeting, this mechanism is probably best utilized in combination with other methods that guarantee better overall results of the programme's targeting system. Demographic targeting by sex or age has proved to be one of the most commonly used mechanisms within the realm of targeting systems.

Self-selection

Self targeting or self-selection is one of the simplest targeting systems to implement. Under self-selection, the social protection programme has universal eligibility, but contains elements that by design encourage only the poor and vulnerable to access the programme's benefits.

The first of the contributory factors designed to assure that the poor are targeted under self-selection is the cost of participation. Private costs of participation are higher for the non-poor than for the poor not because explicit costs of accessing benefits are higher but rather because opportunity costs are higher for the non-poor. Often times, anti-poverty interventions will take the form of public work schemes that require a full day or various days of unskilled labour with low wages. In other cases, the process of applying, enrolling, and collecting the payment or benefit may require long periods of time waiting in lines and public offices. While outwardly free of explicit charges, the time requirements of accessing these benefits have the inherent opportunity cost of lost wages from other activities or limited hours of employment. For the poor and vulnerable, these costs are much lower, if not altogether non-existent, due to the fact that the poor generally have limited or no source of income.

Secondly, stigma surrounding a social protection programme can be used as a self-selection tool by discouraging the non-poor from participating. For example, food stamps, coupons, and vouchers are noticeably different from cash and, therefore, expose those who use them as beneficiaries of anti-poverty programmes. Regardless of the form it takes, stigma will have two effects on a programme: it will impose a cost on the programme's beneficiaries; and it has the good possibility of lowering leakage rates. On the other hand, creating stigma around a programme can also compromise the dignity of its beneficiaries and as such have the negative effect of discouraging participation in the programme. Accordingly, it should only be implemented as a targeting mechanism after careful consideration and analysis of the cultural and social-environmental characteristics of the impact area have been completed.

Finally, preferences about quality can be manipulated by programmes to self-target the beneficiaries. The two clearest examples of this targeting mechanism is the use of subsidized products that are either preferred by the poor or are of a quality that discourages the non-poor from using them. The former is determined from cultural studies made on the preferences of different socio-economic populations.

Combining targeting mechanisms and new paradigms for poverty reduction programmes in Africa

In reality, most CT programmes combine different targeting options in an attempt at enhancing performance. Notwithstanding the advantages that using solely the PMT has, this sort of targeting system cannot be applied in countries where no substantial differences in income are apparent. In countries in SSA including Kenya, where a significant percentage of inhabitants fall below the poverty line, this method is not refined enough to distinguish the truly ultra-poor from the generally poor. On the other hand, while community based methods are appealing in that they empower local actors and harness local knowledge, there are concerns about elite capture, lack of clarity in the use of eligibility criteria, and transparency.

The main disadvantage with using multiple targeting instruments is the inherent complexity, the administrative costs and the possible time delays, especially in low capacity environments. The cost of targeting is typically charged during the first year of programme implementation and compared with the benefits provided in that year or for the short period that the beneficiaries are expected to be in the programme. In Africa, where CTs tend to be unconditional and aimed at addressing chronic ultra-poverty, beneficiaries are expected to remain in a programme for a period from 4 to 6 years. This means that the upfront cost of targeting can be amortized over a longer period of time. Thus, if a good targeting system (from the cost point of view) should not involve more than 5% of the value transferred, and if the transfer will be given for 4 and up to 6 years, then the upfront cost of targeting can be increased significantly and still be maintained within 5% of the total value of the transfer. This is important in Africa where, as mentioned above, programmes aim to reach the poorest 10–15% in a context where more than half the population is poor. With longer amortization periods, there is greater opportunity to explore multiple targeting methods to ensure that programme benefits truly reach the poorest and most vulnerable and assume the additional costs.

The case study presented below demonstrates the use of multiple targeting instruments – categorical, PMT and community methods – in the high poverty and low capacity context of SSA. This relatively new paradigm integrates three elements that are thought to lead to good performance in targeting. First, as suggested by Coady et al. (2004), it makes use of three different instruments which has been shown to improve targeting performance. Second, it incorporates a proxy means element in the targeting process. The strength of the PMT is that is uses multiple indicators which cannot easily be manipulated, are relatively easily to verify, and tend to represent long term or chronic well-being. Third, it takes advantage of local knowledge by incorporating the opinions of the local community, which also builds local capacity, increases 'buy-in' and potentially reduces conflict and resentment within the community.[1]

Targeting in the Kenya CT-OVC

Background

In response to a concern for the welfare of the high number of orphans and vulnerable children (OVC), the Government of Kenya with technical assistance from UNICEF decided to conduct a cash transfer pilot project to study the feasibility of targeting procedures, transaction costs, case management and use of conditions versus no conditions. The main objective of the CT-OVC programme is to provide a social protection system through regular cash transfers to households living with OVC in order to encourage fostering and retention of OVC within their families and communities and to promote their human capital development. The main objective of the pilot evaluation is to assess and evaluate different operational mechanisms and conditionalities in order to select those which prove to be the more effective and to obtain empirical information for designing a valid model to be scaled-up nationwide. This pilot is an innovative experience for Kenya and the region, including the evaluation of the impact of conditionalities before scaling-up.

The eligibility criteria envisaged by the programme for beneficiary households are as follows:

1. Household having orphaned members or vulnerable children (OVC) aged 0 to 17 years old;
2. Ultra-poor households; and,
3. Not being beneficiary of other cash transfer programmes (applies to direct OVC beneficiaries only, not other household members).

A single/double orphan or children having caregivers who are chronically ill are defined as OVCs.

The targeting system

The targeting mechanism used by the programme is based on the combination of categorical, community and individual selection. **Geographical** areas were selected based on poverty levels and HIV/AIDS prevalence (directly related to OVC). The **community based** targeting process is led by members of the community defined as Location OVC Committees (LOC) who are in charge of identifying households within identified geographic areas based on the eligibility criteria indicated above. LOC are instructed to visit all households who may look *poor and have children* to fill out a targeting form. This form is simple and contains the basic variables to check whether the household visited meets the eligibility criteria. Once the field work is completed, all members of the LOC gather to decide which households qualify or not by discussing the identification eligibility criteria for the programme collected in the targeting form. That information is entered in the Management and Information System (MIS) which does the initial cross-checks. With the clean list, enumerators go back to those households identified by the LOC as eligible, and collect systematic information on them. This verification form requests more detailed information on the household, including a number of *proxy variables* which reflect household welfare, and which were identified in focus groups with community representatives as well as through analysis using national household survey data. The programme defines an ultra poor eligible household as one that meets at least 8 out of 15 characteristics from among 9 different categories: *(i)* education of the head of the household/caregiver; *(ii)* not presently working; *(iii)* occupation; *(iv)* construction materials of the dwelling in walls, floor and roof; *(v)* type of toilet; *(vi)* source of drinking water; *(vii)* source of lighting and cooking fuel; *(viii)* farming acres and ownership of property; and, *(ix)* cattle, goats, sheep, pigs, camels.[2]

This information is entered in the MIS which, after doing the respective cross-checks of the categorical as well as poverty criteria (proxy variables), generates the final list of eligible households. The targeting process actually identifies more eligible households than can be covered with actual programme resources. A ranking system is used to identify families having greater vulnerability so they can access the programme first. The age of the household head is used as priority criteria, so those heads who are under 18 and over 60 are more likely to be selected for the programme. The ranking system to prioritize eligible households is the following:

1. Child headed households (under 18 years of age), and within them, households with larger number of OVC.
2. Eldest headed households, and within them, households with larger number of OVC.

Finally, *the lists are validated by a community assembly,* where programme officers explain to the assembly the rules of the targeting system and then each name is announced out loud in the established order according to the priority criteria. This is the moment for concerns, doubts and questions to be raised by the community regarding the ranking of households for programme eligibility. The options for changes are related to the eligibility and the ranking position assigned to each household.

The basic questions in this system include: *(i)* Does the system select the poorest and most needy? *(ii)* How costly is it to implement? What is the cost of targeting relative to the transfer amount? *(iii)* Does the LOCs visit a large percentage of potentially eligible households? *(iv)* Does the cross-checking process meet its objective? How long does it take? *(v)* Does the community accept the results of the process? How many appeals are lodged and how are they handled? *(vi)* Do government and cooperating partners accept this targeting system? Is there public confidence in its effectiveness?

Effectiveness

Table 6.1 addresses the question of whether the LOCs did visit the large majority of households in the selected locations. From the results shown, it appears that the LOCs did not visit the majority of households with children, which may lead to errors of exclusion. According to the numbers below, it seems the LOCs tried to collect information of those households who actually met the criteria. In fact, the LOCs declared as eligible households 91.7% of those which were visited and data collected.

Table 6.2 shows the characteristics of beneficiaries under the pilot exercise, as of 30 September, 2007, when the baseline data included a total of 15,585 eligible households that were duly validated by their respective communities in 7 different programme sites: Garissa, Homa Bay, Kwale, Kisumu, Migori, Nairobi, and Suba. Eligible households have on average 3.1 OVC and 5.9 members.

Out of a total of 17,300 eligible households only 5,038 (containing 15,618 OVC) were prioritized and invited to enter the programme. In other words, 22.3% of all eligible households were incorporated into the programme. Of the total households entering the programme, 58% (that is 2,022 households) had heads of household under 18 years of age or older than 60 – this is directly because of the prioritizing of such households at the central level. The other 42% of beneficiaries correspond to heads of household aged between

Table 6.1 Number of households in the CT-OVC programme in Kenya

Estimated households in programme locations	191,252	100%
Screened households by LOCs	25,563	13.4%
Eligible households defined by LOCs	23,452	12.3%
Eligible households after verification process completed	15,585	8.1%
Beneficiary households	5,038	2.6%

Source: MOHA, Central Programme Unit of the OVC-CT programme, September 2007

Table 6.2 Characteristics of beneficiary households (hhs) under the pilot CT-OVC exercise in Kenya

OVC per hh	Age of Caregiver	Member per hh	Most prevalent poverty indicators
1 OVC:	<18 yrs: 0.4%	1–3 mem: 16.2%	Lighting fuel: 88.6% paraffin/kerosene
18.4%	18–29 yrs:		Cooking fuel: 84.4% firewood
2 OVC:	14.3%	4 mem: 16.7%	Cattle: 76.7% none
23.8%	30–39 yrs:	5 mem: 18.2%	Dwelling floors: 75.6% mud/cow dung
3 OVC:	28.7%	6 mem: 15.5%	Dwelling walls: 73.6% mud/cow dung
22.3%	40–49 yrs:	7 mem: 12.0%	Dwelling roofs: 70.2% iron sheets
4 OVC:	25.8%	8+ mem: 21.5%	Source of drinking: 49.9% river/pond
16.6%	50–59 yrs:		Sanitary solution: 49.7% pit latrine
5+ OVC:	18.3%		
18.9%	60+ yrs: 12.6%		
3.1 OVC/hh		5.86 mem/hh	Average

Source: MOHA, Central Programme Unit of the OVC-CT programme, September 2007

50 and 60 years old because the programme actually prioritized older heads after child headed and heads above 60.

On the other hand, the hypothesis that verification does not add much to the targeting process seems not true in the Kenyan case. A large percentage of households who were originally identified by LOCs as eligible were rejected after verification. Only 67% of households selected by LOCs were considered eligible after verification by the programme. In other words, 1 out of every 3 households was not correctly selected by LOCs, they failed to identify eligible households meeting the eligibility criteria. It is not clear why they did so, either because they made genuine errors or because they intentionally biased the answers. This highlights the importance of the second level of verification (at programme headquarters). Whether the errors were intentional or not on the part of LOCs is not known, but they were sufficiently large enough to possibly justify the programme verification using poverty proxy variables.

Efficiency and overall costs

Programme beneficiaries in the CT-OVC programme are expected to receive about $300 per year and $1,200 in 4 years; therefore, in order for the cost of targeting to be around 5% of the total transfer amount, it should cost around $60. In fact, the costs are running at $50 per beneficiary despite the complexity of the system.[3] This cost includes the entire process, beginning with the visit of dwellings by LOCs until the community validation of the priority lists. LOC members, enumerators and government officers receive transport and lunch allowances for each day of field work. Additionally, the costs analysis includes materials used in the fields and the costs of pertinent training, transport of forms and data entry. It is worth mentioning that this cost does not include the salaries of programme officials but does take into account their transportation to the training and supervising sites.

If we assume that beneficiaries will receive benefits for 4 years, then the total amount transferred will be approximately $1,200 dollars. The current value[4] is translated into $941 real present value. If this benefit lasts 6 years, the present value would correspond to $1,300. Therefore, the cost of the targeting system could fluctuate between 3.8% and 5.3% of the total amount of the transfer at the present value if the per beneficiary cost remains at $50. However the system has just begun and is still moving down the learning curve. It is expected that the cost of later exercises, based on experience gathered by the programme and its operators, will be lowered to around $30. If so, then the cost would correspond to between 2.3% and 3.2%, which is below 5% despite the complexity of the system.

One of the potential concerns of a system like this is the time needed to carry it into effect. If no delays are met between each of the activities, the process would consume approximately 2 months. In practice however there are delays between activities, due to logistic preparation and bureaucratic procedures, and as a result, it can take up to 4 months before the total list of eligible households is ready. Thus if the system continues to be used, the only way in which it will work at scale is if it is carried out in parallel (in the fashion of a pilot activity). LOCs within a district could be trained at a single site and return to their communities to carry out the targeting all at the same time. As capacity is built provincial and district officers with experience will be able to provide technical assistance and support to the district levels reducing the burden of work at the central level and, thus, making parallel processes more efficient.

Transparency

Communities in the selected locations were, in principle, satisfied with the proposed process. Throughout the targeting process, including, at the validation of lists, the complaints related to the eligibility criteria, the targeting process, the actors involved or the selected households were minimal. It seems the communities understood the targeting process.

The next question concerns whether or not the priority list worked; whether or not the community accepted that only a small percentage of eligible households would become programme beneficiaries. As a matter of fact, only 32.2% of the eligible households were incorporated as programme beneficiaries. The entire community gathered in a *baraza* (assembly) to validate the selection. It was explained that there were many more that could be eligible and that priority was attached according to age. The meetings were long, lasting approximately one day at each community. The large majority of them asked that the names of beneficiaries be read out loud, following the priority listing. In this manner, the members wished to verify whether or not an inclusion error was apparent concerning the age of heads of household. According to the district and programme officers, the large majority of validation processes were accepted by communities. Very few appeals were lodged and more often than not, ages were corrected in order to correctly relocate heads of households. The assemblies, of course, accepted the validation process based on the promise that as more resources become available, the same priority list would be followed and that no later changes could be made by outsiders or politicians. As a matter of fact, priority lists remained in the hands of LOCs.

However, after enrolment, when the payment process started, complaints arose. Households that were part of one of the previous steps presented themselves to inquire about their status in the programme. The fact that cash is delivered can work as an incentive for people to try to find their way in. Still, great effort is needed in the design and implementation of clear and comprehensive communication strategies.

Challenges

The targeting system described in this paper is relatively new and still being tested. As mentioned earlier, a social experiment is being carried out to assess the impact of the programme on a range of outcomes, and part of this evaluation will also assess the performance of the targeting system. Even at this early stage there are already some key lessons learned and challenges that can be shared, and these are described briefly in the rest of this section.

Availability and quality of up-dated information. For the geographical targeting, the characterization of poverty is the prevalent indicator, but political realities are at work so that executing units must balance political wishes with technical data. On the technical side, first stage geographic selection of districts or communities requires detailed information which might not be available in the SSA context: poverty maps, geographic information and social indicators, infrastructure coverage indicators and geographic maps of basic needs. The political negotiations can also influence the targeting mechanism in search of balances for all regions or constituencies.

Operational costs and community level acceptance. This type of targeting system implies higher costs and extensive field work requiring more days of work, and allowances to community members helping in the process. The intense participation of community members may not always guarantee transparent selection. Checks and balance mechanisms, transparency of communications and standardization of processes in communities with different cultures and characteristics make the process complex. Heterogeneity of ethnic groups, power influence for inclusion and exclusion of minority groups such as other clans, tribes, stigmatized people make crucial the need of supervision at central level in most processes. The issue of relative or horizontal equity is also a concern with community based mechanisms because of different criteria – poorer households may be included in one community while an identical household is excluded in another community because of heterogeneity in the application of the broad guidelines for selection.

Sustainability of the process as it was designed depends on the buy-in from the Government of Kenya and its capacity. The pilot experience to date has been positive, but it is complex enough that it may not be continued when going to scale, or it might not be adhered to the same degree.

The current targeting criteria and processes have been designed following a rigorous and participative method. The definition has been identified in a way that covers all possible risks with exigency. With the results from the Operational and Impact Evaluation the criteria and processes will be adjusted to fit into the Kenyan reality. Some criteria and processes may be enhanced as well as some may be reduced in order to find the right combination with reasonable cost effectiveness outputs.

Concluding remarks

This chapter has highlighted a novel targeting system being employed in the Kenya CT-OVC. Documenting the experience is useful for other SSA countries since targeted CT programmes are rapidly expanding in the region. The use of multiple selection criteria is reported by Grosh et al. (1998) to be a key factor that improves targeting performance, so the Kenyan model, which uses a mix of various targeting methods, may be a useful model to adopt if results from the impact evaluation are positive.

Despite the complexity of the targeting system being tested in Kenya, the preliminary operational experience is positive. The implementing agency has embraced the system of multiple targeting instruments, involving both community based and PMT instruments, and to date more than 25,000 households have been screened using this system.

The Kenyan experience illustrates that relatively complex targeting systems can be implemented in low capacity environments, although the programme is still in pilot stage and has not yet been scaled-up. Unit costs are high, but fall within acceptable margins due to the longer time horizon that participants are expected to be in the programme. The process of central verification is worthwhile in the Kenyan context, and technology and use of a sophisticated information system has been of great assistance.

Other versions of the model described in this paper will be implemented in the near future. In Tanzania, a CT pilot programme intends to make an initial verification and identify inconsistencies in the selection process carried out by community committees.[5] If these inconsistencies in category variables determining eligibility criteria exceed 10% of total households screened in that community, then a comprehensive verification (similar to that being carried out in Kenya) will be carried into effect at that community only. On the other hand, another cash transfer pilot activity carried out in Bangladesh will include rural locations, and is studying the possibility of using PMT scores as a priority variable.[6] That is, those households having the lowest PMT values (i.e. lowest predicted expenditure level of the household) will be the first to enter the programme. In other words, priority would be attached to the predicted poorest amongst the poor using PMT. Of course, each of these systems poses a different challenge and errors, but in both cases, they contain key elements of what might be considered a new targeting paradigm – the use of combined systems that allowed systematic verifications, and the application of more sophisticated tools, both technical and technological.

These examples of the application of multiple selection tools, along with the Kenyan case, represent a new approach to targeting in low-income settings for CT programmes. Initial experiences from Kenya, documented here, are positive. However it remains to be seen whether targeting performance will improve, and whether such complex schemes can be scaled-up in relatively low capacity circumstances.

Endnotes

1. The Malawi National Cash Transfer scheme uses community based targeting to select participants. The South African Child Support Grant applies means-test. The Mozambican *Programa Seguranca Alimentar* cash transfer programme is the closest to multiple targeting. In that programme, an initial community based selection is verified through a home visit from the central programme office. No quantitative proxy indicators are used.
2. A complete proxy means score has not yet been developed because of the lack of updated national survey data to calculate weights. This may be done once the recent national poverty survey become available.
3. Information provided by MOHA, Programme Coordinating Unit, 2007.
4. 9% per annum is assumed as an average discount rate, 6 annual payments of $47 each (rate of exchange equivalent to Ksh 64 per $1) during a period of 4 years.
5. Community based cash transfer pilot project financed by the Government of Japan and to be executed by the Tanzanian Social Fund under the supervision of the World Bank, 2007.
6. Cash transfer pilot for rural municipalities (Union Parishad) financed by the World Bank under the loan project, Local Governance Support Project, and to be executed by the Ministry of Local Government and Rural Development and Cooperatives, 2006.

References

Castañeda, T., Lindert, K., De la Brière, B., Fernández, L., Hubert, C., Larrañaga, O., Orozco, M. and Viquez, R. (2005) 'Designing and implementing household targeting systems: lessons from Latin American and the United States', *Social Protection Discussion Paper Series* No. 0526, World Bank, Washington D.C.

Grosh, M. (1997) 'Administering targeted social programmes in Latin America: from platitudes to practice', *World Bank Regional and Sectoral Studies*, World Bank, Washington D.C.

Grosh, M., del Ninno, C., Tesliuc, E. and Ouerghi, A. (2008) *For Protection and Promotion: The Design and Implementation of Effective Safety Nets*, World Bank, Washington D.C.

Mkandawire, T. (2006) 'Targeting and universalism in poverty reduction', Social Protection: the role of cash transfers', *Poverty in Focus*, International Poverty Centre, United Nations Development Programme, Brasilia, Brazil.

Valdivia, M. and Dammert, A. (2001) *'Focalizando las Transferencias Públicas en el Perú: Evaluando Instrumentos de Identificación del Nivel Socio-Económico de los Individuos / Hogares*, Perú.

About the authors

Carlos Alviar worked as OVC programme officer in UNICEF, Kenya. He was a member of the team working on Kenya's Cash Transfer Programme for Vulnerable Children.

Francisco Ayala is the Founder and Director of Ayala Consulting Co. in Quito. Over the last decade, Dr. Ayala has been actively working on the development of effective tools for the assessment of social protection programmes in America, Africa, the Middle East, Asia and the Caribbean. Amongst other things, Dr. Ayala is known for his work with Conditional and Unconditional Cash Transfer Programmes. Through this time, he has accumulated extensive experience in working with the most vulnerable and poorest populations in underdeveloped and developing nations.

Sudhanshu Handa is Associate Professor of Public Policy at the University of North Carolina at Chapel Hill. In 2007–2008 he served as UNICEF's Regional Social Policy Advisor for Eastern & Southern Africa where he led a team that developed the agency's regional strategy in Social Protection. An Economist by training, his research areas are in poverty, human development and social policy evaluation.

CHAPTER 7

Institutional issues in scaling-up programmes for meeting the health related needs of the very poor[1]

Hilary Standing and Elizabeth Kirk

This chapter examines efforts to reach the poorest population through health interventions. It identifies the main institutional issues which confront attempts to target the poorest and develop programmes for this hard to reach part of the population. Different kinds and experiences of targeting are discussed in terms of their appropriateness to health programmes. The chapter explores institutional arrangements for ensuring that programmes meet their goals. It then looks at the increasing trend towards demand side financing approaches to reaching the very poor on a significant scale. It concludes by noting some important gaps in our understanding of successful scaling-up, including a lack of empirically grounded accounts of the development of institutional arrangements and how barriers and capacity constraints are overcome as programmes move to scale.

Introduction

Following on from the previous micro-based targeting chapters, we extend the discussion by reviewing current strategies for scaling-up successful interventions to meet the health-related needs of the poorest in developing countries, focusing mainly on institutional issues which affect capacity to scale-up small-scale or pilot interventions which specifically target these populations. Several institutional obstacles to scaling-up small-scale interventions are identified. These include prohibitive or unsustainable costs, problems with scaling-up targeting mechanisms (which often rely on local knowledge to target the poor effectively), and the risks of capture of decentralized resources by local elites. Effective collaboration between local constituencies and local governments or agencies is also harder to replicate on a regional or national scale. The chapter identifies key principles for successful scaling-up. These include a gradualist approach, a serious commitment to shifting power to the local level, a focus on ease of replication, and working within existing structures.

The structure of the chapter is as follows. The next section provides further literature based background on the issue of targeting the poorest. We then move on to consider some institutional arrangements for reaching the very poorest and examine the increasing interest in demand side financing approaches. Finally, we look at the institutional issues involved in scaling-up programmes focused on the very poor.

Background

Overall, while all mechanisms for targeting the poorest suffer from elements of leakage as well as weak institutional and governance structures, findings from a range of studies indicate that these problems are outweighed by the distributive benefits of some schemes. Demand-driven financing (involving the provision of resources directly to users to obtain services for a distinct group) also has potential for reaching the poorest. However, parallel interventions on the supply side are needed to ensure quality is raised in addition to coverage.

Two main bodies of research and documentation are relevant to this chapter. The first is conceptual and methodological. The work of the Chronic Poverty Research Centre (CPRC) has analysed the complex gradations of poverty, or socio-economic rungs, through which people can ascend or descend. This body of work breaks down the category of the poor, indicating the very significant differences in consumption and living standards within the category (Smith and Subbarao, 2002). Of particular relevance to health policy is the implication in some of this work of a correlation between poor households experiencing health-related shocks and their descent into extremely vulnerable/chronically poor groupings (Amis, 2002). As Ravallion notes, 'increasingly, uninsured risk is coming to be seen as a cause of chronic poverty' (2003: 10).

The proxy indicators of chronic poverty identified in the Chronic Poverty Report 2004-5 (CPRC, 2004) can be summarized as certain geographic locations such as remote rural areas, urban slums and conflict zones; certain disadvantaged social groups such as castes, tribes, ethnic groups, refugees; disadvantaged people in households such as elderly, disabled, women, children; poor health (disability, serious illness); life cycle (elderly, children, widows); and economic position (bonded or indentured labour).

An important implication of this classification is that programmes aimed at improving the health of the very poor need to be similarly differentiated in terms of institutional arrangements and capacity to reach these diverse groups. A 'one size fits all' approach to scaling-up for the very poor will not work either.

Second, there is a large body of documentation indicating that standard models of state-provided health services in both low and middle-income countries tend to result in wealthier income groups receiving a disproportionate share of public health spending at the expense of poor and vulnerable sectors of the population.[2] The very poor and vulnerable are widely acknowledged to be the most intractable to reach through mainstream sectoral policies and programmes. This is accepted to prevail 'for a variety of reasons including physical proximity to facilities, leakage of resources away from diseases proliferating amongst the poorest, ignorance of treatment options and cultural and household constraints' (Ensor, 2003: 12). We can add to this, high levels of self-funded resort to self-treatment and unregulated health markets among the very poor as public facilities fail to provide appropriate services to these groups.

Both sets of studies find that health systems have significant ground to travel in meeting the needs of the poorest. However, there is relatively little published or grey material on successful institutional scaling-up of health programmes geared to these groups. There is somewhat more learning from outside the health sector from potentially scaleable experiments through food and cash transfers to the poorest sectors of the population at regional or national levels.

Targeting and targeting mechanisms: Institutional arrangements for reaching the very poorest through expanded programmes

Targeted interventions are the main approach to reaching these groups. This section focuses on targeting mechanisms and the institutional issues they raise for effective targeting.

Mechanisms for dispersing public services can be roughly divided into those aiming to provide them on a universal basis, and those seeking to restrict a benefit or service to a sub-set of the population through the use of some sort of targeting mechanism or targeted transfer.[3] As the ability of universal models to equitably dispense benefits to a population is being increasingly questioned, targeting is enjoying a renewed popularity in mainstream development thinking as the most effective way to reach the poorest and most vulnerable groups.[4]

Here, we are mainly concerned with targeted dispersal systems as it is in these that the most potential for learning appears to be found. As a range of possible targeting mechanisms exist, each with advantages and drawbacks that carry significant implications for the institutional requirements and scale-up capacity of the intervention, the different available mechanisms are outlined below.

Targeting and targeting mechanisms can take a number of different forms. *Direct or individual targeting* refers to a system that performs means-testing of beneficiaries, enabling administrators to directly ascertain the relative wealth (or poverty) of a household (Gwatkin, 2003: 4). Due to the high administrative requirements of such a system and paucity of reliable data about citizens, the use of such targeting in Least Developed Countries (LDCs) is often impractical and expensive (Barrett and Clay, 2001: 2).[5]

Indicator targeting therefore, has often been employed as an alternative. This uses certain agreed characteristics (such as location of residence, level of land ownership, age, etc.) to identify those most in need in a community (Ravallion, 2003: 17). While far less complex administratively than direct targeting, one significant drawback of this approach is its potential for error, due to the diversity of consumption levels that often exists among those displaying outwardly similar characteristics[6] as well as the major difficulties involved in identifying the very poorest. This is a major issue for the health sector where targeting, optimally, needs to take account of health needs at a household and individual level. Alternative ways of dealing with this in the health sector are through burden of disease analysis (conditions which particularly affect the poor), interventions focused on easily discernible conditions, such as pregnancy, and interventions which target marginalized populations such as those in stigmatized occupations, for example sex workers; street dwellers; and those with chronic diseases. All these are vulnerable in terms of trajectories into extreme poverty.

Community-based targeting and *self-targeting* provide alternative means to identify those most in need. In the former, decisions are usually taken by the programme's central administration (national or subnational) on the amount of public good to be distributed to each locality, while distribution within the locality becomes the job of a local authority. These kinds of targeting seek to exploit informational advantages of local knowledge. Community based identification of beneficiaries can often be very effective both in identifying the neediest and gaining local ownership of targeting decisions. However, two primary concerns remain: first, the potential for capture of benefits by local elites due to the degree of discretion afforded them, and second, the likelihood that the experience and results of usage of community-based targeting are likely to be as diverse, and thus as non-predictable, as the communities themselves (Ravallion, 2003: 21).[7]

Self-targeting, requires no administrative selection at all, but rests on making a public good available on terms that are attractive only to the very poor. Food-for-Work programmes are the best publicized examples that make effective use of this mechanism (Barrett and Clay, 2001: 3-4). Within the health sector, examples would include a system that made primary health care services freely available to the self-selecting poorest but that imposed inconvenience on or disincentive to users, such as significant queuing for services, that would give sufficient incentive to those with the capacity to pay for services to do so (Alderman in Ravallion, 2003: 23). An obvious potential problem with such a mechanism is that by seeking to make the costs of participation attractive only to those with no other option, the costs of participation also effectively bar those for whom the service is intended (Ravallion, 2003: 23).

There is another, indirect, way in which self-targeting works in the health sector, namely through market segmentation. One of the key features of Sri Lanka's success in creating a relatively pro-poor health system is through a form of self-targeting. The private sector mainly provides outpatient care to the wealthier, enabling them to select out of the public sector in response to the private sector's better waiting times and less over-crowding. The public sector meanwhile retains a monopoly on in-patient services and on outpatient services for the poorer, through differentials in consumer perceived quality (McNay et al., 2004: 16-19).

A two-tier system can be prevented from developing by ensuring that technical quality in the public sector remains equal to that of the private market, by for instance, training the majority of providers in the public system thus ensuring that professional reputations must be made, and kept, in this sector but allowing part-time private practice. Latin America is one of the few regions to show a similarly pro-poor bias of expenditure due to self-exclusion of the wealthier from certain services (Gwatkin, 2003: 4). However, we have little direct evidence on the extent to which the very poor and vulnerable groups are actually catered for in these relatively pro-poor health systems.

We now turn to programmes which are targeted and discuss what mechanisms are used, and how accurate and cost effective they are. The World Bank International Conference on Local Development (2004) provides useful insights on institutional and scaling-up questions in targeted interventions, while the administrative challenges which targeting presents to LDCs are reflected in a review of World Bank support to vulnerable group programmes. This finds that 'most vulnerable' programmes have a heavy bias towards the Latin American region (Gibbons, 2004: 6), suggesting that large-scale targeted programmes are more likely to emerge in areas with more sophisticated administrative infrastructure and to be most appropriate institutionally to middle income countries.

Despite their imperfections however, targeted programmes in LDCs are widely held to be more effective generally at reaching the poor than those that are untargeted, and this is confirmed by a World Bank (2002) review comparing targeted against untargeted initiatives which covered 67 programmes from different sectors.[8]

Geographical targeting was found to be effective for reaching certain categories of the very poor who tend to be geographically concentrated – such as ethnic groups and war-affected populations (Gibbons, 2004: 14).[9] In the absence of sophisticated data gathering systems to map the necessary demographics, defining proxy indicators for geographical targeting remains an imperfect technique, although recent developments in Geographical Information Systems (GIS) mapping are changing this. One example of the problems inherent in this method is shown in the Malawi Social Action Fund (MASAF) evaluation: 'The experience of MASAF illustrated the difficulties that a scaled-up public works programme would face. There were disputes about the appropriateness of the indicators of a geographical area's need. These indicators would have to be updated frequently to command general support' (Bloom et al., 2005: 2).

From a health perspective, geographical targeting is most relevant *(i)* to contexts where particular types of poverty or vulnerability are known to be spatially highly concentrated, and *(ii)* where there are clear challenges from high levels of diseases which disproportionately affect the poorest.

Targeting to mitigate social exclusion

Language-based targeting through tailored local language promotional campaigns has been used to identify beneficiaries where ethnic/minority communities are targeted recipients (Gibbons, 2004: 17). The Slovak Social Fund successfully used employment-based targeting to engage the marginalized Roma population in its activities in part through the hiring of staff representatives of this group, and ensuring Slovak representation on steering committees (World Bank, 2004: 1)

Another example is BRAC's use of community-based targeting. In Bangladesh, the Income Generation Vulnerable Group Development (IGVGD) Programme aims to reach the most vulnerable groups in the community.[10] It employs a community-based targeting principle in which the overall allocation of benefits to localities is administered at the centre,[11] and allocation to individual households is mediated by elected representatives of unions and wards.[12] Independent assessment of targeting found a minimal amount of leakage to the non-poor: 'on a set of extreme-poor sensitive indicators, the IGVGD fares quite well' (Hashemi cited in Matin, 2002: 17). While no figures of the cost of targeting are available, the use of elected representatives to dispense participation in the scheme to participants would imply this element of targeting administration was on a voluntary basis. Thus the costs of the mechanism could be expected to be low.

While this is encouraging, the community-based targeting mechanism revealed deficiencies arising from the clientelist nature of socio-political power in Bangladesh. While the targeting mechanism efficiently disabled those outside of intended beneficiary groups from receiving benefits, thus leakage levels were low, there appears to have been a lack of equity of selection *among* those in such beneficiary categories. Using local elites to select qualified participants appears to have construed eligibility in favour of the chronically poor who were connected in some way to those elites (through seasonal agricultural employment, or use as election hands) and this group of poor candidates was revealed to enjoy increased chances of receiving repeat benefits through the scheme while a significant percentage of chronically poor households appear to have been excluded from consideration (Matin, 2002: 15-19). Such a finding indicates that closer monitoring and mechanisms for remedial action to ensure equitable distribution of benefits may be needed for programmes employing community-based targeting mechanisms.

There are contexts where targeting should not be tried. A major example is where the majority of the population in an area needs a service, and a non-existent or poor quality private sector exists, then establishment of a targeting mechanism and associated infrastructure may be an expensive and inequitable remedy for the situation (Ensor, 2003: 12).

Targeting the very poorest

The most effective forms of targeting combine different modalities, for instance a first level geographical mapping by district or other administrative unit, combined with selective targeting on household or other criteria. This is complex and also requires data to be both available and reasonably accurate and therefore has to be offset against what is possible and cost effective. There is also likely to be a difference in capacity between, for instance, urban and rural areas. Backing health interventions onto existing targeted poverty reduction programmes is one way of dealing with this. There is considerable potential for doing this in countries such as India and Bangladesh with a fairly developed infrastructure of poverty interventions. Where existing poverty-reduction programmes operate a relatively accurate means of targeting the poorest, linking up with those programmes to make use of, and assist in the refinement of, their poverty targeting mechanisms could be the most effective and economical path to establishing a pro-poor health programme.

An example from Bangladesh is BRAC's experience in annexing a micro-credit programme for the extreme poor onto the World Food Programme's Vulnerable Group Feeding Programme, This demonstrated that adding a longer-term pro-poor intervention onto an emergency relief programme can enable an easy entry point and facilitate the refinement of a targeting mechanism over time (Matin, 2002).[13] In seeking the best entry point to the poorest groups, BRAC deliberately approached administrators of short-term emergency input programmes, with which they sought to dovetail more medium-term interventions. This was in recognition of the constraints that operate against the participation of the extreme poor in longer term projects and the need therefore to facilitate strategic linkages enabling them 'to benefit from other mainstream development projects' (Matin, 2002: 4). Developing institutional means to dovetail between relief and more permanent structures of care may well prove an efficient entry point for health service interventions seeking to target the very poor.

A second possible entry point for health interventions seeking to reach the poorest is suggested by an increasing body of analysis finding that rural work/food-for-work programmes are among the most effective in identifying those from the poorest communities (Lustig, 1997; Ravallion, 1991,; Barrett and Clay, 2001). The self-targeting mechanism employed by such schemes renders them simple to administer, and they are, in part consequentially, enjoying an increased uptake in LDCs.

Other institutional obstacles may need to be taken into account. As many commentators have pointed out, in calculating the costs of health care to the extreme poor, indirect costs, such as transport and lost income, often impose a larger burden than the obvious expenses of paying fees for curative services and purchasing medicines. There may also be substantial social obstacles to overcome, such as stigma, and lack of voice. To truly render health care accessible to the poorest, institutional mechanisms need to consider how to minimize these costs and obstacles.

What the targeting literature shows is that there are no perfect schemes. All suffer to some degree from elements of leakage and weak institutional and governance structures. The larger the scale the more likely this is to be the case. However, in low-income countries struggling with multiple constraints and challenges, this is hardly surprising. The more complex the targeting mechanisms, the greater the institutional challenges. It may be that the trade-off is an agreement on what is an acceptable level of leakage. Overall, the findings seem to suggest that the distributive benefits of at least some types of targeting in the health and social sectors in developing countries outweigh the governance and administrative problems. However, this can only be definitively determined on a case by case basis and with better information on the costs of schemes of different magnitude.

Experiences of demand-side ways of meeting the health needs of the very poor

Interest in what has become termed 'demand-side financing' (DSF) has been growing in the last few years. Falling mainly under the umbrella of targeted transfer mechanisms, demand-side financing systems are increasingly engaging policy makers' interest as potential instruments for delivering services to the poor, including the very poor (Ensor, 2003; Islam, 2003; Standing, 2004), and involving both state and non-state actors in their implementation. Defined by Pearson as 'a means of transferring purchasing power to specified groups for the purchase of defined goods and services' (cited in Islam, 2003: 20), demand-side mechanisms stand in opposition to traditional mechanisms of making inputs to health systems, where suppliers of services are given additional resources to provide services for a distinct group. By contrast, demand-side mechanisms aim to give the resources directly to users or to a body acting on their behalf. Third party purchasing thus has elements of demand-side financing but DSF is more commonly associated with vouchers or cash transfers. These are exchanged for services from a provider, sometimes prescribed or sometimes of the users' choice. Institutionally, DSF requires both a targeting mechanism and an infrastructure for administering the transfers and monitoring providers and recipients.

DSF has been used more extensively in education than in health and has been particularly aimed at increasing utilization (e.g. of school attendance by girls). In health, it is being put forward not only as a way of targeting the poor and vulnerable groups (e.g. very poor pregnant women, people with disabilities) but as way of improving the supply side response to the poor through enhanced competition between providers for clients with purchasing capacity (Ensor, 2003; Standing, 2004).

Experiences of DSF in health and other sectors

A comprehensive review of demand-side financing in health and education (Ensor, 2003) found just 12 cases of DSF within health for which evaluation studies were available. These are mostly from middle or high-income countries. We thus have a very small evidence base on DSF in the health sector of low-income countries.

In Bangladesh, the World Bank supported Educational Stipend Programme is an example from outside the health sector of a highly successful demand-side programme in which tuition and stipends for secondary school students have been able to greatly increase numbers of girls attending school in Bangladesh (Islam, 2003). However, it contains mixed lessons on the possibilities of targeting the very poor. For example, resentment by the less poor of the initially targeted nature of the education intervention led to an extension of the stipend scheme to other rural households. It is not clear to what extent the very poor take advantage of this programme.

Modes of DSF employed within health and targeted at specific poverty and vulnerable groups include:

- Use of a voucher/other form of evidence of entitlement, 'The most common mode of DSF scheme' (Ensor, 2003: 4).
- Group specific transfers to poorest pregnant or nursing mothers/sex workers/young children (Standing and Gooding, 2003: 2).
- Treatment entitlements for people with disabilities (ibid.).
- Cash transfers to households below poverty line conditional upon medical care being obtained (Ensor, 2003: 40).
- Community-based micro health insurance initiatives (Islam, 2003: 8).
- Community-driven development schemes financed under targeted Social Funds.

Cambodian Health Equity Fund

One promising application of a direct targeting mechanism able to identify the poor and administer payment of hospital costs on their behalf is provided by the Sotnikum Health Equity Fund (HEF) in Cambodia (Hardeman et al., 2004, see also Men and Van Pelt, this volume). Avoiding the well-publicized failures that can arise when government health personnel are tasked with identifying and exempting poor patients from hospital fees,[14] the scheme engages a third party agent, here a local NGO, to identify the poorest patients and pay hospital fees on their behalf, as well as indirect costs (food, medicines and transport) direct to the patients. The scheme seeks to reach the 'extremely poor' as well as those 'at risk of falling into extreme poverty',[15] and the contracted NGO used a pre-existing, field-tested questionnaire to score self-reported socio-economic status of patients entering the hospital, together with active identification of poor patients in hospital wards[16] (Hardeman et al., 2004: 24). Independent evaluation reported greatest efficacy in identifying and assisting those in the extreme poor category, lesser efficacy in successful identification of those in the 'at risk' category, and minimal leakage to the non-poor (ibid.: 25-6). A steep increase in the number of overall poor patients accessing hospital services in the second year of the scheme's operation indicates its success in facilitating access for those who would otherwise have been prevented from seeking services (ibid.: 29). The costs of the intervention were deemed to be low, constituting 8.6% of the total annual hospital budget (ibid.: 29) or US$ 0.06 per capital per year (ibid.: 29).

Institutional issues in scaling-up

In the ostensibly successful case of Cambodia's HEF, the existence of a local NGO with a pre-existing, tested mechanism for identifying the poor and poorest, together with pre-existing relations with this constituency, appear to have been a factor in its success. Similarly, the lack of widespread knowledge about the scheme was probably a factor in the accurate patient responses to self-reported socio-economic questionnaires confirmed by evaluation reports of zero leakage to non-poor patients. In seeking to scale-up the scheme, as the Cambodian government was aiming to do, obvious obstacles presented themselves. There were problems of finding third party purchasing bodies with similar capacity, experience and motivation to that of the NGO contracted in the pilot case, alongside incentives for patients to distort responses to wealth assessment tools as knowledge of the scheme and its value increases among the population at large. Additionally, the Sotnikum pilot took place in a context of successful qualitative reforms being made to the service providing environment, a factor behind the high demand for government-run hospital services. Ensuring such reform in all provinces in which a HEF scheme would be introduced was potentially a momentous task.

It is important to note that this variant of demand-side financing, falling under the third party purchaser category, also appears to have required, for its success, two significant inputs. The first was the involvement of international bodies, Médecins Sans Frontières (MSF) and UNICEF, who assisted with establishment and set-up of the scheme. The second was significant improvements to the supply-side environment, negotiated between these bodies and the Cambodian Ministry of Health, in which a 'New Deal' for health workers was put in place to address the causes of poor quality service provision, and which 'immediately resulted in better staff motivation and higher user rates' (Hardeman et al., 2004: 23). The 'simple' introduction of a demand-side initiative in the form of a health equity scheme in the absence of concerted reform to supply side services would therefore have delivered questionable results.

In its establishment of a new government-facilitated health insurance scheme aimed at enabling the poorest sectors of the population to pay for health care, China is employing the innovative step of separating the task of purchase of services from that of providing them, with the purchasing ministry being that of Civil Affairs, which is expected to exert more exacting standards in monitoring the quality of provision, than would the Ministry of Health in monitoring its own services (Bloom, 2004: 5). Analysis on the impact of this division of labour on the quality of care however, is yet to be published.

Conditional cash transfers have also been used in facilitating greater health service use by the poor. For example, the PROGRESA (and subsequently named *Oportunidades*) programme in Mexico is a very large state funded anti-poverty programme with a large health component incorporating health and nutrition related conditions for access to the transfer. This was found to have 'significant positive impact on public health care utilization, nutrition monitoring, health status of adults and children (measured by self-reported illness rates)' (IFPRI report cited in Ensor, 2003: 40).[17] Various evaluations have indicated reasonable success in reaching the poorest groups and households, both through geographical targeting at the poorest states and household level targeting (Latapi, 2005; Menocal, 2005).

Vouchers have had some success: 'International evidence suggests that vouchers have been successful in raising the consumption of key services amongst certain groups. Evidence also suggests that vouchers can be used to target vulnerable groups' (Ensor, 2003: 4). Such schemes are judged to be most applicable for providing health services to the poorest in areas where *(i)* demand is predictable and *(ii)* the targeted group is relatively easily identifiable, for instance in providing maternal health (safe delivery) services (ibid.). This implies they are not appropriate for assisting the poorest to access limited curative services, which are not predictable and where demand for inappropriate treatment may need to be controlled (Standing, 2004).

The evidence is less positive on the effect of vouchers on improving service *quality* through increased competition (Ensor, 2003). Serious concern has been expressed about the quality of the education provided to students benefiting from the education stipend programme in Bangladesh. For example, the Bangladesh Food For Education project managed a spectacular increase in female enrolment in secondary schools, but saw quality of education fall largely due to this success (Islam, 2003), confirming that supply-side interventions were also required.

This is especially the case where demand-side initiatives are introduced in a monopoly-provider situation, where service quality in many LDCs is widely perceived to be low. Thus, significant supply-side inputs are likely to be required also to improve the quality of care and thus demand for service (Ensor, 2003). Significant investment was made in supply of services prior to the introduction of the Cambodian Health Equity Fund (Hardeman et al., 2004).

Evidence also suggests that DSF initiatives must take a comprehensive approach to barriers to health-seeking behaviour among the poorest, including offsetting indirect costs such as transport, income-loss and medication which often exceed the direct costs encountered by the poor when they are considering seeking treatment (Ensor, 2003). We do not know very much about the threshold at which the very poor will find it worth their while to encash their transfers in health DSF programmes.

DSF mechanisms are not a cure for existing institutional weaknesses. They may encourage certain 'perverse' behaviours by providers and administrators. These include collusion between providers to create cartels or exclude certain categories of clients, development of a 'market' in vouchers or other transfers, and over-medicalization where alternative treatments may be more appropriate (Standing and Gooding, 2003). This is particularly a risk in LDCs with weak institutions.

A recent study of delivery mechanisms of cash transfer programmes in Bangladesh found that, on the whole, the schemes work reasonably well, given their size and the kinds of institutional constraints faced by poor countries. But the findings indicate that the schemes are over administered but under governed. That is to say there are too many structures and personnel involved, particularly in the IGVGD scheme, but insufficient checks and balances on rent seeking, inappropriate choice of beneficiaries and leakage. For instance, there is not enough hands-on monitoring of the distribution at delivery, giving too much opportunity for abuse by local officials such as the weighman for distributed grain, and no separate appeal processes for aggrieved beneficiaries. This could be remedied by some carefully targeted changes to the way the schemes are managed. This could include addressing the perceived transaction costs particularly in the non-cash transfers which create a view among agents administering the programme that it is legitimate to reduce the amount of the transfer to the beneficiaries (Ahmed, 2004).

Thus, the development of appropriate administrative and governance institutions is absolutely critical to DSF success. These will vary with the mechanisms adopted, but include:

- Capable monitoring and governance bodies at both national and local level.
- Community bodies able to play an informed and empowered advocacy/watch-dog role (ibid).
- Processes to liaise with communities, engage and win support of the community for the initiative, and set the price of the transfer correctly (Standing and Gooding, 2003).
- Development of competent third-party purchasing organizations where beneficiaries are at informational disadvantages in evaluating which service they require and where best to access it (Ensor, 2003).
- Quality-assurance/standards agencies that can determine and certify providers able to supply services to certain standards (Ensor, 2003).

Different forms of DSF clearly have potential for reaching the poorest through a combination of targeting specific groups and individuals and providing positive incentives to take up services. However, in the health sector, relatively few interventions have been systematically tried and evaluated in low-income countries. We need a better body of evidence to make an informed judgement. Evidence so far suggests that they are better at increasing coverage than ensuring quality unless there are parallel interventions on the supply side aimed at raising quality standards.

Institutional obstacles to scaling-up successful small-scale interventions

There are a number of major obstacles to scaling-up programmes aimed at reaching the poorest to improve health related outcomes:

Costs may be prohibitive or unsustainable

- Likening certain successful small-scale programmes to retail 'boutiques, too costly for the masses' the World Bank summary on scaling-up community driven development points to examples of programmes with large budgets per capita that donors are prepared to finance on a small-scale, but that are impractical at scale (Binswanger and Aiyar, 2003: 5).
- Even where unit costs are affordable, national scaling-up can fail to mobilize the required co-financing from communities or local governments (ibid.). This is particularly the case where the very poorest are targeted as they often lack political agency or representation.

Co-production between local constituencies and local governments/agencies is harder to replicate on a regional/national scale

- While these arrangements may work in particular local contexts, due to the quality of relationships between parties, commitment of key personnel etc, on a larger scale it is harder to ensure that the well-documented institutional problems which can affect co-production (incompatibility of incentives of co-producers, differences in values and experiences of co-producers, lack of clarity of rules and responsibilities) do not render the initiative unworkable (Binswanger and Aiyar, 2003). Loewenson's review of more than 100 cases of attempted state–civil society participation in health, found that many of these were typified by an 'absence of clear mechanisms' to 'enable such relationships between the state and CSOs' (2003: 9).

Problems with scaling-up targeting mechanisms

- Scaled-up programmes aiming to target the very poor face significant data challenges. To target the poorest most effectively, sophisticated demographic information is ideally required. This is highly unlikely to exist in an LDC context (Gibbons, 2004; Barrett and Clay, 2001). Therefore, small-scale programmes in LDCs reaching the poorest often rely instead on sources of local knowledge (CBOs, NGOS, community representatives) to assist targeting, and such sources, being particular to their localities, are not necessarily amenable to being scaled-up.

Risks of elite capture of decentralized resource flows

- This may be an issue where allocation to localities is decided centrally, but dispersal to beneficiaries is determined at local level in order to exploit the information advantages of using some kind of local authority (Ravallion, 2003). Recent work by Das Gupta et al. (cited in Gillespie, 2004: 17), as well that by Galasso and Ravallion (cited in Ravallion, 2003: 22) exploring Food-For-Education community targeting in Bangladesh, finds that where there is more intra-community inequality of wealth, elite capture of benefits is more likely. There is a danger in clientelistic societies that while resources may reach the poorest, clients of the elites dispensing resources may benefit disproportionately and exclude certain sections of the poorest – as was BRAC's experience in the IGVGD programme (Matin, 2002).

Conclusions

While the evidence base is beginning to expand, there are still considerable gaps in our understanding of how to develop appropriate institutional arrangements to reach the poorest through targeted interventions in health. First, there is a lack of empirically detailed accounts of the institutional arrangements and delivery mechanisms in both small-scale and expanded programmes. Without this more detailed information, it is difficult to go beyond fairly general principles such as the need to manage leakage and keep rent seeking within acceptable bounds. We need more information on the substantive ways in which these problems are managed.

Second, little is known about the beneficiary perspective. How do the very poor view these programmes? What factors lead them to participate or to exit? Where are there positive examples of consultation and involvement? To what extent is it possible to create or sustain voice in expanded programmes?

Third, there is very little on the economics of scaling-up. In particular, there is a lack of cost-benefit studies of scaling-up, For instance, what is the trade off between costs of best or good practice on institutional frameworks, targeting and monitoring and regulation of programmes, set against benefits and outcomes for the very poor?

A clearer understanding of the successful factors involved in scaling-up such programmes is however emerging. Recent work on scaling-up of pilot programmes in reproductive health (Simmons et al., 2008) has advanced our understanding of the factors that affect performance. The 'gradualist' principle of scale-up is a point emphasized by several analysts. For example, in an analysis of five separate instances of scaled-up pro-poor programmes, Gillespie asserts that 'scaling-up should always start with one province or district to prove that the scaling-up can indeed be successful' (Gillespie, 2004: 16). The medium to long-term nature of the need to develop capacity is perhaps the most pivotal reason for adopting a gradualist approach, particularly in the context of the challenge to reach the poorest populations, households and individuals.

This echoes Islam's analysis of factors behind the success of the Bangladeshi female students' scholarship programme, one of which he suggests, was the staged approach taken in expanding the programme: 'the large scale of the operation and ultimately universal coverage was done in stages; not at a time. This has also enabled the sector to develop management capacity in phases to undertake such a huge operation' (Islam, 2003: 7).

A number of writers have argued that perhaps paradoxically, scaling-up of poverty reduction programmes requires a serious commitment to shifting power to the local level, facilitated by mobilization of community based organizations with the local knowledge and capacity to reach the poor. Binswanger and Aiyar note that 'Global experience [of scaling-up] ... shows strong political commitment to decentralisation and empowerment is essential, and a local champion often leads the process' (2003: 17) and that applying the principle of subsidiarity also cuts economic costs and improves transfer efficiency (ibid.: 22). Others similarly note that decentralizing authority and resources is central to successful scaling-up (Gillespie, 2004; Simmons and Shiffman, 2008). However, the challenge posed by such decentralization to national level commitments to meet the needs of the poorest requires further scrutiny of the political economy contexts in which programmes are operating.

One illustration of the recognition of the need for more powerful local structures in large-scale programmes targeted at the poorest is provided by China's forthcoming programme of getting health insurance to the most marginalized. In the context of a society which still largely operates through command and control structures, there is nevertheless acknowledgement of the need to strengthen elected structures if they are to monitor service provision (Bloom, 2004).

As a number of the examples quoted above demonstrate, enabling institutional environments are best built up within existing structures however imperfect, rather than creating new ones. Gillespie also argues that parallel structures risk undermining and alienating existing infrastructure, particularly government provision (2004: 19, 35). However, Simmons et al. (2002) argue that public sector bureaucracies tend not to have the characteristics needed to scale up health services based on equity, quality of care and provision of a comprehensive range of services (as in reproductive health, for example). This is because managers working in bureaucratic systems based on command and control typically do not perceive the need or do not have the implementation and resource capacity. They note that especially where health systems are weak, expectations must be kept very realistic.

For rapid scale-up, according to some, ease of replication is key. Binswanger and Aiyar (2003) argue that the simpler the institutional framework and the less complex the relationships between actors, the swifter and more successful the initiative is likely to be. This suggests that complex co-producing arrangements may not fare well in scaled-up versions. On the other hand, others argue that success is conditioned by local cultural and social systems so 'the best practice here may be the absence of a best practice' (Mansuri and Rao quoted in Gillespie, 2003: 35). In this understanding, scaling-up requires continuous adaptation to local circumstances with just a few normative principles, such as informed consent, regarded as universal and non-negotiable (Simmons et al., 2002; Simmons et al., 2008). This again suggests that there is no 'one size fits all' solution to meeting the health needs of the very poorest and that local and national adaptations to political economy constraints and opportunities will provide the best ways forward.

Endnotes

1. This is a revised version of a paper originally prepared for the Department for International Development, Health Systems Resource Centre, in 2005.
2. Cf: Gwatkin 'In brief, even the simplest interventions offered through government facilities usually reach the better off at least somewhat more frequently than they do the neediest' (2003: 3) and 'In Africa ... the top twenty percent of the population gets two and a half times as much benefit from government health expenditure as does the bottom twenty percent (ibid.: 8)'. Cf: also Ensor (2003: 5) and Rannan-Eliya cited in McNay et al. (2004: 16).
3. This can be in cash or kind. The majority of cash transfers are conditional – i.e. they can only be converted into a specific good or service.
4. Ravallion observes that 'conventional wisdom in mainstream development policy circles' which has for a long time discounted targeting mechanisms on account of *(i)* the leakage of benefits to the non-poor and *(ii)* their perverse impact on labour-supply and savings of recipients, is now being fundamentally questioned, if not discounted (2003: 1-2).
5. Gwatkin notes that within health, one particular type of individual targeting has tended to receive the most attention, that of identifying poor individuals who qualify for exemption from health system user fees (2003: 5). While Thailand has encountered some success with this model (ibid.: 6), it is generally seen as a poor way to target: 'Exemptions from fees are unlikely to direct ... subsidies precisely, while provider incentives are weak and distorted' (Islam, 2003: 16).
6. Note also that in the cases of both direct and indicator targeting, once the purpose of data collection is clear, there will be incentives for households to distort it to exaggerate their hallmarks of poverty (Ravallion 2003: 17).
7. Galasso and Ravallion (2005), researching Bangladesh's Food For Education project, found that the higher the levels of inequity of land ownership in a village, the worse that village performed at community-based targeting of the poor, suggesting the perpetuation of inequity where the poor are economically weakest.

8. This review 'found that the poor got more benefits in 70-75 per cent of cases than they would have, had the benefits been evenly distributed across the population (which would in itself be an improvement over the present situation with respect to government health service expenditure programs)' (Gwatkin, 2003: 5).

9. However, as the poverty of certain ethnic populations can be linked to their more general social exclusion, the 'vulnerable group' review report recommended the avoidance of long-term targeting for these categories of the very poor, as it may have the effect of further marginalizing/creating ghettoes (Gibbons, 2004: 25).

10. The programme seeks to reach *(i)* the 'chronically poor', described as those who frequently go without food; *(ii)* 'widows and young women with children abandoned by their husbands' as well as *(iii)* 'occasionally deficit' households who have recently suffered a major shock usually to the male head of household (Matin, 2002: 14).

11. Using food insecurity and vulnerability maps (Matin, 2002: 19).

12. The lowest tiers of local government machinery in Bangladesh.

13. The accuracy of the targeting mechanism in the Income Generation for Vulnerable Group Development (IGVGD) programme has been independently assessed to be high (Matin, 2002: 17), despite issues of equity of access to the programme's benefits among those in the poorest groupings.

14. Such failures are held to arise from health workers *(i)* lacking the skills to objectively assess a patient's incomes and *(ii)* experiencing a conflict of interest between giving exemptions and the pressure to maximize revenue, particularly where fees are officially intended to augment their own incomes (Hardeman et al., 2004: 22).

15. The characteristics used to distinguish between these two categories were: 'Extremely poor = small (thatch house, <0.5 ha land, no cows, food shortage more than 5 months, no savings, live on day-to-day basis, can only borrow small amounts' and 'Poor = wooden house, >1.5 ha land, 2 cows or fewer, bicycle, food shortage less than 4 months, small savings <US$5, borrow regularly' (Hardeman et al., 2004: 25).

16. Identification was based on patients' lack of basic items such as food, utensils, mosquito nets and clothing (Hardeman et al., 2004: 24).

17. However, no details are given on the scale of this initiative and the report contains no reference to attempts to scale-up cash transfer programmes within health.

References

Ahmed, S. S. (2004) 'Study on delivery mechanisms of Cash Transfer Programs to the poor in Bangladesh', Data Analysis and Technical Assistance Limited, report prepared for the World Bank, Dhaka, Bangladesh, 12 June, 2004.

Amis, P. (2002) 'Thinking about chronic urban poverty', *CPRC Working Paper No 12*. Chronic Poverty Research Centre, Manchester.

Barrett, C. B. and Clay, C. (2001) 'How accurate is Food-For-Work self-targeting in the presence of imperfect factor markets? Evidence from Ethiopia', Cornell University, Ithaca.

Binswanger, H. and Aiyar, S. S. (2003) 'Scaling up community-driven development: theoretical underpinnings and program design implications', *World Bank Policy Research Working Paper No. 3039*, World Bank, Washington D.C.

Bloom, G. (2004) 'Health policy during China's transition to market economy', in Gauld, R. (ed.), *Comparative Health Policy in Asia-Pacific*, Open University Press, Maidenhead, UK.

Bloom, G., Chilowa, W., Chirwa, E., Lucas, H., Mvula, P., Schou, A. and Tsoka, M. (2005) 'Poverty reduction during democratic transition: the Malawi Social Action Fund 1996–2001', *IDS Research Report 56*, Institute of Development Studies, Brighton, UK.

CPRC (2004) *The Chronic Poverty Report 2004-05*, Chronic Poverty Research Centre, Manchester, UK.

Ensor, J. (2003) 'Demand side financing for publicly financed services: an international review', Oxford Policy Management, Oxford.

Galasso, E. and Ravallion, M. (2005) 'Decentralized targeting of an anti-poverty program', *Journal of Public Economics* 85: 705–727.

Gibbons, C. (2004) 'Reaching vulnerable groups through demand driven programmes', powerpoint presentation to the World Bank Social Funds Group, 17 June, 2004.

Gillespie, S. (2004) 'Scaling up of community driven development: a synthesis of experience', *FCND Discussion Paper 181*, IFPRI, Washington D.C.

Gwatkin, D. R. (2003) 'Free Government Health Services: are they the best way to reach the poor?', World Bank, Washington D.C.

Hardeman, W., Van Damme, W., Van Pelt, M., Por, I., Kimvan, H. and Messen, B. (2004) 'Access to health care for all? User fees plus a Health Equity Fund in Sotnikum Cambodia', *Health Policy and Planning* 19(1): 22-32.

Islam, M. K. (2003) 'Health financing options for the poor', an assessment prepared for the World Health Organization (WHO), Bangladesh.

Latapí, A. E. (2005) 'Progresa – Oportunidades: Where do we go from here?' CIESAS Occidente, paper prepared for *Poverty and Poverty Reduction Strategies: Mexican and International Experiences*, Monterrey, Mexico, January, 2005.

Loewenson, R. (2003) 'Annotated bibliography on civil society and health: civil society – state interactions in national health systems', report CSI/2003/BI2, World Health Organization, Geneva.

Lustig, N. (1997) 'The safety nets which are not safety nets: Social Investment Funds in Latin America', Available from: http://www.iadb.org/sds/doc/764eng.pdf [accessed 22 July 2009].

Matin, I. (2002) 'Targeted development programmes for the extreme poor: experiences form BRAC experiments', Chronic Poverty Research Centre (CPRC), Manchester, UK.

McNay, K., Keith, R. and Penrose, A. (2004) 'Bucking the trend: how Sri Lanka has achieved good health for all at low cost – challenges and policy lessons for the 21st century', Save the Children Fund, London.

Menocal, A. R. (2005) 'Less political and more pro-poor? The evolution of social welfare spending in Mexico in the context of democratisation and decentralisation', presentation to the DSA Poverty Study Group, London, 2 June 2005.

Ravallion, M. (1991) 'Reaching the poor through rural public works: arguments, evidence and lessons from South Asia', *World Bank Research Observer*: 153–175.

Ravallion, M. (2003) 'Targeted transfers in poor countries: revisiting the trade-offs and policy options', World Bank, Washington D.C.

Simmons, R. and Shiffman, J. (2008) 'Scaling up health service innovations: a framework for action', in R. Simmons, P. Fajans, L. Ghiron (eds) *Scaling up health service delivery: from pilot innovations to policies and programmes*, World Health Organization and ExpandNet, Geneva.

Simmons, R., Brown, J. W. and Diaz, M. (2002) 'Facilitating large-scale transitions to quality of care', *Studies in Family Planning* 33: 61-75.

Simmons, R., Fajans, P., Ghiron, L. (eds) (2008) *Scaling up health service delivery: from pilot innovations to policies and programmes*. World Health Organization and ExpandNet, Geneva.

Smith, J. and Subbarao, K. (2002) 'What role for safety net transfers in very low income countries?', *Social Safety Net Primer*, World Bank, Washington D.C.

Standing, H. and Gooding, K. (2003) 'Demand-side financing in the Bangladesh Health Sector – issues and knowledge gaps', background paper prepared for the DFID demand-side financing mission, Dhaka, July 2003.

Standing, H. (2004) *Understanding the 'demand-side' in service delivery: definitions, frameworks and tools from the health sector*, DFID Health Systems Resource Centre, London.

World Bank Operations Evaluations Department (2002) *Social Funds: A review of World Bank Experience*, World Bank, Washington D.C.

World Bank International Conference on Local Development (2004), Washington D.C., 16-18 June 2002. Available from: http://info.worldbank.org/etools/docs/library/136160/tslg/conference/description.html [accessed 22 July 2009].

About the authors

Hilary Standing is a social scientist specializing in health and development. She is a Fellow of the Institute of Development Studies at the University of Sussex, UK, where she is involved in a number of international research programmes on health systems, reproductive health, and gender and health. Recent publications include (with Gerald Bloom) guest editing of, and contributions to, a 'Special Issue of Social Science and Medicine on Future Health Systems' (June 2008). She is currently based in Dhaka, Bangladesh, where she is a Visiting Professor at the BRAC University James P. Grant School of Public Health and Adjunct Scientist at the International Centre for Diarrhoeal Diseases Research, Bangladesh (ICDDR,B).

Elizabeth Kirk is Team Manager in the Ethical Trading Initiative. She works on Project Strategy and is currently working on various projects, such as Homeworkers and Garments Project in Sri Lanka.

PART III

Policies and Programmes for the Poorest: Case Studies

CHAPTER 8
Eradicating extreme poverty: The Chile Solidario Programme

Armando Barrientos

In 2002, the Chilean Government introduced Chile Solidario, a programme aimed at eradicating extreme poverty in the country. The design and scope of the programme are highly innovative. It is based on a multidimensional understanding of poverty and on the capability approach, and it focuses on lifting social exclusion for the poorest households. It targets seven dimensions of poverty and provides sustained support for households in extreme poverty. The chapter outlines the factors that led to the implementation of Chile Solidario, describes its main features and draws lessons for other countries.

Introduction

In this first chapter of the policies and programmes section we start by focusing on the role social protection has on eradicating extreme poverty, specifically in Latin America. The social protection system which developed from the 1930s onwards in Latin America combined three main components: social insurance funds which provided formal workers with protection against life course and health contingencies; employment protection focused on male breadwinners in formal employment; and social assistance (Barrientos, 2004). Policy designers assumed that, following the example of European countries, social insurance would eventually include the vast majority of the population. Social assistance was therefore residual and lacked a focus on the poor and poorest. As a consequence, commentators have described social protection in Latin America as 'truncated' because the majority of the population who depended on informal employment was excluded (de Ferranti et al., 2000).[1]

New forms of social assistance have emerged in the last decade, as a response to the rise in vulnerability which followed acute economic crises and structural adjustment in the 1980s, usually referred to in the region as the 'lost decade'. The headcount poverty rate increased in Latin America from 40.5% in 1980 to 48.3% in 1990 (CEPAL, 2007). The recovery that followed has been insufficient to reduce poverty to the 1980 level. By 2002, the headcount poverty rate was at 44%. Indigence rates, the share of the population with incomes below those needed to purchase a basic basket of food, rose from

18.6% in 1980 to 22.5% in 1990, and then declined to 19.5% in 2002. Despite some economic growth in the years since the 'lost decade', close to one in two Latin Americans is in poverty, and one in five is in extreme poverty.

The new forms of social assistance have focused on income transfer programmes targeted on the poor and poorest, and focused on breaking the intergenerational cycle of poverty by facilitating investment in human capital, especially nutrition, health and schooling. *Bolsa Escola*, which has become *Bolsa Familia* in Brazil, and *Progresa*, later *Oportunidades* in Mexico, are well known examples. *Bolsa Familia* reaches over 11 million poorest households in Brazil with an income transfer which increases with the number of children of school age in the household. *Oportunidades* reaches 5 million households in Mexico. It began as *Progresa* in 1997 in marginalized communities in rural areas, and combines income transfers, rising for children of school age and girls, with supply side support for health and education providers. These programmes provide regular and reliable transfers of around 20% of household consumption, conditional on children attending school and household members accessing primary health care providers. Transfers are paid to the mother. Two key features characterize these new forms of social assistance. They are strongly focused on the poor and poorest, and understand extreme poverty as intrinsically multidimensional and intergenerational.

More recently, the emergence of integrated anti-poverty programmes, such as Chile Solidario with the ambitious aim of eradicating extreme poverty, provide an example of even broader, and more innovative, forms of social assistance. Chile Solidario provides a range of cash transfers and coordinated support along seven dimensions of well being: health, education, income, employment, housing, registration, and intra-household dynamics. At the basis of the design of this programme is an understanding that social exclusion is a key factor in the persistence of poverty, and of the need to bridge the gap that exists between those in extreme and persistent poverty and their rights and entitlements. Although most international policy discussion has focused on the income component of new forms of social assistance in Latin America (cash transfers), the main innovation of new forms of social assistance in Latin America is that they combine a range of interventions around regular and reliable income transfers. Chile Solidario provides a very good example of this crucial point.

The rest of the chapter is organized as follows. The next section outlines the main perspectives on poverty and anti-poverty policy that inform the design and orientation of new forms of social assistance in Latin America, and Chile Solidario in particular, followed by a section that describes the factors behind the introduction of Chile Solidario. The penultimate section introduces the main features of the programme and a final section concludes and draws out some lessons for other developing countries.

Explaining the focus on the poor and poorest in Latin America?

There is evidence from attitudinal studies that Latin Americans share a strong concern about poverty, and perceive poverty as arising largely from social and economic factors. Graham (2002) discusses the significance of public attitudes on public assistance and the emergence of 'social contracts'. She contrasts public perceptions of the causes of poverty in the USA and Latin America, and finds that Latin Americans are more inclined than the USA public to see poverty as due largely to factors outside the control of the poor.[2]

Poverty reflects deficits in well-being. The capability approach developed by Sen argues that well-being should be understood and evaluated in terms of a capacity to lead the lives we value. He argues that the well-being of a person mainly depends on the life that s/he values and what s/he succeeds in doing or being (Sen, 1985). Focusing on capability expands and refocuses the approach to poverty in a multidimensional direction and pays due attention to agency. Anti-poverty policy takes its cue from this broader understanding of well-being and agency deficits. Supporting those in poverty to break out from their situation involves addressing a wide range of deficits, and ensuring they have the capacity to lead the lives they value.

It is a failing of the current international policy debate on poverty that the focus is overwhelmingly on the efficiency implications of focusing on the poor and poorest. Some policy approaches take it for granted that focusing resources on the poorest may generate lower social pay-offs, or that social protection is most effective in addressing the needs of the moderately or transient poor. The empirical and conceptual bases for these assumptions has been challenged (Barrientos et al., 2005). Ultimately, a focus on the poorest must be justified on the shared vision of a fair society. Focusing on the poorest is consonant with ethical theories of justice. Rawls' (1971) theory of justice relies on two main principles. The first principle states that each person has an equal right to a fully adequate scheme of equal basic liberties which is compatible with a similar scheme of liberties for all. The second principle states that social and economic inequalities are to satisfy two conditions. First they must be attached to offices and positions open to all under conditions of fair equality of opportunity; and second, they must be to the greatest benefit of the least advantaged members of society. The first principle applies particularly to political liberties and citizenship; while the second principle applies more specifically to social and economic spheres. The implication for social protection is that alternative social states must be evaluated from the perspective of their effects on the least advantaged.

The implications from these perspectives on poverty are increasingly informing the design and orientation of new forms of social assistance emerging in Latin America. With Chile Solidario in particular, an understanding that poverty is rooted in structural social and economic institutions and relations, that it can best be understood in terms of deficits in capability, that is deficits in well-being and agency; and that, in a fair society, addressing poverty involves a paramount concern with the least advantaged – have directly informed its design and orientation.

Explaining the introduction of Chile Solidario

Chile Solidario was introduced in 2002 with the aim of eradicating extreme poverty in Chile. Its full title is Social Protection System Chile Solidario (*Sistema de Protección Social Chile Solidario*). Chile Solidario aims to provide intensive support to the 225,000 poorest households in Chile (considered to be in extreme poverty) along seven dimensions: education, health, income, employment, household dynamics, housing, and registration, so that at the end of a two year period these households have the capacity to lift themselves above extreme poverty (MIDEPLAN, 2003).

Why Chile Solidario? Chile has experienced a sustained period of economic growth since the mid 1980s, averaging annual rates of growth of GDP in excess of 7%. Economic growth has created the conditions for a significant reduction in poverty incidence and gap. In the region, two poverty lines are commonly used. Indigents are those living in households in which income or expenditure is at or below the value of a basic basket of food ensuring minimum nutrition, the indigence line. Indigents are those with insufficient food intake, and can be considered to be in extreme poverty. The poverty line is conventionally twice the indigence line. This assumes that, in addition to food, a minimum socially acceptable living standard would require that the same amount spent on food is spent on non-food items. Figure 8.1 shows the incidence of indigence and poverty in Chile 1990–2003.

As can be seen from the figure, the poverty headcount declined from 38.6% in 1990 to 18.7% in 2003. The indigence headcount declined from 12.9% to 4.7% in the same period.[3] These figures show that growth is a key driver for poverty reduction, and at the same time they demonstrate that growth is not enough. Policy makers looking at these figures in the year 2000 were concerned that the headcount poverty reduction had slowed down, and, critically, that headcount indigence had stagnated. The need for a pro-active stance on poverty and indigence was evident.[4]

Assessments of the poverty reduction (in)effectiveness of existing public programmes had correctly identified several weaknesses. An exercise mapping public programmes with poverty reduction objectives in 1999 found 134 such programmes delivered by 25 different agencies. The same exercise was repeated in 2002 and found the number of programmes had risen to 142 with 33 agencies involved (MIDEPLAN 2003). The multiplicity of programmes reflected a piecemeal, fragmented, and sectoral approach to poverty reduction, which greatly undermined its effectiveness. The supply mode of provision was also problematic, in that it was largely passive and paid no attention to the higher access costs faced by poor households, and to their social exclusion.[5] Evaluation of these programmes, such as there was, suggested they failed to reach the poorest, and focused instead on the moderately poor. For the

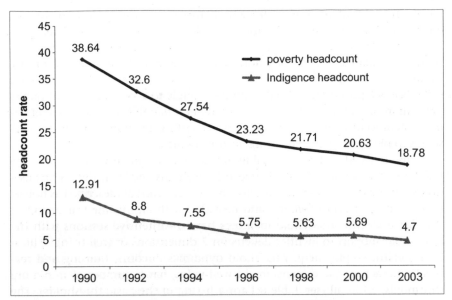

Figure 8.1 Incidence of poverty and indigence in Chile (1990–2003)
Source: Estimated from CASEN survey data, taken from Santibanez 2006

designers of Chile Solidario, the main barrier to effective poverty reduction was the social exclusion experienced by the poorest in securing access to public programmes delivering social protection.

The insights into the nature of poverty and vulnerability shared by policy-makers are quickly noted here (MIDEPLAN, 2003). Policy design acknowledged the multidimensional nature of poverty, to a much greater extent than conditional income transfer programmes elsewhere in Latin America (which are mainly focused on schooling, health and nutrition). It explicitly adopts a capability approach in the sense that it aims to bring about greater equality in the capability space through ensuring that 'all can access a minimum of basic capabilities' (MIDEPLAN, 2003: 17). It defines the household as the focus of support, based on the view that in the context of social protection, agency largely lies with the household. It also reflects a rights approach to human development, and pays attention to local development and participation. Some of these insights will be taken up in the discussion below.

The main features of Chile Solidario

Figure 8.2 provides a trajectory description of the operation of Chile Solidario. This is discussed briefly below. Analysis of the National Characterization Socio-economic Survey (CASEN, 2000) household survey identified 225,000 indigent households, who became the target population for Chile Solidario. Chile has for sometime used a proxy means test to identify poor households eligible for support by public programmes. Households applying for support receive the visit of an enumerator who completes a brief questionnaire covering housing conditions, education, employment and income. This questionnaire is known as *Ficha CAS*.[6] Using the responses to the questionnaire, a score is calculated for the household. This score ranks households according to their level of deprivation, a proxy for their poverty. Households who have a score below a poverty threshold point are eligible to access all relevant public programmes. This score is valid for two years. *Chile Solidario* uses this targeting system to identify the extreme poor by setting a threshold point for CAS scores to pick up the 225,000 indigent households.[7]

Households identified as eligible are contacted and invited to join the PUENTE programme (BRIDGE between households and their rights).[8] Households joining the programme are allocated a social worker (described as household support or *apoyo familiar*) and provided with an income transfer. Over the first 6 months household members have 14 intensive sessions with the household support to identify deficits on 7 dimensions of well-being: education, health, employment, household dynamics, income, housing and registration. Each of the dimensions of well-being has a number of minimum thresholds, 53 in all (see Table 8.1 for a listing of the basic thresholds). The sessions not only identify households' deficits but also cover how to overcome these deficits, leading to specific commitments (*compromisos*) on the part of the households and the household support. Achievement of the basic thresholds are acknowledged and recorded. The household support is responsible for coordinating access to the relevant public agencies and programmes; while household members are responsible for fulfilling their commitments. After the first six months, sessions are fewer. Households are expected to exit PUENTE after two years, and the main target for the programme is that 70% of households exit the programme having successfully reached all 53 basic thresholds. Over the subsequent 3 years households continue to be entitled to access to public programmes and the cash transfer. Households that fail to reach all 53 basic thresholds when exiting PUENTE continue to work to achieve these during this period.[9]

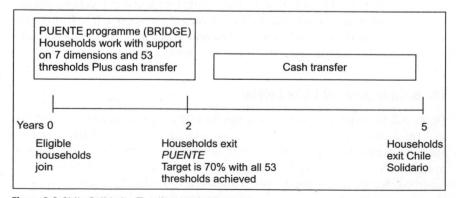

Figure 8.2 Chile Solidario: Timelines and outcomes

Table 8.1 Chile Solidario's basic thresholds, by poverty dimension

Dimension	Basic threshold (social minima)
Registration	Recorded in the Civil Registry Have identity card Valid CAS form with municipality Up to date with military service Up to date criminal record documentation Disabled are registered as such
Health	Registered with primary health care unit Up to date with pregnancy checks Children below 7 up to date with immunizations Children with up to date health check-ups Women 35+ up to date with Papanicolau test Contraceptive methods up to date check-up Older people up to date check-ups Up to date check-up if suffering from chronic illness Disabled are participating in a rehabilitation programme All members are aware of preventative health measures
Education	Pre-school children attending or applying for pre-school If mother working and no adult carer in the household, that pre-school children access child-care Children below 15 attend school Children of school age access demand subsidy Children over 12 can read and write Disabled children are in an educational establishment One adult is responsible for the education of the children and liaises with school Adults have a positive and responsible attitude to education Adults can read and write
Household dynamics	Daily communication about practices, leisure, time Have effective mechanism for dealing with conflict Clear norms for sharing and living together Fair distribution of household work (for all, independent of sex or age) Knowledge about community resources and networks Linked to support programmes if violent behaviour Regular visits to children if in care Regular visits to youth if incarcerated and support for their rehabilitation
Housing	Regularized occupancy of land and housing Applying for housing if in need Safe drinking water Access to energy sources, electricity, gas, etc. Adequate sewage Housing protected from leaks or threat of flooding At least two habitable rooms Bed and bedding Cooking equipment and facilities Effective disposal of rubbish Non-contaminated environment Access to water subsidy
Work	At least one adult in regular paid employment No child below 15 not attending school because in work If unemployed, registered with the labour bureau
Income	Access to family subsidy (SUF) Access to Family Allowance (Asignación Familiar) Access to non-contributory pension (PASIS) Household income above the indigence line Household budget in-line with resources and priorities

The information available indicates that in the main the programme has been implemented as planned. By September 2005, 86.9% of eligible households had been contacted (189,534 out of a target 218,217 households), and 51,441 had exited PUENTE. A CEPAL evaluation of PUENTE in the first quarter of 2003 raised a number of detailed issues concerning implementation, but reported a very positive assessment from beneficiaries and programme officials (CEPAL, 2003). A subsequent attitudinal and progress evaluation done by the University of Chile in 2004 also reported high levels of satisfaction and achievement among those interviewed (Canales, 2004).[10] A full scale evaluation of Chile Solidario with a survey recently collected will help assess outcomes more reliably.[11]

Chile Solidario explicitly aims to strengthen capabilities by ensuring the poorest can achieve a minimum set of basic thresholds. In this respect, it is highly unusual if not unique among anti-poverty programmes. The programme documentation refers to capabilities (*capacidades*), which were described above as the range of beings and doings that a person values. In Chile Solidario, these are described by the basic thresholds listed in Table 8.1. It can be argued that this set of thresholds corresponds in some way to achieved capabilities, as that together they provide what the programme designers understood as a minimum or basic set of capabilities. The assumption here is that making sure the poorest have a basic set of capabilities, they would be in a stronger position to overcome persistent poverty. The purpose of the programme is therefore to enlarge the set of capabilities of the poorest, so that at least a basic set of capabilities is within their reach.[12]

It is important to note that the list of 53 thresholds was set by the programme designers without any involvement of the beneficiaries. Some important issues arise in this context.

Firstly, it can, and should, be questioned whether the list of thresholds provides a comprehensive set of basic capabilities. There is a weighty literature on this issue which cannot be reviewed here (Doyal and Gough, 1991; Nussbaum, 1999; Alkire, 2002). There is no consensus on a possible list of basic capabilities, and perhaps such consensus on this would not be feasible or desirable. It is very likely to differ across societies, and across communities, households and individuals.

Secondly, it should be questioned whether the basic thresholds adopted by the programme designers do ensure beneficiary households reach a minimum socially acceptable level. In the context of Chile Solidario, capability is not measured directly, but indirectly through binary indicators of achievement of basic thresholds as listed in Table 8.1. For many of the thresholds reported, their content admits to different levels of achievement, which are not fully captured by a yes/no evaluation (Santibañez, 2006).

On ethical foundations, Chile Solidario clearly demonstrates a Rawlsian concern with the poorest. This shows that a Rawlsian ethical standpoint is capable of gathering sufficient political support and that it can be successfully operationalized. However, there are some issues at the margins, literally. As noted above, identification of eligible households is based on scores in the CAS form. The scores rank households according to their deprivation along a range of variables. It was also noted above that the identification of the aggregate of eligible households at the national and regional levels was based on estimates of the incidence of indigence. However, the identification of beneficiary households was based on the CAS form. There is a large overlap in the identification of eligible households through these two measures, one based purely on income, the other based on income, housing, employment and education. However, there are also differences around the upper-bound. The CEPAL study found that among households participating in the programme to December 2003, 37% had household income above the indigence line, and therefore would not have been eligible if the income eligibility alone had been used (CEPAL, 2003). Conversely, the regional allocations based on income alone produced a situation where the cut-off point in CAS scores differed across regions. A household with score points around the upper-bound could have been eligible in one region but not in another.[13] Operationalizing Rawls' 'difference principle' needs considering carefully, especially as regards to setting the upper-bound of the 'least advantaged' group (Pogge, 1989).

This section has reviewed the main features of the Chile Solidario programme, noting how these reflect the key perspectives on poverty identified above (the structural factors behind poverty, the focus on capability and on the least advantaged) and how they are operationalized. To an important extent, Chile Solidario does attempt to implement these perspectives on poverty in the design and operation of the programme, making it a uniquely innovative anti-poverty programme. A full evaluation of the programme will be needed before we can be certain that the programme has been successful, but to date the programme has managed to reach its target population and exit rates from the PUENTE component of the programme are in line with expectations. The Government of Chile has already taken steps to expand the target population of the programme to incorporate those among the poorest who do not live in established households, street dwellers for example, and the poorest older persons living on their own. Chile Solidario is rapidly being emulated in other countries in the region, especially through the integration of additional interventions to existing income transfer programmes.

Conclusions and main lessons

The rise in poverty and vulnerability which followed the 1980s economic crisis and structural adjustment in the region has made it urgent to develop innovative responses. Social protection institutions in place before the 1990s in Latin America were 'truncated' in that they excluded the majority of the population who are dependent on informal employment. In the last decade new forms of social assistance have emerged, focusing on the poor and poorest, and increasingly reflecting an understanding of poverty as essentially multidimensional and persistent over time. *Bolsa Escola/Família* and *Progresa/Oportunidades* are the largest and best known such programmes. More recently, innovative and integrated anti-poverty programmes are being developed. Chile Solidario provides the best example. Chile Solidario goes some way to extending the scope of social assistance programmes in Latin America in a multidimensional direction.

Other countries wishing to develop similar approaches will need to take note of the fact that Chile Solidario was implemented on the basis of a large number of pre-existing public interventions focused on poor households, which needed integrating. It also benefited from the 'fiscal space' generated by sustained growth, and strong delivery capacity. Whether programmes of this type could be implemented in low-income countries with weak financial conditions and poor delivery capacity is an open question.

The scope of the programme should alert policymakers to the fact that monetary transfers are not enough, by themselves, to lift extremely poor households out of extreme or persistent poverty. These should be accompanied by basic services – such as education, health, and childcare – and protection against contingencies which may push households back into extreme poverty. A key lesson from *Chile Solidario* is the need to think in terms of integrated programmes as opposed to isolated interventions.

Chile Solidario has a strong focus on lifting social exclusion, and reconnecting the extreme poor with their rights and entitlements, and to full participation in economic and social activities. Effective poverty reduction and eradication requires strengthening the agency of poor households. The programme adopts a 'contractarian' approach to strengthening agency, with poor households identifying their deficits and setting in place strategies to overcome them. There are alternative approaches to strengthening the agency of poor households, especially in conditions where they concentrate geographically or occupationally, through strengthening 'communitarian' processes and institutions to enable agency. It is likely that the conditions which would make one or the other approach most effective will vary from country to country.

Endnotes

1. Only a handful of the most developed countries in the region, Uruguay, Argentina and Chile, managed to achieve high levels of coverage for their social protection institutions, but even there the poorest were excluded.
2. Only 21% of USA respondents agreed with the view that lack of effort by the poor themselves is not an important cause of poverty; while 63% of Latin American respondents agreed with the view that poverty is due to bad circumstances, with only 36% agreeing with the view that lack of effort by the poor themselves was a major cause of poverty (Graham, 2002).
3. The fall in the poverty gap for the same period was from 14.8% to 6.3% and for the indigence gap was from 4.33% to 1.74%.
4. In 2000, Ricardo Lagos was elected President of Chile, the third centre left administration since the ending of dictatorship in 1990 and the second

socialist President since Salvador Allende. His manifesto placed strong emphasis on social development and poverty reduction.

5. MIDEPLAN eloquently refers to this mode of provision as 'modelo de espera'(MIDEPLAN, 2003), a 'sit and wait' attitude among service providers commonly observed across the highly bureaucratic public service agencies in the region.

6. A revised and expanded new version of this tool, the *Ficha de Protección Social* is currently being introduced.

7. This method of identifying eligible households raises some issues as regards targeting. CASEN identifies indigents solely on the basis of household income, but the CAS score covers four dimensions with income contributing only around 11% of the score. Put another way, CASEN identifies the income poorest but CAS identifies the most deprived. There is no guarantee these will be the same, and in practice Chile Solidario targets the extreme poor (poorest 5% of households) rather than the indigent (those with income below the indigence line). Another issue is that the threshold CAS score for the Chile Solidario is estimated at the region level, so that two households with the same scores in different regions may have different eligibility status (CEPAL, 2003).

8. The PUENTE Programme is managed by a long standing social fund FOSIS and the municipalities.

9. Programme figures show that 75.3% of 51,441 households exiting PUENTE by September 2005 had managed to reach all 53 thresholds, but this rate seem to have declined over time (Santibañez, 2006).

10. Government satisfaction with the progress of Chile Solidario is reflected in the plans under discussion to expand the programme, to street dwellers, and to older people living alone (*La Nación,* 6 April 2006). This is also the route recommended by a World Bank study of social protection in Chile (World Bank, 2005).

11. The design of the programme includes the collection of panel surveys, but to date only the 2004/5 wave has been completed.

12. It is questionable whether the proliferation of alternatives, say branded pharmaceutical products as opposed to generic ones, does imply a wider set of capabilities.

13. The CEPAL study also points to the presence of standard targeting problems, measurement errors and lack of information on beneficiary households (CEPAL, 2003).

References

Alkire, S. (2002) 'Dimensions of human development', *World Development* 30(2): 181–205.

Barrientos, A. (2004) 'Latin America: towards a liberal-informal welfare regime', in I. Gough, G. Wood, A. Barrientos, P. Bevan, P. David and G. Room (eds), *Insecurity and welfare regimes in Asia, Africa and Latin America*, Cambridge University Press, Cambridge.

Barrientos, A., Hulme, D. and Shepherd, A. (2005) 'Can social protection tackle chronic poverty?', *European Journal of Development Research* 17(1): 8–23.

Canales, M. (2004) 'Evaluación del estado de avance del sistema *Chile Solidario'*, Informe Final Report, University of Chile, Santiago.

CEPAL (2003) 'Análisis de Resultados del Programa Puente 2002', report, CEPAL, División Desarrollo Social, Santiago.

CEPAL (2007) 'Panorama Social 2006', CEPAL, División Desarrollo Social, Santiago.

de Ferranti, D., Perry, G. E., Gill, I. S. and Servén, L. (2000) 'Securing our future in a global economy', *Viewpoints*, The World Bank, Washington D.C.

Doyal, L. and Gough, I. (1991) *A Theory of Human Need*, Palgrave Macmillan, London and New York.

Graham, C. (2002) 'Public attitudes matter: a conceptual framework for accounting for political economy in safety nets and social assistance policies', *Social Protection Discussion Paper 0233*, World Bank, Washington D.C.

MIDEPLAN (2003) '*Chile Solidario*: El desafío de crear un sistema de protección y promoción social', powerpoint presentation, MIDEPLAN, Santiago.

Nussbaum, M. (1999) 'Women and Equality: the capabilities approach', *International Labour Review* 138(3): 227–245.

Pogge, T. W. (1989) *Realizing Rawls*, Cornell University Press, Ithaca.

Rawls, J. (1971) *A Theory of Justice*, Harvard University Press, Cambridge, MA.

Santibañez, C. (2006) 'Pobreza y desigualdad en Chile: Antecendentes para la construcción de un sistema de protección social', report, Inter-American Development Bank, Washington D.C.

Sen, A. (1985) *Commodities and Capabilities*, North-Holland, Amsterdam.

World Bank (2005) 'Household risk management and social protection in Chile', World Bank Country Study, World Bank, Washington D.C.

About the author

Armando Barrientos is Professor and Director of Research at the Brooks World Poverty Institute at the University of Manchester and a Senior Researcher with the Chronic Poverty Research Centre (CPRC) coordinating research on vulnerability and social protection. His most recent book is *Social Protection for the Poor and Poorest* (edited with David Hulme and published by Palgrave in 2008).

CHAPTER 9

Assisting the poorest in Bangladesh: Learning from BRAC's 'Targeting the Ultra Poor' Programme

David Hulme and Karen Moore

This chapter examines BRAC's Challenging the Frontiers of Poverty Reduction/Targeting the Ultra Poor Programme, or CFPR-TUP. The programme aims at reaching the poorest in Bangladesh and assisting them (through assets and skills) to overcome their vulnerability and move out of poverty. The chapter follows the evolution of the programme (launched in 2002) and describes the context in which it was initiated. It explores two of its main strategies: (i) the 'pushing down' of development programmes to reach the poorest and (ii) the 'pushing out' of existing poverty alleviation programmes from conventional approaches. The analysis also reviews what is known about the impacts of TUP and explains its achievements in the areas of vulnerability, child development and graduation to mainstream BRAC microfinance. It draws lessons from TUP about the types of programme design features and the processes required in order to develop such ambitious initiatives. The chapter concludes that the programme has in fact succeeded both in reaching significant numbers of Bangladesh's poorest people and in improving their economic and social conditions.

Introduction

Social protection seeks to reduce the deprivation and improve the future prospects of poor and vulnerable people and households. However, even when such policies and programmes are working well, assisting the poorest and most socially marginalized people can be very difficult. This is a particularly important issue in countries with mass poverty, where a large minority, or sometimes a majority, of the population live below the poverty line. In such contexts, effective social protection policies may benefit millions of poor people but do little or nothing for the very poorest (CPRC, 2004).

This chapter commences with an examination of the evolution of a programme designed to reach the poorest people in Bangladesh, to improve their immediate situation and to give them the assets and other skills to move out of poverty and dramatically reduce their vulnerability – BRAC's Challenging the

Frontiers of Poverty Reduction/Targeting the Ultra Poor Programme, or TUP. It then reviews what is known about the impacts of TUP, and finds evidence that the programme is both reaching significant numbers of Bangladesh's poorest people and improving their economic and social condition. The concluding sections draw lessons from the TUP about the types of programme design features and the processes required to develop such ambitious initiatives.

The context of the 'Targeting the Ultra Poor' (TUP) Programme

As noted in the first chapter of the book, Bangladesh has been doing well in recent times (Drèze, 2004) with reasonable rates of economic growth, improving social indicator levels and strengthened resilience to environmental shocks (floods, storm surges and drought). The headcount poverty index dropped from 52% in 1983/84 to 40% in 2000, although the fall in extreme poverty has been more modest (Hossain et al., 2000). The UN's Human Poverty Index (HPI), based on income poverty, illiteracy and health deprivation measures, fell from 61% in 1981/82 to 36% in 2004. Despite these improvements, life for many remains characterized by severe deprivation and vulnerability, with around 31% of the rural population trapped in chronic poverty and 24% of the entire population experiencing extreme income poverty (i.e. with consumption expenditure at less than 60% of the government's official poverty line). Between 25 to 30 million Bangladeshis have seen little or no benefit from democracy or the country's significant and consistent economic growth.[1]

Chronically and extremely poor people – the 'ultra poor' to use BRAC's terminology – 'face a complex structure of constraints that mainstream development approaches [including the country's social protection policies][2] have found difficult to address' (Hossain and Matin, 2007: 381). Ultra poor people have not been able to improve their lives through *(i)* accessing employment opportunities created by the growth of the formal sector (e.g. garment industry, fisheries, services); *(ii)* benefiting from the 'green revolution' that filtered across the country in the 1980s and 1990s; or *(iii)* participating in the self-employment and casual employment opportunities of the dynamic informal economy that has been supported by Bangladesh's much-praised microfinance industry (Hulme and Moore, 2007). Market-related opportunities, governmental social policies, and non-governmental organization (NGO) programmes miss the ultra poor because they lack the material, human, financial and social assets to engage, and/or they live in areas or belong to ethnic/social groups that are bypassed or excluded.

In particular, rural people living in remote areas or difficult environments (e.g. the seasonally eroded *chars* or seasonally flooded *haors*) and disadvantaged women are likely to be ultra poor. The ultra poor are not a distinct group, but a heterogeneous assemblage of different people usually experiencing multiple deprivations (see Sen and Begum, this volume, for a detailed discussion). Commonly they are casual labourers (in agriculture or services), migrants or displaced people, ethnic or indigenous minorities, older people and those with severe impairments or ill-health.

For analytical purposes we can recognize both the economically active ultra poor, commonly surviving through their precarious, multiple livelihoods, and the economically inactive or dependent ultra poor (frail old people, the physically or cognitively impaired, chronically sick or destitute).[3] BRAC's TUP has chosen to focus on the economically active ultra poor. The inactive ultra poor remain dependent on ultra-marginal economic activities and support from family, relatives, neighbours, NGOs and community-based organizations and, sometimes, government social policies such as old-age pensions.

BRAC[4] was established in 1972 to provide humanitarian relief to the tens of millions of Bangladeshis suffering after the war of independence and later environmental disasters. Subsequently it moved on to development work, and has evolved into the world's largest service delivery NGO. As of June 2006, BRAC was working in over 65,000 villages and over 4,300 urban slums, in every district of Bangladesh. It claimed over 5 million members, almost entirely women, and an annual expenditure of over US$250 million. Nearly 1 million children were enrolled in a BRAC school, and almost 3.5 million have graduated. The NGO employs over 37,000 full-time staff, over 53,000 community school teachers, and tens of thousands of poultry and community health and nutrition workers and volunteers. There are now international programmes in Afghanistan, Sri Lanka, East Africa and the United Kingdom (BRAC, 2006a). In Bangladesh, BRAC's major programmatic foci are the promotion of self-employment (microfinance, and technical support) and human development (non-formal education and health services). BRAC, the NGO, is at the centre of a corporate network including BRAC University, BRAC Bank, BRAC Printers, the country's largest cold store company, and several other businesses.

Three key points must be noted:

1. BRAC has the capacity to manage operations across Bangladesh that rivals the business sector and often outperforms the government;
2. BRAC has substantial experience in programme experimentation and learning; and
3. BRAC's economic programmes are heavily loan driven and envision poor people as microentrepreneurs.

The evolution of the TUP Programme

BRAC launched the TUP Programme in January 2002 as an experimental initiative that recognized two key findings from BRAC field experience and research:

1. BRAC's highly regarded microfinance programme rarely reached the poorest women.[5] This was partly because of self exclusion – the poorest women report being very worried about the consequences of not being able to make weekly loan repayments (*kisti*) and so do not join BRAC's

village organizations (VOs). Partly it was due to social exclusion – many VO members do not want to associate with the very poor for both economic and social reasons. And partly it was because BRAC's loan driven approach to microfinance does not match the needs or preferences of the poorest. BRAC has been aware of this issue since the mid-1980s when it began to experiment with new programmes to reach the poorest (see next section).

2. For many years the World Food Programme (WFP) operated a Vulnerable Group Feeding (VGF) scheme that provided poor women with 31.25kg of wheat per month for two years. In 1985 BRAC began working with WFP to create a 'laddered strategic linkage', the Income Generation for Vulnerable Group Development (IGVGD) programme, that would allow food aid recipients to climb out of poverty by graduating to BRAC's microfinance groups and self-employment initiatives. WFP's food aid would be complemented by BRAC-provided savings programmes, social development, income generation training and, eventually, microcredit. The IGVGD has received favourable evaluations and continues to operate,[6] but at least 30% of IGVGD participants do not progress to microfinance programmes and these are usually from the poorest and most vulnerable households (Webb et al., 2001). In addition, a significant minority of 'new' IGVGD participants have taken part in the programme previously but have failed to improve their livelihood security (Matin, 2002).[7]

These two experiences indicated that BRAC's programmes were having problems assisting the poorest. TUP was launched to build on existing knowledge and the organization's commitment to the very poor. TUP was overseen by BRAC's founder-director, Fazle Abed, and systematically monitored by BRAC's Research and Evaluation Division (RED).[8]

The TUP programme also used the concept of a 'laddered strategic linkage', however, its approach was 'more systematic, intensive and comprehensive, covering economic, social and health aspects' (Hossain and Matin, 2007: 382). The idea behind the TUP approach is to enable the ultra poor to develop new and better options for sustainable livelihoods. This requires a combination of approaches – both promotional (e.g. asset grants, skills training) and protective (e.g. stipends, health services) – as well as addressing socio-political constraints at various levels. TUP employs two broad strategies: 'pushing down', and 'pushing out' (Matin, 2005a):

1. 'Pushing down': TUP seeks to 'push down' the reach of development programmes through specific targeting of the ultra poor, using a careful methodology combining participatory approaches with simple survey based tools. Within geographically selected areas, certain exclusion and inclusion conditions must be met. The selected households are then brought under a special two year investment programme involving asset transfer, intensive social awareness and enterprise training, and health services.

2. 'Pushing out': TUP also seeks to 'push out' the domain within which existing poverty alleviation programmes operate by addressing dimensions of poverty that many conventional approaches do not. This involves a shift away from conventional service delivery modes of development programming to a focus on social-political relations that disempower the poor, especially women, and constrain their livelihoods. Building links and support networks with other groups and organizations is key to 'pushing out'.

It is important to note that the TUP Programme in fact targets two groups of ultra poor people:

- the 'Specially Targeted Ultra Poor' (STUP), who are supported with the complete package (called the 'Special Investment Programme'), which includes asset grants; and
- the 'BDP (BRAC Development Programme) Ultra Poor', changed to 'Other Targeted Ultra Poor' (OTUP) in the second phase of the Challenging the Frontiers of Poverty Reduction/Targeting the Ultra Poor (CFPR-TUP), who do not receive asset transfers, only skills development, more intensive staff support, and health support.

The STUP are organized into microfinance groups after 18–24 months, while those OTUP who are not already BDP microfinance members join groups immediately. In this chapter we are only concerned with the STUP, who receive asset transfers as a key part of the programme.

By late 2003, after experimentation and redesign, the programme had nine main components (Table 9.1) that were carefully sequenced and linked.

Table 9.1 Targeting the Ultra Poor Programme (TUP) in Bangladesh: Its components and their purpose

Component	Purpose
Integrated targeting methodologies	Identify and target ultra poor
Monthly stipends	Consumption smoothing, reduce vulnerability, and reduce opportunity costs of asset operations
Social development (functional literacy)	Confidence building, and raise knowledge and awareness of rights
Health support	Reduce morbidity and vulnerability
Income generation training and regular refreshers	Ensure good return from the asset transferred
Income generating asset transfer (e.g. poultry, milch cows, horticulture)	Significantly increase the household's asset base for income generation
Enterprise input and support	Ensure good return from the asset transferred
Technical follow-up and support of enterprise	Ensure good return from the asset transferred
Establishment of village assistance committee and mobilization of local elites for support	Create a supportive and enabling environment

Source: Adapted from Hossain and Matin (2007: 383)

Table 9.2 TUP programme targeting indicators for the Specially Targeted Ultra Poor (STUP) in Bangladesh[9]

Exclusion conditions (all selected households must satisfy all conditions)	Not borrowing from a microcredit-providing NGO. Not receiving benefits from government programmes. At least one adult woman physically able to put in labour towards the asset transferred.
Inclusion conditions (all selected households must satisfy at least three conditions)	Total land owned less than 10 decimals. Adult women in the household selling labour. (In Phase II, changed to 'Household dependent upon female domestic work or begging'.) Main male income earner is disabled or unable to work. (In Phase II, changed to 'No male adult active members in the household'.) School-aged children selling labour. No productive assets.

Source: Matin (2005a)

It carefully targets the poorest[10] (Table 9.2), provides them with a monthly stipend and health services to provide basic security, provides social development and income generation training,[11] transfers assets to participants (e.g. poultry and cages, milch cows and stables), and provides technical support, inputs and advice.

The initial TUP plans envisioned that TUP members would graduate to joining BRAC VOs, but a number of problems in the field led to a redesign (Hossain and Matin, 2007: 383). In particular:

1. TUP members became heavily dependent on BRAC staff for assistance and advice, rather than on VOs, effectively treating BRAC as a patron;
2. Many VO members resented TUP beneficiaries, as they had not received 'gifts' but had to repay BRAC for assets and services; and
3. The assets transferred to poor women experienced relatively high levels of theft or damage, sometimes due to such jealousy.

This led to the design of Village Assistance Committees[12] (VACs) that are to enlist the energies of local elites to support TUP participants, and the poorest more generally, in their village. The VACs have seven voluntary members – a BRAC fieldworker, a TUP participant, two VO members, and three members of the village elite.[13] The contribution of these committees to TUP performance, and more broadly to local level social and political change, are complex and difficult to assess. However, Hossain and Matin (2007: 390) judge them to be a 'modest success' and a challenge to those who automatically assume that the involvement of local elites in development programmes will always be negative.[14]

The present status of the TUP

The TUP aims 'to build a more sustainable livelihood for the extremely poor, by providing a solid economic, social, and humanitarian foundation, which would enable this group to overcome extreme poverty' (Hossain and Matin, 2007: 382). By mid-2006 the TUP was operating in 15 of Bangladesh's 64 districts, with a geographical focus on the north of the country and especially areas experiencing seasonal hunger (*monga*) on an annual basis. At that time the cumulative number of TUP participants was 100,000, and there are plans to recruit 300,000 new STUP participants over the next five-year phase (BRAC, 2006b).[15] The entire CFPR-TUP programme is funded by a donor consortium[16] which has contributed about US$65 million over the period 2002 to 2006 and committed a further US$155 million over the next five years. By 2006, the high initial costs of the 'Special Investment Programme' were reduced by over 40% to US$268 per recipient (BRAC, 2006c) as the programme scaled-up and found ways of reducing costs.

TUP already receives a flow of international visitors, usually funded by aid agencies, who are keen to learn from it. Interestingly, the TUP has already begun to influence other programmes in Bangladesh, with DFID's *Chars Livelihood Programme* redesigning itself from a broad-based capacity building initiative to an asset transfer programme.

The achievements of the TUP

The large majority of data collection and assessment of TUP performance is undertaken by BRAC-RED. This includes the maintenance of a panel dataset that tracks key indicators for a sample of selected ultra poor households (SUPs) who have participated in the TUP since 2002, and non-selected ultra-poor households (NSUPs) who have not participated in the TUP. At the pre-programme baseline study stage, both SUPs and NSUPs were objectively ranked in the 'poorest' group in the villages. However, NSUPs were not selected for the programme because their household scores were close to the cut-off line between the 'poorest' and 'poor' categories – i.e. NSUPs had higher welfare scores than SUPs. In addition to the panel dataset of objective indicators, BRAC-RED (2004) also conducts regular subjective assessments of SUP and NSUP poverty and welfare indicators and change.

Rabbani et al.'s, (2006) analysis of the TUP panel dataset provides evidence of TUP recipients (i.e. SUPs) improving their livelihoods more rapidly than the NSUP control group.

Asset accumulation: Over the period 2002 to 2005, TUP participants had a greater rate of asset accumulation than non-participants in all asset domains – financial assets (savings and credit), physical assets (a range of livestock, household and productive assets), natural assets (access to cultivable and homestead land), social assets (social and legal awareness), and human capital (household demographic structure, education, health and sanitation). Figure 9.1

provides a diagrammatic comparison of SUP and NSUP asset pentagon dynamics. Although the human capital picture is relatively complex and overall improvements are very small for both groups, as many of these changes can take longer to emerge, nutritional improvements are already apparent. Figures 9.2

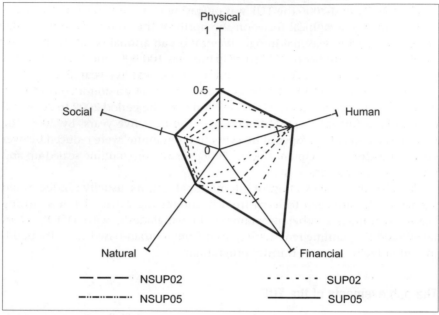

Figure 9.1 Asset pentagon dynamics for BRAC charts in Bangladesh: Comparing SUPs and NSUPs over time.
Source: Rabbani, Prakash and Sulaiman (2006: 16)

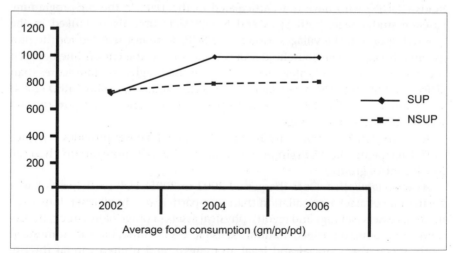

Figure 9.2 Change in food consumption: Comparing SUPs and NSUPs over time.
Source: Matin (2006)

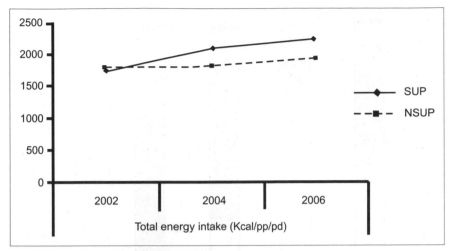

Figure 9.3 Change in energy intake: Comparing SUPs and NSUPs over time.
Source: Matin (2006)

and 9.3 illustrate the dynamics for human capital in terms of food and calorie intake; SUP households also have improved the quality of their food intake to a greater extent than NSUPs (see also Haseen, 2007). It is also notable that a greater proportion of SUP households have been able to improve their situation in terms of combinations of multiple types of assets than NSUP households, suggesting that improvements may be more sustainable over time.

Vulnerability: In 2002, SUP household's self-reported higher levels of food insecurity (occasional and chronic deficit) than NSUP households. In 2005 both groups reported improvements in food security. But the food security of NSUPs had improved only a little while SUP food security had been significantly ameliorated, with food deficit reports reducing from 98% to 70% (Figure 9.4). The TUP was associated with a reversal of SUP and NSUP status – SUPs now reported greater food security than NSUPs. Further, while both SUPs and NSUPs are equally vulnerable to various crises – with the newly asseted SUPs perhaps more vulnerable to livestock death – subjective assessments suggest that the SUPs can expect to recover from shocks sooner than the NSUPs.

Subjective poverty dynamics: Community-level assessments of changes in household poverty status reported SUPs as having experienced significant improvements in their welfare. This contrasted with NSUPs who were reported to have experienced a downturn in their circumstances (Figure 9.5).[17]

Graduation to mainstream BRAC microfinance: By 2004, the first TUP participants had completed the two-year special investment phase and were organized into separate village organizations. They were being offered a full range of BRAC's development services, including microfinance. Based on previous experience, BRAC takes a flexible, experimental and member-driven approach to credit provision, and it generally seems to be working – about 70% of these women had taken and regularly repaid a first loan. BRAC continues to strive

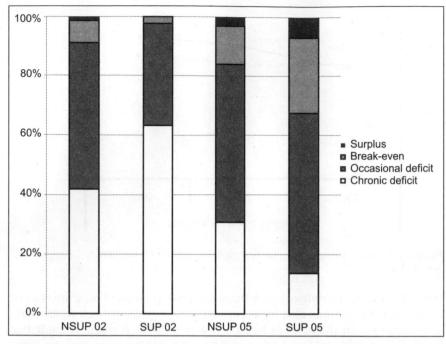

Figure 9.4 Self perception of food security: Comparing SUPs and NSUPs in terms of changes in availability of food in one year over time
Source: Rabbani, Prakash and Sulaiman (2006: 24).

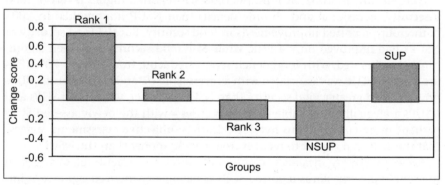

Figure 9.5 Average change score over period 2002–2005 of households in different wealth rankings as assessed by community meetings
Source: Sulaiman and Matin (2006: 8)

to assist those 30% who were unable or unwilling to take a small loan, or had trouble repaying.

Child development: Not all of the indicators for TUP have shown improvements, and there has been particular concern about the lack of progress for children in TUP households. Nutrition status among the under-fives and primary school enrolment rates have changed little or not at all. This may be because of time lags associated with changes in such indicators, or patterns of intra-household resource allocation. These findings have led to deep debates in BRAC, concerned about interruption of intergenerational poverty, about modifications to the TUP approach.

Independent verification: An independent review of the TUP in 2004 concluded that the programme had resulted in extremely poor women improving their livelihoods, had been relatively cost effective, and had been more effective than comparable initiatives targeting the poorest (Posgate et al., 2004 in Hossain and Matin, 2007). In addition, our limited fieldwork and interviews with TUP participants provides support for these generally positive assessments and has not yielded any data to challenge such conclusions.

Learning from the TUP

The most obvious lesson from the TUP is that the very poor can be reached and supported through carefully designed and targeted programmes. Moreover, with appropriate support, the poorest households can develop the capacity to engage with the economy in ways that permit them to sustain their improved welfare position without further subsidies or transfers. The poorest are not a residual group to be ignored or put on permanent social assistance until the growth process 'trickles down' to them: with a strategic 'hand up' they can engage in the economy and share in the benefits of growth.

However, one needs to be cautious about drawing wide-ranging conclusions from the TUP, as it is a highly context specific initiative. It is very dependent on the capacity of BRAC to experiment, innovate, learn and develop service delivery systems that can operate across the country. This demands high level analytical and management skills, alongside the ability to 'win' substantial financial resources to run the programme. In particular, BRAC's technical capacity to advise on poultry, dairy and horticultural activities should not be taken for granted. The broader environment in Bangladesh has also been supportive – steady economic growth, improving physical infrastructure (e.g. the Jamuna Bridge, easing access to the north for people and goods, as well as local roads and electrification), high population density, and socio-political stability.[18]

For analytical purposes we can divide the potential lessons into two main types – the design features that are TUP's 'context' and the 'process' features that describe how the TUP evolved. In practice, successful programmes need to integrate both of these elements – an effective process has to generate content that can develop into a standardized package for delivery at scale.[19]

Design features

1. *Laddered, strategic linkages*: At the heart of TUP is the idea that the poorest people cannot benefit from a single 'magic bullet' (microcredit, bed nets, women's groups). Rather they need a carefully sequenced set of supports that provides livelihood security; confidence building and busi-

ness/technical skill development; asset transfer; and support for and institutionalization of their improved position within the local economy and society. BRAC's experience suggests that programmes for the poorest need to be relatively complex, involving several different elements of social protection, income generation and local organization building, which are carefully related to each other.

2. *Asset transfer*: One of the highly innovative features of the programme is that it involves the transfer of what is in local economic terms, a substantial asset grant to each poor household. The relatively low level of initial assets of the poorest, allied to their ability to accumulate assets because of the frequency of adverse shocks that they experience, requires that they be given a 'hand up'. In effect, this means a 'one off'[20] gift of a micro-business so that they have both the material (e.g. poultry, cages, veterinary support) and non-material (technical skills and social standing) resources to engage with the economy. Organizations learning from TUP will need the ability to identify and support such micro-businesses and the financial capacity to meet the costs involved.

3. *Financial costs and impact assessment*: The unit costs of the Special Investment Programme – running at US$280 in 2005, 84% of which is asset transfer (Matin, 2005b) – are relatively high. For an aid donor or charity that works out at 3,571 households assisted per US$1 million. To encourage donors and sponsors to meet such costs, organizations maintaining such programmes will need to be able to demonstrate that there are substantial benefits occurring and that, to a high degree, these are sustained after the initial investments. Similar programmes will only be feasible *(i)* in contexts where there is substantial donor commitment, and *(ii)* for organizations that have the capacity, or can contract the capacity, for high quality programme monitoring and evaluation that can be externally validated.

4. *Local institutional development*: Perhaps the most challenging aspect of TUP, and the one that demands the most 'acting out' in the field, is the institutionalization at the local level. This is not about the service delivery agency but about 'new' village level organizations and the modified social norms and practices that are needed to ensure that short-term programme gains continue into the future. BRAC's early design – the TUP participants will join existing BRAC village organizations (VOs) after two years, access services through these and have an enhanced social position because of VO membership – proved to be problematic. Their revised approach – developing the TUP VOs that can work directly with BRAC, and establishing local committees that enlist the support of the local elite to assist TUP participants economically and socially – shows substantial promise, but success is by no means guaranteed. It is highly original in challenging the entrenched idea that in Bangladesh local elites are always exploitative and must be bypassed and/or disempowered (Hossain and Matin, 2007). In effect,

the TUP assumes that local elites are segmented and that while some may mirror the well-substantiated, rapacious stereotype of academic and popular literatures, others are more humane and socially-minded. Further, this second group can be developed by promoting the pre-existing social norms of cooperation and the better-off helping the less well-off (Uphoff, 1992).

This local institutional development component is perhaps the most context specific and least transferable of the TUP design. It is highly dependent on the programme 'process'.

The TUP process

1. *A process approach*: The processes out of which the TUP has evolved is akin to the idealized notions of adaptive management and learning process approaches that have been written up in the development management and rural development literatures over many years (Bond and Hulme, 1999; Johnston and Clark, 1982; Korten, 1980; Rondinelli, 1993). BRAC diagnosed a problem with its existing programmes, systematically reviewed its own experience and that of others, and moved into a carefully monitored experiment with a new programme. This experiment was 'learned from' by encouraging field staff to voice concerns and propose ideas about what might be done, through both process documentation and baseline studies by RED and the guiding hand of Fazle Abed. Uncomfortable 'errors' were embraced – such as the admission that existing VOs were not keen to admit the ultra poor to their organizations – and the programme modified. From a strong knowledge base the TUP was expanded (from 5,000 to 50,000 new households per annum) and cost-reduction measures made to permit increased staff caseloads and reduced financial costs. The programme continues to experiment with the frank admission at head office that the VACS are by no means a proven social technology.

   The main difference between the TUP experience and the idealized process approaches relates to the balance between technical analysis and beneficiary participation. The TUP has been driven by the technical analyses of BRAC's directors and field managers. BRAC listens carefully to TUP participants and documents their experiences; indeed, they are encouraged to use their 'voice'. But this is not a participatory approach as envisioned by Robert Chambers (1997) and others. It is much more akin to the private sector model of having a 'customer orientation'. BRAC also listens carefully to field staff and elicits their ideas about how the TUP could be improved. However, data analysis is a task for the head office, and decision-making for a small handful of staff.

2. *A service delivery approach*: The TUP is managed by a standardized business-type approach, with clear organizational structures, lines of responsibility, financial controls, and input, output and outcome

monitoring. As knowledge is gained, it is routinized in the programme through documentation, training and supervision. BRAC operates a tight administrative 'machine' which seeks to reward performance (especially through promotions within expanding programmes), reduce costs and encourage poorly performing staff to move on. This is not a worker cooperative, it is an effective business with a strong social goal.

3. *Partnerships*: 'Partnerships' is such an all-embracing term that it can become meaningless. However, BRAC has built on a set of strategic partnerships that allow it both to pursue its goals and acquire support where it lacks capacity. Its partnership with donors, and especially with DFID and CIDA through its AKF-C partnership, provides the finance it needs but permits the flexibility and learning for TUP that is essential. A whole set of other donors, who would want a blueprint and would engage in micro-management, are strategically avoided by BRAC – they have the money but lack other qualities!

The most adventurous partnership of TUP is its engagement with local elites. Conceptually this is an extraordinary step; hopefully as the experiment unfolds the news will continue to be positive.

Conclusion

BRAC's TUP programme started out from earlier attempts to combine social protection programmes (food aid) with economic promotion schemes (micro-credit, and business and technical services). Its recent performance demonstrates that the poorest people can be reached and, with a carefully sequenced set of programme components, supported to a position in which they have a high probability of sustaining their enhanced levels of welfare and assets.

There are many potential lessons that might be drawn from TUP including both its design features and the process from which it has evolved and continues to evolve. On the 'content' side its major innovations are *(i)* the transfer of a substantial set of assets to very poor households – in effect, a redistribution of assets from the taxpayers of aid donor countries to the ultra poor in Bangladesh, and *(ii)* the recruitment of village level elites to local committees to support TUP participants and other very poor people. The latter is a radical idea in terms of the social engineering of a more pro-poorest context in rural Bangladesh.

In terms of 'process', the TUP, like most of BRAC's other programmes, has benefited from many of the elements idealized in 'learning process approaches' and 'learning organizations'. It has built on experience, mounted carefully monitored experiments, standardized and scaled-up its delivery systems, and gradually reduced the programme's unit costs. While this process has listened carefully to TUP participants and field staff it is far from the 'participatory' approach lauded by some development theorists. The experiment is closely controlled by BRAC's upper echelons.

In the future it will be important for other agencies – NGOs, donors, governments, pro-poor elites – to learn from the TUP experience, but two notes of caution must be sounded. First, the TUP is a very complex programme and only organizations, or partnerships of organizations, with high levels of analytical and management capacity are likely to be able to mount such initiatives at scale. Secondly, the TUP cannot reach all types of ultra poor people. The economically 'inactive' ultra poor (frail older people, AIDS orphans, people in chronic ill-heath) and socially excluded or adversely incorporated people (bonded labourers, refugees, indigenous people in remote areas) will need more conventional forms of social protection – old-age provisions, humanitarian aid, 'free' health services, and child grants.

Acknowledgements

Our thanks to Bangladesh's poor people and BRAC's staff for helping us learn from their experiments and experiences. Particular thanks to Fazle Abed, Founder-Director of BRAC; Imran Matin, Munshi Sulaiman and the entire BRAC-RED team involved in research on CFPR-TUP; and Rabeya Yasmin, CFPR-TUP Programme Coordinator.

Endnotes

1. For more detail on economic, social and poverty indicators in Bangladesh, see Sen and Hulme (2006).
2. For an inventory see World Bank (2005).
3. When this division is empirically operationalized then it is often found that the 'economically inactive' are actually heavily involved in low or no-pay work such as gleaning, caring for children or older people, and begging.
4. Formerly known as the Bangladesh Rural Advancement Committee.
5. This is true for most of the country's microfinance institutions (Zaman, 2005) and may be the situation internationally (Hulme and Mosley, 1996).
6. In its 2003/4 annual cycle the IGVGD model took on 44,000 new beneficiaries (Hashemi, 2006: 5).
7. For detailed discussions of BRAC's learning from the IGVGD, see Matin and Hulme (2003) and Matin (2005a).
8. This 'Learning Partnership' is supported by the Canadian International Development Agency (CIDA) via the Aga Khan Foundation-Canada (AKF-C). Working papers can be downloaded from www.bracresearch.org
9. The social development component focuses on functional literacy, but BRAC fieldworkers believe its main contribution is to build the confidence of TUP participants.
10. The targeting parameters for OTUP are slightly wider, particularly in terms of the maximum land ownership requirement of 30 decimals.
11. The 2002 baseline survey found that of the ultra poor, 54% were totally landless, 50% ate two meals or fewer a day, 70% were dependent on

irregular, casual labour and 95% lived without sanitation facilities (BRAC-RED 2004).

12. In Bangladesh these are known as *Gram Shahayak Committees* (GSCs). For a detailed description and analysis of these see Hossain and Matin (2007).

13. These are described as 'respected individuals in the local community [chosen] through a process of guided selection' (Hossain and Matin, 2007: 384–5). Often they have strong religious beliefs and reputations for being publicly-minded.

14. We must confess to being rather cynical about this innovation when we heard of it in 2003 – 'is this an act of desperation?' we wondered. However, fieldwork in 2004 revealed its potential – in effect, empowering some local elites to pursue a social mission that for religious and other reasons they valued.

15. In fact, the proposal for the second phase of CFPR-TUP proposes greater differentiation for effective targeting and learning purposes, with a total of 800,000 beneficiaries:

- STUP Model I (full package): 200,000
- STUP Model II (full package, but with a lower average asset value, a lower daily subsistence allowance, and a lower staff:client ratio): 100,000
- OTUP Model I (as STUP Model II, but with soft loans rather than asset transfers, and a lower staff:client ratio): 100,000
- OTUP Model II (as OTUP Model I, but with a regular loan, no subsistence allowance, and a lower staff:client ratio): 400,000

16. Made up of the United Kingdom's Department for International Development (DFID), the Canadian International Development Agency (CIDA), the European Commission, Novib (Oxfam Netherlands), and the World Food Programme (WFP), and recently joined by AusAid. During the first phase, BRAC itself contributed over US$4 million, and plans to contribute US$5 million over the 2007–11 period.

17. It should be noted that while the objective assessment of assets (Figure 9.1) and subjective assessment of poverty dynamics (Figure 9.5) are consistent for SUPs, with both showing an improvement, there is inconsistency for NSUPs.

18. Many might challenge this latter point, but compared to many other countries with high levels of ultra-poverty – Afghanistan, Nepal, Democratic Republic of Congo, Sierra Leone, Somalia – Bangladesh's recent political problems and violence are enviable.

19. See Korten (1980) who recognized BRAC's capacity for innovation and service delivery at an early stage, and Johnston and Clark (1982) who eloquently explain the need for effective programme development to both 'think through' and 'act out' its components.

20. One of the design features of the TUP that is not yet clearly specified is how it deals with women whose TUP projects fail (e.g. their milch cow dies, their horticultural products cannot be marketed). Our own fieldwork indicates that such women are usually given a 'second chance', but this seems to be at the discretion of field level staff rather than as a formal programme component.

References

Bond, R. and Hulme, D. (1999) 'Process approaches to development: theory and Sri Lankan practice', *World Development* 27(8): 1339–58.

BRAC (2006a) BRAC at a Glance June 2006. Available from: www.brac.net/downloads_files/June_06_AAG_BW.pdf [accessed 13 July 2009]

BRAC (2006b) *CFPR II Project Proposal*. Unpublished.

BRAC (2006c) *CFPR Progress Report*. Unpublished.

BRAC-RED (2004) 'Towards a profile of the ultra poor in Bangladesh: findings from CFPR/TUP baseline survey', BRAC-Research and Evaluation Division, Dhaka and Aga Khan Foundation, Canada. Available from: www.bracresearch.org/highlights/cfpr_tup_baseline_survey.pdf [accessed 13 July 2009]

Chambers, R. (1997) *Whose reality counts? Putting the last first*, ITDG, London.

CPRC (2004) *The Chronic Poverty Report 2004–05*, Chronic Poverty Research Centre, Manchester. Available from: http://www.chronicpoverty.org/cpra-report-0405.php [accessed 13 July 2009]

Drèze, J. (2004) 'Bangladesh shows the way', *The Hindu*, 17 September 2004.

Haseen, F. (2007) 'Change in food and energy consumption among the ultra poor: is the poverty reduction programme making a difference?' *Asia Pacific Journal of Clinical Nutrition* 16/Suppl.(1): 58–64.

Hashemi, S. (2006) 'Graduating the poorest into microfinance: linking safety nets and financial services', *CGAP Focus Note 34*. Available from: www.cgap.org/portal/binary/com.epicentric.contentmanagement.servlet.ContentDeliveryServlet/Documents/FocusNote_34.pdf

Hossain, M. and Matin, I. (2007) 'Engaging elite support for the poorest? BRAC's Targeted Ultra Poor Programme for rural women in Bangladesh', *Development in Practice* 17(3): 380–92.

Hossain, M., Sen, B. and Rahman, H. Z. (2000) 'Growth and distribution of rural income in Bangladesh: analysis based on panel survey data', *Economic and Political Weekly* December 2000: 4630–37.

Hulme, D. and Moore, K. (2007) 'Why has microfinance been a policy success? Bangladesh (and beyond)', in A. Bebbington and W. McCourt (eds) *Statecraft in the South: Public Policy Success in Developing Countries*, Palgrave MacMillan, London.

Hulme, D. and Mosely, P. (1996) *Finance against poverty, Volumes I and II*, Routledge, London/New York.

Johnston, B. F. and Clark, W. C. (1982) *Redesigning Rural Development: A Strategic Perspective*, Johns Hopkins University Press, Baltimore.

Korten, D. (1980) 'Community organisation and rural development: a learning process approach', *Public Administration Review* 40: 480–511.

Matin, I. (2002) 'Targeted development programmes for the extreme poor: experiences from BRAC experiments', CPRC Working Paper 20, IDPM/Chronic Poverty Research Centre, Manchester. Available from: http://www.chronicpoverty.org/pubfiles/20Matin.pdf [accessed 13 July 2009]

Matin, I. (2005a) 'Addressing vulnerabilities of the poorest: a micro perspective from BRAC', paper presented to the Annual Bank Conference in Development Economics, Amsterdam, May 2005. Available from: www.BRACresearch.org/publications/addressing_vulnerability_of_the_poorest.pdf [accessed 13 July 2009]

Matin, I. (2005b) 'Delivering the "fashionable" [inclusive microfinance] with an "unfashionable" [poverty] focus: experiences of BRAC', presentation to ADB Microfinance Week, Manila, 14–18 March 2005. Available from: http://www.adb.org/Documents/Events/2005/ADB-microfinance-week/presentation-day1-03-matin.pdf [accessed 13 July 2009]

Matin, I. and Hulme, D. (2003) 'Programs for the poorest: learning from the IGVGD program in Bangladesh', *World Development* 31(3): 647–65.

Posgate D., Craviolatti, P., Hossain, N., Osinski, P., Parker, T. and Sultana, P. (2004) 'Review of the BRAC/CFPR specially targeted ultra poor (STUP) programme: mission report', BRAC Donor Liaison Office, unpublished report, Dhaka.

Rabbani, M., Prakash, V. A. and Sulaiman, M. (2006) 'Impact assessment of CFPR/TUP: a descriptive analysis based on 2002–2005 panel data', CFPR/TUP Working Paper Series No. 12, BRAC Research and Evaluation Division, Dhaka and Aga Khan Foundation, Canada. Available from: www.bracresearch.org/workingpapers/impact_tup.pdf [accessed 13 July 2009]

Rondinelli, D. (1993) *Development projects as policy experiments: An adaptive approach to development administration*, Routledge, London.

Sen, B. and Hulme, D. (eds) (2006) *Chronic Poverty in Bangladesh: Tales of Ascent, Descent, Marginality and Persistence*, Bangladesh Institute of Development Studies, Dhaka, and Chronic Poverty Research Centre, Manchester. Available from: http://www.chronicpoverty.org/p/438/publication-details.php [accessed 13 July 2009]

Uphoff, N. (1992) *Learning from Gal Oya*, Cornell University Press, Ithaca.

Webb, P., Coates, J., Houser, R., Hassan, Z. and Zobaid, M. (2001) 'Expectations of success and constraints to participation among IGVGD women', report to WFP Bangladesh, (Mimeo) School of Nutrition Science and Policy/DATA Bangladesh, Dhaka.

World Bank (2005) 'Social safety nets in Bangladesh: an assessment', report No. 33411-BD, Human Development Unit, South Asia Region, World Bank, Washington D.C. Available from: http://siteresources.worldbank.org/BANGLADESHEXTN/Resources/FINAL-printversion_PAPER_9.pdf [accessed 13 July 2009]

Zaman, H. (2005) *The Economics and Governance of NGOs in Bangladesh*, consultation draft, Human Development Unit, South Asia Region, World Bank, Washington D.C. Available from: http://www.lcgbangladesh.org/NGOs/reports/NGO_Report_clientversion.pdf [accessed 13 July 2009]

About the authors

David Hulme is Professor of Development Studies at the University of Manchester and Executive Director of the Brooks World Poverty Institute and the Chronic Poverty Research Centre. His recent publications include *Poverty Dynamics: Inter-disciplinary Perspectives* (2009, Oxford University Press with T. Addison and R. Kanbur), *Social Protection for the Poor and Poorest: Risks, Needs and Rights* (2008, Palgrave with A. Barrientos), *The Challenge of Global Inequality* (2006, Palgrave with A. Greig and M. Turner), a Special Issue of the *Journal of Development Studies* (2006) on 'Cross-disciplinary Research on

Poverty and Inequality' and many articles in leading journals. His research interests include rural development; poverty analysis and poverty reduction strategies; finance for the poor and sociology of development.

Karen Moore joined Education for All Global Monitoring Report (GMR) team at UNESCO (Paris) in February 2009. A poverty specialist, the majority of her research focuses on understanding the intersections between childhood, youth, intergenerational, life-course and chronic poverty, and policies to interrupt these, primarily in South Asia. Prior to joining the GMR, Karen worked as a Research Associate with the Chronic Poverty Research Centre; she was based first at the University of Birmingham and then at the University of Manchester. She was a key author of both Chronic Poverty Reports.

CHAPTER 10

Unconditional cash transfers to the very poor in central Viet Nam: Is it enough to 'just give them the cash'?

Peter Chaudhry

This chapter presents the preliminary results of Oxfam's unconditional cash transfer project in Central Viet Nam. It examines whether just giving cash transfers unconditionally to the poorest can lead to a fundamental and sustainable transformation of their lives. The chapter explains why Oxfam sought to engage in this 'just give the cash' project as opposed to more traditional development assistance projects. It also analyses how the recipient households used the cash transfers and how these cash transfers can lead to change, not only at the household but also at the communal level. The analysis demonstrates how the poor can use money responsibly when given the chance; how this money can help the poor address some structural aspects of their poverty and finally how it can lead to social transformation in the focus villages. The chapter studies this project in light of the growing international literature on cash transfers and their impact on chronic poverty within a general social protection framework.

Introduction

In 2003 Lord Meghnad Desai, then of the London School of Economics, observed that:

> We are giving fifty billion dollars of overseas aid. There are a billion poor people in the world. Why don't we just find the poor and give them one dollar a week and do nothing else. No questions asked. What they do with the money is not our concern. That would probably do more to relieve poverty than anything else. (Hanlon, 2004: 375)

This is an oft-quoted belief, frequently made by development practitioners, politicians, academics and 'lay' observers alike and is borne of frustration with the perceived failures of international development assistance. Making unconditional cash transfers to the very poor challenges many of the assumptions under which development organizations work, with traditional development projects often favouring a high level of outside technical assistance, and the delivery of often highly technocratic solutions to perceived poverty 'problems'. Beneficiary's participation is actively sought, but this is often 'framed' within the context of the kind of assistance the project is seeking to provide (i.e. agricultural extension support, education or health service provision). Implicit in this (whether conscious or not) is a belief that development agencies know what's best for the poor.

In 2007 Oxfam Great Britain in Viet Nam set out to test, under 'real world' conditions, the hypothesis that just giving cash unconditionally can lead to a fundamental and sustainable transformation in the lives and livelihoods of the very poor. This chapter discusses preliminary findings from the research project. It describes how recipient households used the one-off unconditional cash payment, and how the project challenged the existing ascribed roles of the poor and the non-poor in village politics. The chapter follows on from the social protection chapters in this volume, and considers the Oxfam project in the light of a growing international literature on cash programming and an increasing policy interest in Viet Nam and elsewhere in the potential of cash transfers to address chronic poverty within a social protection framework. In the next section the cash transfer project is described, after which some of the methodological and other issues associated with such a system are discussed. The penultimate section outlines the results, one year on, before drawing some conclusions.

Oxfam's unconditional cash transfer project in central Viet Nam[1]

In early 2007, Oxfam Great Britain in Viet Nam gave a one-off cash payment to around 500 households on or below the official poverty line in all 8 villages of An Loc commune, Can Loc district of Ha Tinh province in Viet Nam. The payment of around US$375 was equivalent to more than half of the average annual income of a poor household in the commune, and was provided with no conditions attached on how the money was to be used. Ha Tinh was selected on the grounds that Oxfam had a track record of working with the provincial authorities (an important consideration in Viet Nam) and that, given the sensitivity and relative uniqueness of the project, an area which Oxfam knew, and were known in, would best facilitate establishment of the research project.

Ha Tinh province is located on Viet Nam's central coast and is particularly disaster prone, with frequent floods and typhoons. The tough climate and poor quality of land make rural livelihoods challenging for farmers, who make up the overwhelming majority of the province's inhabitants. Although a poor province of Viet Nam, Ha Tinh is not considered to be amongst the very poorest, according at least to official poverty measurements. But the poverty landscape of Viet Nam is changing, and inequality gaps in particular appear to be widening. These gaps are appearing between provinces, but also within provinces and districts too. So it is possible to see very poor communities even in districts where the aggregate poverty indicators are not so low. This is the case for Can Loc district, where the research project is located, and particularly for An Loc commune, which had a poverty rate of 55% according to People's Committee estimates at the time of project design (against the national poverty rate of 19.5% in 2004). Within the eight villages of the commune, four had poverty rates of above 59%, with the highest rate 84% in one village.[2]

The commune's eight villages had an estimated 3,358 people living in 758 households and according to official poverty data at the time of project design, there were four households that could be considered rich, and 84 that were better-off with incomes of at least VND 400,000 per person, per month (double the official income-poverty line).[3] Oxfam gave VND 6 million (approximately $375) to 400 households below the official poverty line, and VND 3 million to around 100 households just above the poverty line. The money was delivered as a one-off cash payment into a savings account, requiring joint signatures of both male and female householders to withdraw cash. Oxfam imposed no conditionality upon the use of the cash, other than it should not be used for illegal purposes, and required only that beneficiaries participate in the monitoring of the use of the money over a three-year period.[4]

By 'just giving cash' to the poor and observing the impact, Oxfam hoped to benchmark, in broad terms, what the net poverty reducing effect of a project would need to be, to outweigh simply giving the poor a lump-sum cash payment. The design of the project was predicated on the assumption (borne out of Oxfam's experience with unconditional cash transfers in emergency contexts) that the poor can use money responsibly when given the chance, and that they themselves are best placed to prioritize investment choices. This is not to say that the only obstacle to people escaping poverty is a lack of cash. The project recognized from the beginning that there are significant structural obstacles facing the poor in Viet Nam; that the rural poor often have a marginal voice in processes of decision making and an inability to exert influence over how village resources are allocated, and that processes of exclusion extend to perceived 'cultural' norms too; through ascribing secondary roles to women in decision making, for example, or in characterizing ethnic minority groups as 'backward' or 'unmodern' and therefore unable to take advantage of economic opportunities proffered. These obstacles cannot necessarily be overcome through a straightforward injection of cash. Rather, the project sought to understand what role the cash could play as a potential catalyst in wider change processes, and what sort of complementary measures were necessary in order to help address some of these underlying 'drivers' of deep seated, chronic poverty.

Identifying the poor

Methodological issues

As with all programmes that want to reach the poorest one must first identify who they are. For this Vietnamese case study when comparing the eventual list of project beneficiaries in An Loc against the official poverty list for the commune, there were significant differences. This was because at the commune level in Viet Nam, administrative methods of poverty classification are used, whereby local officials have a great deal of flexibility in deciding who is included in the official list of the poor and is therefore eligible for state benefits under targeted poverty reduction programmes. Whilst the poor are nominally expected to be living below the official poverty line, in practice compiling the poverty list is a highly political process. Commune officials are subject to pressure from below to include households, and are under pressure to reduce the number of households classified as 'poor' from authorities higher up. Compiling the list is also subject to conceptions of who are the 'deserving poor' and rotation of households on and off the list is quite common, irrespective of their poverty status.[5]

For the project, it was important that a more objective method was used to identify households eligible for the cash transfer. For this reason, a baseline socio-economic survey of household income and consumption patterns, and household assets, was completed, in November 2006, and identification of the poorest households through the survey was subsequently validated through village discussions and with the commune people's committee. Discussion groups also took place with project beneficiaries every six months after dispersal of the money, to monitor both how it has been used, and what wider changes are noticeable in the community (a follow-up household survey will take place in year three, to analyse the medium term impact upon household income and assets of the cash payment).

By adopting such a methodology, Oxfam hoped to capture some of the relational and non-economic dimensions to poverty that often approach the missing from the recognized narrative. Furthermore, adopting such a project recognizes within the communities that poverty is experienced in different ways. There are those, for example, with some assets, who are extremely vulnerable to shocks over time, and those in a deep and chronic state of poverty, whose circumstances seem to change little over time.[6] By adopting the aforementioned methods, the project sought to capture both a large (and therefore representative) group of the poor within the commune, whilst ensuring also that the available resources for the cash payment were not spread too thinly – that the money could still be potentially 'life changing'.

In passing we should also note the alternative targeting scenarios that were considered, which included giving money to all households from the three poorest villages in the commune; targeting the very poorest in all villages in the commune with a large payment to each; and covering both the very poorest and poor in all villages, but with a smaller cash payment. However, eventually, it was decided to make the payment to all households in all eight villages that were below the poverty line in the baseline survey, and make a smaller payment to those households just above the poverty line, who nevertheless face a significant risk of falling into poverty periodically. This was seen as being least divisive, and a flexible cut-off point for the payment also ensures that the project is not creating a new 'underclass', by simply catapulting those who are currently poor, above those who are marginally better off.

Nevertheless, and despite a high level of transparency in arriving at a final list of beneficiary households for the project, the list was still contested by a few. Information about the project was not publicly released until the poverty classification exercise had been completed, but inevitably there was some leakage of information so that households and officials knew that those identified through the ranking exercise could anticipate benefits.[7] There were consequently some attempts at hiding household assets, and a few cases of collusion between households who agreed to validate neighbours as 'poor', in return for a share of the benefits. Conflict arose between these households later when it was felt that recipient households were not honouring their 'debt'.

Attempts to challenge the list were a legacy of the 'official' poverty classification system, through which it was perceived by some that the demarcation of being eligible for benefits is essentially a political, rather than necessarily objective process. This shaped the expectations of influential households who assumed they would be able, as usual, to manipulate access to some or all of the investment funds from the project. But the exhaustive process of wealth ranking, discussion and community validation carried out by the project meant the final list of beneficiaries under the project was widely considered to be accurate and a true reflection of the poor households in the village, a view shared by most villagers, by district level officials who observed the process, and by the implementing partner, PPC, who had extensive experience of working with the community.

Concerns about risks inherent in 'windfall gains'

Some early reviewers of the project concept warned against the dangers inherent in 'windfall gains' – that there is a significant risk in giving money to people when they have not budgeted for, or anticipated this money. They are less likely then to use the cash in a productive way, as they would not consider it to be a part of their everyday household budget. There was certainly an acknowledged risk that the money may not be used for productive purposes, and may well be spent on consumption. But the boundaries for what constitutes 'frivolous' or 'non-productive' expenditure are blurred and, to a degree, culturally loaded – is the purchase of a karaoke machine frivolous, for example, if it is periodically hired out for weddings and other social events, and so offers an (unpredictable) economic return? Is money spent on entertaining influential business people and officials mis-spent, if it results in a good business opportunity?

In the event, the project premise that the poor are not *inherently irresponsible* in using money seems to have been borne out, as the discussion in the next section shows. Even where money was used for non-productive purposes, such as house improvements, there was a clear rationale behind the choice and a significant perceived social benefit to how the money was used. In fact, 'misuse' of money by the poor in other contexts may be as much about mistargeting (i.e. giving money to those who don't really need it) than any inherent incapacity of the poor to make sensible investment decisions.

Results: 'One year On'

How the cash was spent

Funds were eventually released to households in late February 2007, after the traditional lunar New Year holidays. A follow-up survey of beneficiaries one year on showed that households had used the cash in a variety of different ways.[8] Approximately 34% of funds overall were used for income generating activities, most notably animal husbandry; 70% of these funds were spent on buying a cow, buffalo, pigs, chickens, or were invested in aquaculture. About 22% was invested in farming to buy fertilizer, seeds, and to hire machines for ploughing, and about 8% was invested for business; either buying farm machines to rent, or buying stock for stalls or other similar small enterprises. Overall, 76% of all project beneficiaries reported spending some money on generating income, and 85% overall reported that the project had a significant impact upon their incomes.

The second most significant area of expenditure overall was in buying assets or repairing houses, in which 19% of project money overall was invested. This is unsurprising given that, from the baseline survey, a third of all houses had no latrine and 14% of houses had an earth floor. 56% of households overall reported using funds for this purpose during the first six months after receiving money, and 73% overall reported that the project had increased their household's inventory of assets. Interestingly, one of the most important areas of expenditure listed by the elderly was the purchase of a coffin; this was important for their security of mind, that they would be buried properly, and also that their funeral would not be a financial burden upon their families.

Approximately 19% of the money overall was spent in paying off debts. 60% of beneficiaries reported spending money in this way in the first six months of the project, and reflects the very high level of indebtedness of households in An Loc commune, which is reflective of poor rural households throughout Viet Nam. Once previous debt burdens were repaid, households were free to borrow money again for a variety of purposes, and relieving debt was considered a significant project impact for 68% of households in the first six months of the project. Project funds were also used to meet immediate household expenses, with nearly half of all households using the money for this purpose and 18% of the cash overall spent on consumption. This included meeting food shortfalls, and investing in education and health for the household. Consequently more than half of all beneficiary households reported overcoming food shortages in the first year, and overall expenditure on health care for poor households in the commune doubled, on average, on the previous year.

A very small amount of the money (1%) was kept in the bank, with only 3% of beneficiaries reporting they kept the money to earn interest. This reflects on the one hand the critical urgency to use the money for production and consumption purposes; that they simply couldn't afford to leave the money in the bank to accumulate interest. But it also reflects a high level of uncertainty amongst project beneficiaries over whether they would be able to keep the money at all, because the project was subject to a concerted effort by village leaders and the better off to appropriate the money and redistribute to everyone, as well as to use the money to fund 'social' projects such as road building, and the construction of village halls. In the event, many households were subject to pressure to surrender some of the money for communal projects, with about 9% of the funds overall spent on 'transfers', and 51% of all households reporting that they spent some money on either 'supporting others' or as a 'social contribution'. This also undoubtedly dictated how quickly most of the money was spent, with almost all of the funds gone within the first six months of the project.

Safeguarding access to the cash: Why the poor needed allies in high places

Attempts to pressure beneficiaries and seize the project funds were driven by village elites, both within the commune government structure, and from better off villages within the commune that had relatively fewer beneficiaries from the project.[9] Cash transfer schemes are particularly vulnerable to this form of pressure for redistribution, as experience from elsewhere in the region shows. For example, in Indonesia, education subsidies intended for the poorest households immediately after the economic crisis in the late 1990s were often appropriated by village heads and redistributed through their own patronage networks. (Mukherjee et al., 2002). And a recent review of the Indonesian Government's unconditional cash transfer programme to the poor to offset the effects of the removal of the national fuel subsidy has highlighted how, in some incidences, communities forcibly redistributed the cash assistance intended for specific poor households to a general subsidy to all villagers, irrespective of their wealth (SMERU, 2006).

Recipients of the cash in the better-off villages of An Loc were particularly prone to pressure to fund communal projects, to repay taxes owed, or to redistribute the cash to all households in the village. Leaders of this movement at the time cited village traditions of sharing all benefits equally and of having 'looked after' the poor in the past, so that they were now due some repayment in recognition of this. There was also a strong narrative constructed which stigmatized the poor as being 'lazy' and always benefiting without working hard, whereas the better off contributed to social projects in the commune and always paid their taxes. Leaders of the better-off villages in the commune were under pressure to secure for 'their' villages a bigger share of the resources available, which they were expected to be able to do as a function of their prominent role in commune politics.

The project therefore challenged the traditional networks of patronage in the commune and caused something of a crisis in identity for village elites and village leaders who were accustomed to being able to manipulate the system of distribution of benefits in the way that they chose. It also highlighted how poor households are seldom in a position to be able to influence the distribution of resources at village level, how this lack of voice is an important dimension in how poverty is experienced, and how it acts as a powerful force in sustaining and reproducing poverty.

The situation was resolved through the intervention of provincial and district level authorities, who sent an investigative team and exerted pressure upon commune officials to fulfil the obligations originally agreed with the project. PPC, the local partner, and Oxfam expended a great deal of time and effort in liaising with higher level authorities in bringing this to pass, and faced determined opposition from commune and village leaders and elites who clearly felt that higher authorities would not intervene, as the cash had already been distributed and officials were a long way away.[10] Ultimately then, the poor of An Loc commune needed powerful advocacy on their behalf even just to access freely the assistance they had been ascribed. But once this had occurred, a positive outcome of the project was a reported increase in voice and confidence amongst beneficiaries, with 96% reporting feeling 'more confident' and 83% reporting a sense of having 'more voice in the community'. These figures were unchanged in the second half of the year, when most project funds had been spent, and it will be interesting to see whether this reported increase in voice and confidence is sustained into the future.

Conclusion: From social protection to social change

Experience from the project will, it is hoped, feed into wider policy discussions within Viet Nam around the appropriateness of making unconditional cash grants to support the poor in the future, particularly as Viet Nam seeks to build a comprehensive system of social protection for the poor and vulnerable. Social protection, broadly defined, refers to income or consumption transfers that protect the weak against shocks and risks (adapted from Devereux and Sabates-Wheeler, 2006). Examples of other unconditional cash transfer mechanisms as social protection measures include pensions, social and disaster insurance payments, and child and family support grants.[11] Devereux and Sabates-Wheeler (2006) have, though, taken the concept of social protection further, to talk about 'transformative social protection'; interventions that also address problems of social exclusion and marginalization, for the chronically and structurally poor particularly. As they note:

> Vulnerable people need protection not only against obvious livelihood shocks such as illness or drought, but also against exploitation, discrimination and abuse … By challenging power hierarchies and inequitable social

relations, social protection can contribute to social transformation, which in turn will reduce economic vulnerabilities. (ibid.)

It was in this context of 'transformative social protection' that the cash project was designed – a single cash payment large enough to catapult poor people out of their existing condition and into a new socio-economic milieu. But in order to realize transformative potential, more than just cash is required.

Poverty is not simply a lack of income but a condition deeply embedded in existing relations of power and social control, relations which are unevenly stacked against the poor. To challenge these relationships the poor need not just material support, but also new allies and alliances able to intervene decisively on their behalf, and new avenues and modalities through which to voice their interests. To this end, cash transfer projects like this provide a vehicle for change, a means to an end, rather than an end in themselves. NGOs like Oxfam can play a key role as advocates for change, and as facilitators in alliance building, but this means engaging deeply with the politics of power, in order that what John Harriss describes as the 'social and political-economic relationships that bring about the effect of poverty' (Harriss, 2006) can be renegotiated and cast anew.

Endnotes

1. The Oxfam GB team responsible for the development of this research project is Nguyen Quang Quynh, Kate Raworth, Ashvin Dayal and Steve Price-Thomas. This chapter has benefited enormously from their comments, though responsibility for remaining limitations rests solely with the author.
2. The poverty rate for Ha Tinh province overall was 35% and for Can Loc district 38.5%.
3. The official income poverty rate of VND 200,000 per person, per month, was equivalent to approximately US$12.5 in 2007.
4. The project's implementation, monitoring and management were carried out by a local partner, the Pro-Poor Centre (PPC), in collaboration with the commune, district and province people's committee's.
5. All observations here are drawn from fieldwork discussions with local villagers and officials in An Loc commune in September, 2008.
6. Emerging panel survey data from the region shows evidence of a significant 'churning' in and out of poverty, reflecting both increased economic opportunity in a booming region, and a related high level of vulnerability and insecurity. A recent study in Cambodia, part of the World Bank's global 'Moving Out of Poverty' study, has more than half of the households slipping into poverty at some point over a four year period (CDRI, 2006). See also Baulch and Scott (2006) on the importance of Panel Surveys and Life History methods.

7. PPC, the local partner, disguised the ranking exercise as an evaluation for a past project in order to try and gain as objective a picture as possible of households' poverty status.
8. All data and information in this section is taken from the six month and annual reports of the project in 2007 and 2008.
9. All observations made here reflect discussions held with PPC, Oxfam staff and district officials during the course of September 2008.
10. The situation was complicated by an administrative reorganization through which An Loc commune was moved to a new district. This enabled commune officials to claim that all agreements previously made with the project were invalidated.
11. It is worth noting that these kinds of payments made to the poor are well established in most western European countries, and are considered essential 'rights' that guarantee a minimum standard of living for those least well-off.

References

Baulch, B. and Scott, L. (2006) 'Report on CPRC workshop on panel surveys and life history methods'. Available from: http://www.q-squared.ca/pdf/CPRC.pdf [accessed 22 July 2009]

Cambodia Development Resource Institute (CDRI) (2006) 'Moving out of poverty: Cambodia National Synthesis Report', CDRI, Phnom Penh.

Devereux, S. and Sabates-Wheeler, R. (2006) 'Transformative social protection', *IDS in Focus* issue 01.3, Institute of Development Studies, Brighton, UK.

Hanlon, J. (2004) 'It is possible to just give money to the poor', *Development and Change* 35(2): 375–383.

Harriss, J. (2006) 'Why understanding of social relations matters more for policy on chronic poverty than measurement'. Available from: http://www.eldis.org/cf/rdr/rdr.cfm?doc=DOC11754 [accessed 13 July 2009]

Mukherjee, N., Hardjono, J. and Carriere, E. (2002) 'People, poverty and livelihoods: links for sustainable poverty reduction in Indonesia', Department for International Development (DFID), London.

SMERU Research Institute (2006) 'The implementation of direct cash transfer in Indonesia', *SMERU Bulletin No. 17.* SMERU, Jakarta.

About the author

Peter Chaudhry has been working in and around South East Asia for the past 10 years. He was previously a researcher with Oxfam Great Britain and is currently working as a UNDP adviser to the Ministry of Labour and Social Affairs in Viet Nam, supporting the national target programme for poverty reduction.

CHAPTER 11

Exclusion to empowerment: Women of the Siddi community in Gujarat (India)

*Somnath Bandyopadhyay, Apoorva Oza and
David Nygaard*

*The chapter considers excluded communities, namely the Siddi community in
Gujurat, and outlines the lives and livelihoods of this group of 20–30,000 people.
The process of recognizing the need for basic infrastructure and service support like
shelter, livelihoods, education, drinking water supply and sanitation, health care
and modern communication systems is identified. However, in order to benefit
from these in any sustainable manner, these communities need to be prepared – to
be aware of the value of these amenities, make demands and share responsibilities for their maintenance and quality. The lessons from the Siddis help us realize
the importance of building confidence through hard work leading to incremental
gains, of spotting and nurturing local leadership that is able to motivate others,
of creating a structure that provide spaces for individuals and collective decisions
in a transparent manner, and of maintaining a positive and humane outlook in
the face of considerable uncertainty. When services are provided in response to the
incremental development aspirations of the community, these will be valued, and
even augmented through local efforts.*

Introduction

This chapter continues the section of the book highlighting specific case studies of what programmes have 'worked' for the poorest. In this case we focus
on the Siddi community of Gujarat, India. The Siddis are a tribal community
lying outside mainstream political and socio–economic development. Their an-
cestors were brought from Africa around 500 years ago and were sold by Arab
merchants to serve as soldiers or slaves under the Portuguese and British authorities, or as servants to the *Nawabs*.[1] Prior to the British rule in India, the
Siddis were going through a phase of assimilation. British policies, however,
segregated the Siddi groups from each other as well as from indigenous Indians
leading to 're-tribalization' (Lodhi, 1992). As a consequence, the Siddis became,
and have remained, a highly marginalized group, largely isolated and unac-
cepted by society (Kaushik, 2004). This marginalization has affected them both
socially and economically. They have low development indicators in a wide

range of areas, for example, a falling literacy rate and lack of jobs. Government indifference and little effort to preserve their culture have pushed them to the brink of ruin (Kaushik, 2004). This type of pressure has led to a society with prevalent social vices such as alcoholism and gambling. Women particularly suffer the effects of this as they are marginalized not only outside of but also within the community.

The chapter highlights the processes that have occurred within the livelihoods of Siddis, particularly in relation to women and the empowerment process, through development actions. In achieving this we structure the chapter as follows. We provide further background on the lives and livelihoods of the Siddis in the next two sections, specifically focusing on how communities have been engaged in development actions. In the following section we outline the basics that were put in place for firstly analysing livelihoods and then enhancing incomes and well-being, before outlining some of the micro-enterprise activities that formed the basis of prospering and empowerment of the Siddi women.

Background: The lives and livelihoods of Siddis

Rough estimates put the Siddis population at around 20–30,000, spread over the States of Andhra Pradesh, Gujarat, Karnataka and Maharashtra. In Gujarat, the Siddis reside largely in the periphery of the Gir Forest – the last abode of the Asiatic lion. There are 1,089 Siddi households, spread over 19 villages in Talala block of Junagadh district. Except in the villages of Jambur and Sirvan, the Siddis constitute a minority among other groups.[2]

These settlements were created before independence (1947) by the Nawab of Junagadh and the British to provide for the labour needed to extract forest resources. In 1972, 1,412 sq km area of the Gir Forest was declared a protected area. There are two Siddi villages that now happen to be located inside the protected area (Sanctuary), where certain rights and concessions are granted by the Forest Department for subsistence. Although the Aga Khan Rural Support Programme (AKRSP, India) has been granted access to work in these villages as well, no construction activity is permitted.

Even in the periphery, the Siddis have few options or opportunities for livelihood. Their traditional natural resource was the Gir Forest, from which they collected dry wood and other non-timber forest produce (NTFP). Many Siddi women still engage in 'head loading', collecting dry wood from the forest and selling it in nearby markets. While this is now 'illegal', the practice persists, but is on the decline due to increased law enforcement, dwindling supplies and now the AKRSP (India) Gir Periphery Management Project.

Conflicts between the villagers and the Forest Department over the cutting of fuel wood, grazing and traversing the protected area for commuting to nearby villages are common. The Siddis are a primary concern for the Forest Department as the community has little choice but to engage in illegal cutting for livelihood purposes. Coupled with the lack of opportunities, skills and reduced or no access to the forest, even subsistence poses a major challenge. Nevertheless, the Siddis rarely migrate.

From an employment perspective, the primary source of income for the Siddis comes from agricultural labour. However, this is seasonal (revolving around sowing or harvesting) and unreliable, taxing and with relatively low remuneration. Temporary labour with the forest and railway departments also provides opportunities for further valuable income, although the temporary nature of this work means that long-term stability is lacking. More recently, the Eco-Development Project (1999–2004), funded by the World Bank, attempted to generate alternative employment opportunities by providing a variety of tools such as sewing and embroidery machines, carpentry tools, threshers etc. to a number of families, along with grant and training support delivered through village level committees. However, in the absence of a long-term sustainable empowerment strategy, these efforts have not been very successful (Robinson, 2005).

Of the prior employment/cash generation linked schemes, perhaps one of the most significant occurred in the 1970s when the government gave many Siddi households 2.5 acres of land, along with supplies of seeds and other agricultural inputs. However, much of the land was stony and undulating and therefore unsuitable for cultivation. This generated meagre annual returns from grazing animals, as low as Rs500 (US$11). The Government Tribal Welfare Office, or Adim Juth, allotted up to Rs20,000 ($444) to each Siddi household to support economic development. While several households have been able to access these funds, the complicated and lengthy loan application process and exploitation by middlemen – who take up to half of the loan amount from them – has prevented many Siddis from accessing these funds (Kaushik, 2004).

Initial efforts of AKRSP (India) focused on land treatment and agriculture enhancement. About a third of the 156 households registered as beneficiaries of this project were women, many of them Siddis. The project negotiated with the Adim Juth to enhance the provision of funds for poor beneficiaries, particularly women, and simultaneously encouraged the beneficiaries to work hard on their fields and take advantage of the knowledge of the staff on agriculture enhancement. Interestingly, and compared with many women 'owning' land in India, some of the land owners among the Siddis are women.[3] Of the alternative activities that women undertake, these include, cleaning animal sheds, cattle grazing and working as agricultural labourers, which are temporary, seasonal and low-paying jobs – only Rs50–60 ($1.5) per month. Such a low base offered both a challenge and an opportunity for empowerment-oriented development outcomes.

Engaging the community and federating the Siddi women's organization

Though AKRSP (India) was already working in the location from the late 1980s mostly on alternative energy projects, from 2002 an integrated and targeted approach began to develop and gather momentum, under the Sustainable Community-based Approach for Livelihoods Enhancement (SCALE) Project.[4] From mid-2004, this momentum almost took on the shape of a movement that bode well for the community and provided impetus to AKRSP (India) to strive harder.

Considering the prior experience[5] of forming multi-community self-help groups (SHGs)[6] had proved counter-productive, this time these organizations were crafted for Siddi women alone. The first two such SHGs were launched in 1994 in Jambur village. Initially, working with these groups was challenging. There was considerable internal conflict, and the members had no exposure to any banking processes. Low literacy levels also meant that the women themselves could not undertake many of the administrative aspects of the SHGs.

Around 1997, the SHG members began to feel that while savings/credits were all very well, they needed to earn money. This is when the idea of making and selling organic compost emerged. The SHG members were taken on an exposure visit to Surendranagar district where women were already making organic compost under another AKRSP (India) programme. This encouraged the Siddis to start making compost themselves – a process, as outlined later in this chapter, that has proved very successful. By 2002, there were 16 SHGs covering 10 villages functioning as user-owned savings and credit groups. However, AKRSP (India) had yet to develop a comprehensive approach for the Siddi community. Access to all Siddi households continued to be limited.

Under the SCALE Project, sustainable alternative livelihood options for the Siddis were found. The range had to be expanded to include the entire Siddi population. A survey had previously indicated that only 210 of the 1,089 households in 10 villages had been involved in programme activities so far. 7 villages had not even been approached. Efforts had to be streamlined and responsibilities had to be defined.

A meeting was organized with SHG groups, and the objective of reaching out to all Siddi households was discussed. The para-worker model, wherein community members are identified, mobilized and trained from within the community, was initiated. Meanwhile, the SHGs had begun to improve their performance and were urged to take on more responsibility. While the SHGs proved to be effective at the village level, there was a need for women from the Siddi community across villages to come together. This is when the idea of forming a Federation gathered momentum and subsequently an Advasi Mahila Sangh (Siddi Women's Federation) was formed in January 2004.

The objectives of this Federation was to reach out to all 19 villages inhabited by the Siddis and to organize and network the Siddi community for social and economic empowerment, the latter through experimentation and support for various micro-enterprises. This Federation could also widen the canvas available to these women by providing access to larger loans, liaise with the government, provide training, offer a platform for sharing experiences and provide an opportunity to members from different SHGs to work together on micro-enterprises.

The Federation that was formed, was governed by representatives of the stakeholder community, managed by committees formed of highly committed individuals (providing honorary services) and administered by a set of individuals with a high degree of professional skills (working for a fee). The policy decisions at the governance levels set the broad agenda for the Federation's priorities, be it community facilities, essential services, enterprise development or liaising with the government.

The Federation was initiated with an initial endowment of Rs481,000 ($10,690) given by AKRSP (India) as well as the bank interest on the amount and interest generated from loans sanctioned for various income-generating activities. In order to cover its operating costs, an annual contribution of Rs10 ($0.2) is collected from all its members, currently numbering around 555. The Federation provides loans with interest (at 7%) which is presently used in asset creation and the conduct of special events. In the future, this interest (along with a higher contribution from members) will be used to cover the operating costs of the Federation, when AKRSP (India) withdraws.

The Federation is currently supported by a community organizer (CO) from AKRSP (India) who works with the Federation on financial management, savings and credit structures and income-generating activities. The CO is also responsible for fostering a sense of group identity and identifying and mitigating conflicts within and between the groups. There is also an institutional organizer (IO), employed by the Federation and paid through funds granted by AKRSP (India), who assists in conducting meetings, planning training programmes and record keeping as well as engaging with individual households when necessary.

Analysing livelihoods and establishing the basics

The method adopted for analysing the livelihoods of Siddi women, was the Nine Square Mandala exercise (Hogger, 1994) and marked a significant turning point, after being conducted with the Siddi women. The exercise has been designed as a practical tool for livelihood system analysis to suit the Indian context. It puts livelihoods within the framework of the entire socio-economic and cultural ecosystem. It defines the interconnectivity between the self, family and community, the past and the future, emotions, and the base and space available. It attempts to analyse rural livelihood systems from various perspectives, ranging from outer (material) to inner (non-material) realities and from tradition-bound to the more future-oriented perspectives (see Table 11.1).

Thus, a livelihood system is more than just a set of physical-economic preconditions for survival. It is a multidimensional whole, embracing all forces and constraints, material and non-material, which determine a family's existence. It is within these contexts that decisions are made.

AKRSP (India) staff applied the concept of the Nine Square Mandala with the Siddi women in April 2004, with surprising results. These women were not only able to understand the whole concept but also apply it in their own context.

Table 11.1 The Nine Square Mandala for livelihood systems analysis

Future Orientation		
9. Inividual	*8. Family*	*7. Collective*

• Vision
• Hopes and aspirations
• Fears
• Self-image/respect
• Models looked up to
	• Ancestors
	• Caste, social status
	• Education, jobs
	• Aspirations to leadership
	• Aspiration to social
	  mobility, wealth, power
		• Subsistence agriculture
		• Food security
		• Religion, tradition
		• Common property
		  resources, state laws
		• World views and ideology

Future Orientation		
6. Inner	*5. Family*	*4. Socio-economic*
• Identity, integrity • Awareness • Selfishness, compassion • People orientation • Courage, curiosity • Responsibility	• Gender relations • Nutrition distribution • Health and family planning • Work distribution • Solidarity	• Production relations • Community organizations • Patterns of cooperation • Markets, land, labour, capital • Government institutions
Traditional Base		
3. Emiotional	*2. Knowledge and activity*	*1. Physical*

• Memories
• Attachments
• Feelings
• Anxieties
• Boredom
	• Technology
	• Agricultural patterns
	• Experiences, skills
	• Traditional knowledge
	• Labour, crafts, services
	• Modern profession
		• Natural environment
		  (climate, topography,
		  location)
		• Natural resources (land,
		  water, forests, population,
		  trees)
		• Wealth distribution
		• Wealth accumulation

Source: Author

They recognized their assets and their limitations. For instance, these women recognized AKRSP (India) and the Gir Forest as their assets. They felt that even though they were marginalized, they had sweet water to drink (unlike Mangrol, a nearby AKRSP (India) project area with saline groundwater). They realized that while they worked as servants for others and kept their employer's house clean, little attention was paid to their own households. This whole process set them thinking and roused aspirations to improve 'their lot'. They realized that much could be gained if they worked together as a community and that their future lay largely in their own hands.

The exercise also laid the foundation for the Siddi Sahiyar Yatra, the first of which was conducted on 1 July 2004, with over 800 women and 160 men participating. The idea was to focus on livelihood issues for women, with prominent Siddi leaders like Hirbaiben giving inspiring speeches. Messages on the importance of voluntary savings, afforestation and women's empowerment were communicated through plays, slogans and songs. At the end of the event, the women took an oath to save collectively in groups, by August 2004, 12 new savings and credit groups were formed.

On 1 July 2005, the Siddi Women's Federation opened an office in Talala with a 10% contribution from the Federation and a 90% contribution by AKRSP (India). The second Siddi Sahiyar Yatra and Sammelan was organized by the women themselves. This again drew an overwhelming response. Due to the mass awareness drives, two Siddi villages from the adjoining Veraval block showed interest in joining the Federation. By July 2006, 42 SHGs comprising 555 members covering all the Siddi villages had been formed. Of these, 26 SHGs are engaged in various income-generating activities. Collective savings have jumped to Rs343,680 ($7,637) in July 2006, from Rs113,065 ($2,513) in 2004.

Two members from each of the SHGs were selected to be represented at the Federation. These representatives are responsible for attending meetings and liaising between their groups and the Federation. They complete a formal membership application that includes a resolution stating that they will abide by the principles and regulations of the Federation. A membership fee of Rs100 ($2) per SHG is paid as well. By paying this fee, each SHG effectively purchases a share of the Federation, wherein they will be entitled to a portion of all profits once it is registered as a co-operative.

The Federation had to define its tasks clearly and develop capacities to execute these well in order to position itself as a credible institution responding to the development needs of the women of the Siddi community. These services include access to larger loan amounts and assistance in record keeping, involvement in awareness raising and training activities, opportunity to learn from (and work with) other members of the Federation, and provide a platform to collectively negotiate (and work with) the government agencies, notably the Adim Juth.

In keeping with its objectives, the Federation has reached out to all 19 Siddi villages and succeeded in forming SHGs in all of them. It has undertaken street plays, campaigns, discussions, workshops and has engaged the print media to generate awareness. A quarterly newsletter, *Safar* (voyage), is published as well. However, it is the successful identification, training and deployment of the para-workers that has led to the sustained enhancement of the quality of SHGs and their linkages with the Federation.

Enhancing human capacities through development actions

Para-workers play a vital role in the successful functioning of SHGs and their linkages with the Federation. These are usually women who have displayed leadership qualities in their SHG and are selected from among the member groups through an informal process. They are currently paid by AKRSP (India) but will be paid by the Federation in the future, and are responsible for record keeping of individual and group savings and loan amounts, facilitating SHG monthly meetings, assisting with the loan application and sanctioning process as well as group formation and development. In addition to providing technical support, they have a social role to play as they help motivate women and act as a mediator within the group.

Each para-worker is responsible for three or four villages and attends all SHG meetings in those villages. On a meeting day, the para-worker arrives in the village half an hour before the meeting and goes to every household requesting people to attend it. Both SHG members and non-members are encouraged to attend. During the meeting, a fixed agenda, planned in advance by the para-worker, is covered. Issues such as savings levels, loans, loan recovery, debtors and group dynamics are discussed. After the meeting is over, the para-worker personally contacts everyone who did not attend the meeting. This interaction provides an opportunity for people to talk to the para-worker and be guided through the process to join an SHG.

Each SHG meets within the first 10 days of every month. The para-worker attends as a Federation representative. During this meeting, savings are collected from each member. The savings of all these groups are consolidated into the Federation account. This is also the time when SHG members can approach the Federation for credit. These meetings provide an opportunity to discuss various issues like whether or not children are going to school, income-generating issues and planning of special events. Women are encouraged to share their experiences. Para-workers and AKRSP (India) representatives also use this opportunity to share the experiences of other women's groups including those engaged in income-generation activities.

In between meetings, para-workers meet at the Federation office to discuss pertinent issues, go over their records, ensure that all transactions have been recorded properly, review any issues that arose during the last meeting and plan the agenda for the next month. The para-workers review committee comprises four women for the different areas in which they work. They oversee the performance of the para-workers, identify if and when they need support and, if necessary, recommend that they be replaced. Each member of the committee is responsible for a different para-worker and has received special training on social issues such as group dynamics, leadership and interacting with the women that they are evaluating.

Enhancing savings and increasing incomes

The Federation currently maintains the savings of all the 26 new SHG member groups as a special service. Individual records are kept of the savings made by all women. It is through this fund that internal loans to new SHG members are disbursed. The income for this account is accrued from the bank as well as from the interest on the loan (1.5% per month). This income is distributed as credit to the members of the SHGs in relation to their individual amounts of savings.

The AKRSP (India) has developed a financial management system that can be operated by the Siddi women themselves. The system is being managed by a para-worker from Jambur village, who has studied till Class VIII. A simple Excel programme gives a monthly update of savings and credit, individual savings, loan recovery status, interest pending, Federation savings and loan status. The SHG and Federation members are encouraged to go to the Talala office and check the status of their savings or loan. They have been taught how to take a print-out. While this has made the system entirely transparent and easy to use, it has instilled confidence in the members and they can see that their accounts are being faithfully kept and monitored.

These activities have helped to grow the savings of the community, allowing for a variety of credits ranging from their children's school uniforms, school fees, expenses for their daughters' weddings and improvements in their households. In fact the availability of credit itself has been a boon to the Siddi community. In 2005, Rs101,005 ($2,245) was given for consumption, where the women took loans to meet some unplanned or emergency expenditure or to improve their homes.

But by far the most significant activity that the Federation is engaged in is that of experimenting and supporting various microenterprises to generate income. More importantly, these are proving to be invaluable incubators for developing confidence, skills and linkages – essential ingredients for inclusion and empowerment.

What worked: Micro-enterprises, mega-empowerment

To reduce pressure on the Gir Forest, alternative livelihood models were necessary, which would in turn improve the socio-economic status of the Siddis. Cultivating land was not an option as a majority of them are landless. Therefore, various non-farm-based activities with the potential to generate income were initiated.

Such activities were conducted largely through the Federation because it could give them access to credit and provide a common platform to share and learn. Each income-generating activity was initiated only when the women showed an interest in it and contributed something of their own. Training programmes and exposure visits were also organized. The Federation experimented with 16 different microenterprises, piloted through a group of four women community leaders, that include provision of handcarts, neem oil packaging and marketing, bulk purchase and retail of cloth, selling of dry and fresh fish, opening a grocery shop, selling fruits and a *paan-bidi* (betel nut and cigarette) shop, among others.

The women were encouraged to take small risks and small loans that would yield modest results. Para-workers would also try to convince the women during their meetings to make small investments. To demonstrate that a business can be started with as little as Rs500 ($11), a couple of para-workers sold snacks during the *Urs*[7] festival, making a profit of Rs200 ($4) in a day.

However, the enterprise that has involved the most number of women and achieved considerable success has been the production and marketing of organic compost by the Jambur group, a collective of 24 women from 5 SHGs.

Prospering from compost

The Siddi women involved in producing organic compost adopt rustic yet effective production, marketing and management practices. Some of these women have not even gone to primary school. Yet they have devised systems and assigned responsibilities to ensure a smooth production and marketing process, quality control and payment to workers. Manufacturing of organic manure compost has turned out to be a viable activity for the Jambur group.

Over the years, these women have optimized production costs by reducing raw material stocks. Their credibility has been established in the market and the suppliers respond immediately when contacted over the phone. As a result, the loan amount has declined from between Rs350,000–400,000 ($7,778–8,889) to Rs150,000 ($3,333). Interestingly, along with better stock and financial management, the women have also organized their midday meal together to save time and ensure they eat nutritionally.

The group has five products, all marketed under the brand *Panchtatwa*.[8] The unique bad odour of wet organic compost is used as its selling point. The group has also launched a range of products that cater to different market segments. These include an odourless dry powder, a mix of *neem*[9] cake with dung and vermi-compost[10] and a formulation to capture the large *kesari* mango market. Diversification allows more employment opportunities as the production of organic compost runs on an annual cycle lasting four months a year, providing 60–70 working days to each member.

In spite of eight other competitors within a 20km radius and a price tag higher than most others, the *Panchatatwa* brand sells because of its quality. The women serve as quality monitors for each other and for themselves. They keep pebbles and for every measure of raw material added into the compost pit, one pebble is kept aside. This helps them track the quantity of raw material added in order to ensure a uniform product. These women have, since, learnt to count, make entries in the register and calculate different inputs of raw material and labour.

The product is sold through the AKRSP (India) network of extension volunteers (EVs) who are paid 10% of the product cost as a commission for sales. Two dealers have been finalized at Mangrol and Talala and commission rates fixed at 23%, subject to the condition that they purchase a minimum of 1,000 bags of organic manure, bear transportation as well as the EV cost. These dealers are responsible for stocking the manure. This arrangement has eased the transportation problems for the Siddis.

All sales are recorded using a voucher, filled out in triplicate, that records transaction details such as amount, price, driver, stock number, dates and delivery. For sales of over Rs500 ($11), cash is not accepted. The purchaser is given a deposit slip that he then takes to the bank for deposit and brings back as proof of payment. Women are paid Rs80 ($2) per working day after verification of the number of days they have worked. After the product is sold, profits are calculated and, based on consensus, an amount is deposited in the group account. The remaining profit is divided among the women.

The Jambur group was assigned a contract for bag filling at the Gujarat Agro Industries Corporation, Junagadh, where 16 women worked for several days, filling 20,000 bags at a rate of Rs1.10 ($0.02), earning Rs19, 600 ($422) as profit. From this profit, the group has purchased a sewing machine for Rs4,000 ($89) for stitching bags. SHGs are also entering into buy-back deals amongst themselves as a mechanism to hedge risks for start-ups. The Gabensah SHG in Surwa village is exploring the option of producing vermi-compost. If Gabensah SHG decides to manufacture vermi-compost and is not able to sell it in the market successfully, the Nagarchi SHG in Jambur village has agreed to purchase the product from them for use in the group's organic compost at a rate of Rs2/kg ($0.04).

These women have also developed systems to test their products and track the feedback from their customers. This enables them to respond to specific needs of groundnut farmers and mango orchards, among others. They are also able to refer their potential customers to those who have had a satisfactory experience.

Venturing to diversify

Experience with one business enterprise has enabled the Siddi women to spot business opportunities and invest in them. Neem oil purchase and packaging was initiated in Talala in 2003 by 26 women from Maysabma and Habaspir SHGs,[11] and is still being continued by the Maysabma SHG. Marketed primarily as an insecticide, neem oil is being sold through the EVs and the women through door to door sales in villages. The EVs continue to support the SHG since they are able to travel more and can reach a wider market. Moreover, the women are still not entirely confident about their marketing abilities.

A couple of enterprising women decided to venture into a partnership in mid-2004 for marketing dry fish. The women received a loan of Rs3,000 ($67) from the Federation in addition to training and motivational support form AKRSP (India). After initial losses, the activity soon became profitable at a consistent Rs30 ($0.6) per day. The loan has since been returned, but the activity is only a moderate success.

One of them has now approached the Adim Juth for a grant to purchase a handcart so that she can expand her business. She is pleased with her income-generating investments and efforts and is confident in her abilities to continue to expand her business. The idea of procuring handcarts emerged from the Nine Square Mandala. When discussing their socio-economic space, the women felt they did not have the means to enter markets. The humble handcart served this need.

There are currently six women who have purchased handcarts with a 90% subsidy from the Adim Juth. These handcarts are used to set up small shops as a short-term, festival-based activity, while others rent it out to farmers during the farming season for crop collection and transport.

Elements of empowerment

The impact of AKRSP's (India) efforts with Siddi women can be measured in terms of the SHGs formed, the setting up of the Siddi Women's Federation, increase in savings[12] and applications for loans, and successful income-generating activities. There has been a decline in the dependency on the Gir Forest as perceived by the community, though a quantitative survey is yet to be undertaken.

What is more important, however, is to discern the intangible outcome of these efforts, even as trends. These have emerged from discussions with the Siddi women: Today the Siddi women are more confident. The esteem in which they help themselves and their community has increased. They now want to improve themselves, their homes and the community. The SHGs have increased the space within which women can now interact. They have started visiting banks and are getting exposed to different types of businesses and activities.

With the social support available through the SHGs and the Federation, the women now know that they are not alone. In some cases, men have also supported their activities. For example, in Gabenshan SHG, most women are landless. Although there are some opportunities to rent land, landlessness still poses a barrier to income generation. While this issue was being discussed in a meeting of Gabenshan SHG, Abdulbapa, a landed member of the SHG, announced that if a group of landless women are interested in vermi-compost, he will provide free land and water for them, because he appreciates that landless people need special help.

Social concerns are now being appreciated. Whereas education may have been cast aside earlier, this is no longer the case. Children's education is strongly encouraged among the Siddi women. A part of this results from the increasing social pressure regarding the importance of child development. The childcare centre in Jambur village, initially supported by AKRSP (India) and now managed by the Siddi community, has over 25 children. Almost invariably, they want their children to complete school and are willing to support them financially. In fact, many Siddi women have taken loans for school fees, uniforms and other associated education costs. The president of the Federation – Hirbaiben – has sent her son to college, setting an example for her community. Her dream is to see a member of her community earn a professional degree.

A study on the promotion of income-generating activities of the Federation, conducted in November 2005, revealed that these women are now fairly grounded in economic realities. They appreciate the need to build savings and explore different income-generating options so that they are less vulnerable to unforeseen events and less dependent on others, particularly the moneylenders, for their livelihoods. There is a distinct development of an entrepreneurial spirit. Learning mostly from experience, the women have a basic understanding of business practices. As the Federation develops into a more complex financial institution, the Siddi women are becoming increasingly capable of dealing with more complex economic activities.

The women realize the need to protect the Gir Forest. They readily admit that they would not like to do anything that is illegal but indicate their helplessness in times of emergency. There is a perceptible change in the attitude of others towards the Siddi women. A growing financial security has relieved many psychological pressures on the women and their families. Apart from supplementary income, it has facilitated better domestic financial management and increased their creditworthiness in the market as well as the financial institutions.

Summary of findings

No doubt excluded communities like the Siddis need basic infrastructure and service support like shelter, livelihoods, education, drinking water supply and sanitation, health care and modern communication systems. However, in order to benefit from these in any sustainable manner, these communities need to be prepared – to recognize the value of these amenities, make demands and share responsibilities for their maintenance and quality. The lessons from the Siddis help us realize the importance of building confidence through hard work leading to incremental gains, of spotting and nurturing local leadership that is able to motivate others, of creating a structure that provides space for individuals and collective decisions in a transparent manner, and of maintaining a positive and humane outlook in the face of considerable uncertainty. When services are provided in response to the incremental development aspirations of the community, these will be valued, and even augmented through local efforts.

Learning to aspire

For a community that had accepted its fate, dreaming was a luxury they could ill-afford. A marginal existence and general acceptance of a life of ignominy weighed heavily on their collective identity, stoked continuously by a society that seemed reluctant to accept any possible change in the status quo. Constitutional laws and government policies were more accommodative, but too generic and distant for them to truly benefit. For instance, the poor quality land given to some of them fed their cynicism rather than their aspirations.

Under such circumstances, it was indeed a challenge to be able to learn to dream meaningfully. The Nine Square Mandala was one tool that allowed for such self-introspection and analysis. It also raised aspirations. But a few successes were needed – be it converting rocky terrain into productive lands or conducting a large event in a planned and disciplined manner – to instil confidence, to encourage and to turn acceptance into action.

Having tasted the fruits of their own endeavours, these women are now looking towards their next generation. They are increasingly getting interested in what their children are learning in school. Aspirations that their children attain higher levels of education are growing as are efforts to enable this to happen.

Ultimately a structure and space was needed for concerted development action, and this was provided through the various groups and the Federation. An accepted method was now available for savings, taking loans, sharing experiences, making decisions and resolving conflicts. It helped them develop their own vision, decide where they wanted to go and instil in them values and a sense of commitment for the entire process.

Even now, there are some members who regularly attend the SHG and Federation meetings but do not have the confidence. In such cases, attempts are made to strengthen their confidence still further through hand-holding and direct and indirect support. Interactions are sensitive, keeping in mind the low self-esteem of the women. Street plays, *yatras* (marches), meetings and workshops are used for raising the knowledge and skill levels of the Siddis so that they become a better informed community. In fact, all efforts are being made keeping in mind the cultural identity and sensitivity of the Siddis.

They have also realized that they need to play a greater role in the local government: Hirbaiben is now an elected member of the *Taluka Panchayat*, the middle tier of the local self governance structure in India.

Value-based development

A lot of the work with the Federation members has been based on values. The women are encouraged to adopt a requesting rather than complaining and accusing attitude, not be aggressive, to stop quarrelling and talk calmly. The women are asked to reflect on the fact that there will always be problems. As a result, for them, subsidy and financial support though vital, are now secondary. They have realized that they lag behind other communities and try to understand why this is so. But they want to find solutions to them rather than just complain. With this realization has come change. They now know what is right for them and will stand up for themselves if needed.

The trust and space provided across the organization in AKRSP (India) allowed for the growth of the staff as well as an incentive to perform better. It is important to reflect on the experiences from working with the Siddi women. It is about compassion – treating the very poor and marginalized people with the respect and trust that they deserve but are routinely denied. It is about belief in your own ability and that of the community to make a difference – and it is about perseverance and dedication.

Endnotes

1. However, the Siddi generally have little knowledge of their ancestry and feel little connection to it, identifying themselves as Indian rather than African.
2. The Government of India classifies Siddis as a primitive tribal group (PTG), who have a pre-agriculture level of technology and stagnant or declining population.
3. Women's ownership of land is generally 'strategic' in India, meaning that the land has been transferred to her name in order to avail some sort of subsidy. In contrast, the Siddi women landowners generally have real control over their land. However, the majority of the Siddi women are landless.
4. The present rural development programme of the Aga Khan Foundation, co-financed by the European Commission.
5. Through the Community Managed Natural Resources (CMNR) Project – an earlier rural development initiative of the Aga Khan Foundation, co-financed by the European Commission.
6. These were, and are still, largely referred to as Mahila Vikas Mandals (SHGs) or Women's Development Groups by the programme. This is because AKRSP's (India) work with women's organizations have always encompassed a broader domain to cover a set of social issues that are of direct concern and elements of empowerment that lead to building and nurturing leadership qualities, rather than be limited to only savings and credit activities.
7. A religious festival associated with saints.
8. *Panchtatwa* – the brand under which the compost and other related products are marketed – is selling, in spite of it being more costly than other brands. *Panchtatwa* is made from five different materials – poultry manure, neem oil, castor oil, tobacco dust and farm yard manure – which are combined and kept in a composting pit for 90 days. Starting modestly in 1999 with the production of 200 bags and a buy-back guarantee from Hirbaiben, one of the members of the SHG at Jambur, production had reached nearly 750 tonnes by July 2006: 15,315 bags weighing about 48kg each had been produced at a cost of Rs1,912,560 ($42,501) and sold at Rs2,664,000 ($59,200), making a clean profit of Rs752,440 ($16,721) or Rs31,315 ($696) per member.
9. *Azadirachta indica* – an evergreen tree endemic to the Indian sub-continent. Oil and cake are derived from its seeds and are variously used for their germicidal properties.
10. Nagarchi SHG is manufacturing vermi-compost as a part of its overall organic compost activities. Before launching vermi-compost production, the group went on an exposure visit to a farm in Anand. This SHG is also using vermi-compost as an ingredient in certain types of organic compost that it produces. Vermi-compost costs Rs1/kg ($0.02) to produce, inclusive of all costs. The market rate for this compost is Rs3/kg ($0.06).
11. In the first year, 1,050 litres of neem oil was purchased and packed by the women and sold through the AKRSP (India) EV network at a profit of Rs19,000 ($422), or Rs654 ($15) per woman.

12. In 2003, 210 SHG members had collectively saved Rs113,065 ($2,513); in 2004, 376 members had saved Rs176,620 ($3,925); in 2005, 495 members had saved Rs284,230 ($6,316) and by July 2006, 555 members had collectively saved Rs343,680 ($7,637).

References

Hogger, R. (1994) 'The family universe, towards a practical concept of rural livelihood systems', *Working paper NADEL,* Swiss Federal Institute of Technology, Zurich, Switzerland.

Kaushik, H. (2004) 'Siddi stray from tradition', *Times of India,* Sunday 5 December 2004.

Lodhi, A. Y. (1992) 'African settlements in India', *Nordic Journal of African Studies* 1(1): 83–86.

Robinson, L. (2005) 'A study of the promotion of income generating activities through the Siddi women's federation', report of IDM Fellow, Aga Khan Foundation, Canada.

About the authors

Somnath Bandyopadhyay is a Senior Programme Officer of the Aga Khan Foundation (AKF) in India. Presently he is involved with the design and implementation of a multi-input area development in the state of Bihar.

Apoorva Oza is the Chief Executive Officer of the Aga Khan Rural Support Programme (India), an established organization dealing with participatory development processes in western India, which is now moving into Bihar and Uttar Pradesh. AKF has published 'Development in Bihar: overview, appraisal and approach' that is guiding the process in the new state.

David Nygaard was formerly the Director of Rural Development at the Aga Khan Foundation at Geneva and is presently engaged in documenting lessons in community-based development from different countries.

CHAPTER 12

The NREGA and rural women in poverty: Entitlements, issues and emerging concerns

*Rina Bhattacharya, Meera Pillai and
Ratna Sudarshan*

*In September 2005, the Government of India passed the National Rural Employ-
ment Guarantee Act (NREGA). The scheme based on this law was launched in
February 2006 in 200 of the country's poorest districts. The chapter explains the
background of the NREGA and provides an overview of the entitlements outlined
under its scheme. It focuses on the expected outcomes and implications of the
scheme, especially on women's participation. The chapter then presents some preliminary findings in Abu Road on various aspects of the scheme, such as (i) the
number of participating households; (ii) the extent to which the scheme helped
in building up durable assets to promote local development; and (iii) the workers'
entitlements at the workplace. The chapter concludes that significant numbers of
households (many of them women) have participated in the NREGA public works
scheme. Nevertheless, the conditions of work on site and the wages earned still
do not meet the intended standards. In sum, so far the success of NREGA has
been mainly confined to providing some cash transfers to the needy rather than
articulating the needs of local communities and building durable assets in their
villages.*

Introduction

In this chapter we focus on the issue of public works, and more specifically
the National Rural Employment Guarantee Act (NREGA) in India. Public
works have a long history in India and have been particularly associated with
a form of cash transfer to ameliorate distress of the poorest, at times of famine. NREGA builds upon the experience of earlier programmes, such as Maharashtra Employment Guarantee Scheme (MEGS), but is different in that it is
designed as a statutory obligation of the state and a right of the citizen. It also
seeks to be distinguished from cash transfers by emphasizing on the one hand
the link between productivity and earnings, and on the other the building up
of assets that would in due course contribute to local development. The focus

of this chapter is to provide a background on the NREGA and the next section, in particular, highlights some of the entitlements under the scheme and its poverty impact on rural women. We then move on to focus on the rural women dimensions before reviewing some of the preliminary findings from Rajasthan, which suggest recognition of ground realities and early corrections are both crucial to future impacts. In the penultimate section we highlight some of the concerns associated with such a programme before concluding.

Background

NREGA was enacted by the Indian Government in September 2005. The act was significant as an attempt to address issues of livelihood security faced by the non-working and working poor in the rural areas of the country. It became one of the first legal instruments to recognize the right to work and earn a reasonable minimum wage in the sub-continent. The Act envisages a working partnership between the Central and State Governments, the panchayats and local communities to provide wage employment to people in poverty in rural India. Operational guidelines to implement the Act, specifying parameters and non-negotiables were formulated by the Central Government, based on which the State governments designed schemes about works to be undertaken. The actual execution of works, provision of worksite facilities and supervision of payments were to be overseen by implementing bodies, primarily, elected local governments and government officials.

The Prime Minister, Dr. Manmohan Singh launched the Rural Employment Guarantee Schemes in 2006. These were to be implemented, to begin with, in 200 of India's poorest districts. A sum of Rs11,300 *crores* was allocated for the year 2006–07. The following year (2007–08), another 130 districts were added, of which 113 districts have already been notified, i.e. brought under the purview of the Act, and Rs12,000 *crores* allotted.

NREGA is built on a long history of wage employment programmes in India. Some of its important predecessors at the national level include – National Rural Employment Programme (NREP), 1980–89; Rural Landless Employment Guarantee Programme (RLEGP), 1983–89; Jawahar Rozgar Yojana (JRY), 1989–99; Employment Assurance Scheme (EAS), 1993–99; Jawahar Gram Samriddhi Yojana (JGSY), 1999–2002; Sampoorna Grameen Rozgar Yojana (SGRY), since September 2001; and, the National Food For Work Programme (NFFWP), since November 2004.

In addition, the Maharashtra Employment Guarantee Scheme (MEGS), a famine/drought relief programme that was the first statutory effort at providing guaranteed employment as a means of alleviating poverty in India, has been an important source of inspiration for NREGA. Initiated in 1972, MEGS aimed at providing adults in rural areas with guaranteed employment and wages, creating assets in rural areas in the bargain, including roads, and land and water conservation projects. The MEGS experience was mixed. On the one hand, it offered employment and income earning opportunities, food security for the poor, income stabilization and parity of wages for men and women (Krishnaraj et al., 2003). On the other, there were lacunae such as gaps between work and payment, non-availability of continuous employment, poor awareness of entitlements, non-payment of unemployment allowance throughout the history of the scheme, absence of linkages between MEGS works and larger plans for the district, etc. (Krishnaraj et al., 2003).

Consequently, despite the scheme, a perceptible impact on rural poverty in Maharashtra did not happen. As Kannan (2005) points out, notwithstanding the increases in capital formation, real wages for agricultural labourers in Maharashtra have remained one of the lowest in the country. Other academic literature focusing on issues associated with employment guarantee schemes is also worth noting, for example, Scandizzo et al. (2009) modelled the choice between Employment Guarantee Schemes (EGS) and other activities. They found volatility of wages in the rural labour markets has important implications for switching, and retaining workers already, in the EGS, with a higher EGS wage increasing the attractiveness to relatively skilled and affluent workers. Hence selection may be impaired by several biases in favour of higher income individuals.

Entitlements under the NREGA

The Act guarantees 100 days of employment in a financial year to rural households in notified districts. Work is to be given to adult members of households from these districts (who do not have to belong to 'below poverty line' (BPL) families) who demand employment, and are willing to do unskilled manual work. The work for the household may be split between different adult members of the household, who live in the gram panchayat, or have returned after migrating. The household is defined as a nuclear family, and hence a joint family may constitute multiple households, with equivalent entitlements for employment.

The Act explicitly seeks to make the process of registration for work simple and accessible to the possibly illiterate and marginalized among the rural poor. Hence, the guidelines specify that even oral requests for work should be honoured, with the implication that the gram panchayats, the elected local governments at the primary level, should facilitate the formal registration of people who seek work in this fashion. Likewise, applications for registration on plain paper rather than on official forms, which provide the relevant information about the registrant, are also to be accepted. Further, the Act recognizes the need for promptness in responding to the needs of the rural poor. Details such as establishing local residence, the household as an entity, the eligible adult members of the household, etc., are to be verified by the gram panchayat within a maximum of two weeks, and the household given a registration number. Within a week of registration, households are to receive job cards, which indicate the details of eligible adult members of the household who can seek employment under the NREGA.

Once job cards have been received, single applicants, or several applicants together may apply for work, indicating the date of application and the number of days of work sought. In practice, through the decades, the rural poor have not always commanded priority with the bureaucracy. Seeking to introduce responsiveness and transparency, the guidelines specify that panchayats should provide a receipt which indicates the date on which an application for work has been received. Within 15 days of making an application, applicants should either receive work, or be paid an unemployment allowance. Information about the work provided, and wages or unemployment allowance paid are to be entered on the job card.

While wages are to be notified by the state government, they are not to fall below the 'national floor' of Rs60 per day. The NREGA also tries to ensure the basic dignity of labour, and specifies that the implementing agency has to provide worksite facilities, including medical aid, drinking water and shade and childcare support.

The stated ideological commitment of successive Indian governments towards strengthening local government, however diluted in practice, appears to undergird the NREGA's insistence that the Panchayats at each level will be primarily responsible for the planning, implementing and monitoring. To address this dilution, and perhaps anticipating the problems that are likely to be posed by established socio-economic and political systems and structures to the implementation of the Act, the NREGA has not only created spaces for community participation, but actually demanded it to a hitherto unprecedented level. The guidelines specify that even the initial implementation of the scheme is to begin with a *gram sabha* (community meeting), which has been widely publicized in advance using multiple methods (including 'local cultural forms') which do not require literacy, in order to encourage people's participation, and in particular, participation by people in poverty and likely beneficiaries in large numbers. Panchayats are enjoined to take into account work seasons and migration times while planning the timing of the *gram sabha* to ensure maximum participation of possible beneficiaries. *Gram sabhas* are to be used to share information about the scheme and invite people not only to register in order to benefit from it, but also to recommend what works should be taken up to create useful public assets for the community. *Gram sabhas* are also conceptualized as an important part of the monitoring process, together with local monitoring committees: for public verification that applicants for both registration and participation in works are *bona fide*, monitoring the implementation of works, procurement of materials, quality of works, etc., full and timely payment of wages, and identification and plugging of leakages.

The elected local governments too have been assigned multifarious responsibilities under the Act: to conduct *gram sabhas* after wide publicity, estimate the demand for labour over the course of the year, determine the development works to be undertaken and prioritize them, and plan and propose them to the higher levels of government so that a list of works is ready for use when a demand for work arises. Apart from being responsible for the important documentation and administrative processes like registration of applicants, issuing of job cards and allocation of work, they also have significant financial and executive responsibilities: no less than 50% of works undertaken under NREGA are to be carried out at the gram panchayat level, with the rest being shared by other bodies, including elected local government bodies at the intermediary and district levels. The elected bodies are to be assisted by government officials to be specially appointed for this purpose at the intermediate and higher levels of local government.

Asset creation works that have been suggested under the Act include water conservation and harvesting, drought proofing, afforestation and tree plantation, building irrigation canals, flood control and drainage works, land development, improving rural connectivity by building roads and culverts, etc. The guidelines also specify the anticipated outcomes:

> Investments made under NREGA are expected to yield an increase in employment and purchasing power, participation of women workforce, strengthening of rural infrastructure through creation of durable assets, regeneration of natural resources that provide the livelihood resource base of local rural economy, increase in productivity, and reduction in distress migration. (Government of India, 2006)

Thus, there are multiple reasons why this employment guarantee scheme holds out great promise: unlike earlier schemes designed to assist the rural poor, this is backed by law, and hence government is liable in the event of failed or inadequate implementation, and it is not reversible with any changes of government. Further, the guidelines hold out the hope, and have included many provisions to try and ensure, that 'this legislation becomes a "People's Act"' (Government of India, 2006). It provides scope for implementation by local groups and agencies, confers extensive powers to local panchayats, lays down standards for quality of conditions of work at the worksite such as medical aid, drinking water, shade and crèches for childcare, and provides for allowances and free medical treatment in the event of workplace injuries, and compensation in the case of work-related permanent disability or death. The NREGA has also been designed to work in tandem with the Right to Information Act: 'The objective is to make the planning, implementation and evaluation of the Employment Guarantee Scheme (EGS) more participatory, transparent and accountable through facilitating the exercise of people's right to information. By encouraging social audits, it involves ordinary citizens in vigilance and enforcing accountability in a very tangible and direct manner'. (Government of India, 2006).

Rural women in poverty and NREGA

Entitlements for women

NREGA is also path-breaking in that it provides for several explicit entitlements for women. Perhaps the most significant is that it specifies equal wages for men and women according to law. NREGA also takes into account and addresses explicit and implicit limitations to access that women generally have to face in government wage employment schemes. It provides that a third of the beneficiaries should be women, and that they should be allocated work as close to their homes as possible. The Act recognizes the reproductive work burdens of women, and specifies that if there are more than five children under the age of six at a worksite, a crèche should be made available to take care of them. The Act also recognizes women as valuable members of the community, with a stake in ensuring that benefits conceptualized under the scheme actually do reach beneficiaries and create assets. Thus, women are enjoined to be members of the monitoring and vigilance committees to ensure that planning and implementation of works and payment of wages happens properly.

In addition to these explicit entitlements, several of the guidelines provide spaces for increased claims by women. For example, specific guidelines includes issues such as the 'household' also meaning a single member family. This implies that abandoned and destitute women, widows and other single women in poverty will count as a household, and can apply for and get 100 days of employment. Self help groups (SHGs) can also take up works under the scheme. Thus, women's groups can make representations to the gram panchayat or concerned government officials to take up and execute works under the scheme. In addition regulations also state that training must be provided to local governments as well as to local monitoring and vigilance committees on core issues related to NREGA, on both generic skills and functional skills related to tasks. In particular, training must focus on the relationship between NREGA and the Right to Information Act. This implies that women panchayat members can ask to be trained in the relevant skills so as to be able to undertake public works under the scheme, as well as supervise and monitor implementation, and take on more responsibilities.

Women's participation in earlier wage employment programmes

Although these provisions in NREGA are positive about promoting women's participation at all levels – as beneficiaries, executors of public works and supervisors and monitors, it is also useful to briefly examine the evidence related to women's participation in the Maharashtra Employment Guarantee Scheme (MEGS). Evaluations by scholars like Devaki Jain (ISST, 1979), Dattar (1987), and Krishnaraj et al. (2004) found that the level of participation by women was higher than that of men in most observations, with more women than men being seen on sites, and more women reporting for work than were registered. However, the reasons for this high participation were not necessarily positive. Work provided under MEGS was usually unskilled, short-term and discontinuous work, and more women are casual and subsidiary workers. Hence, much MEGS work was perceived as 'women's work'. From 38% in 1995–96, women's employment as a percentage of the total employment in person days in the scheme went up to 73% in 1998–99, but fell to 57% in 1999–2000. (Krishnaraj et al., 2004).

There were also issues related to the wages received by women. Typically women were not aware of the prevailing norms and wage schedules. Since the work under the MEGS had to be sought in groups, and the leaders of the work gangs were invariably men, they tended to act as arbiters of the rates paid to women, which became subjective. Besides, different wage rates prevailed for different activities; women were typically allocated to unskilled tasks, and paid according to the norms for those activities. Thus, many of the benefits such as equalization of wages, which were part of the scheme's design, did not survive in the actual implementation. Similarly women could not claim maternity benefits without proving 75 days of work and this was difficult because of shifting worksites and poor record keeping (Krishnaraj et al., 2003). Skilled women workers did not participate in MEGS, and the scheme did not provide for acquisition of any new skills by women. The majority of the women participants belonged to landless, small or marginal farming families. However, unlike the men, who were quick to consider migration as an option for improving the family's economic status, women looked on schemes like MEGS as an important component of basic survival strategies (Krishnaraj and Pandey, 1990). They reported an improvement in family nutritional status as a result of participation in the scheme (ISST, 1979) as well as improved status in the family because of an increase in core income.

The majority of the women who participated in the MEGS scheme were between 30 and 35 years of age (ISST, 1979), that is women with very young children with greater reproductive work burdens. Elderly women, participated in smaller measure. There is also no evidence that women played any part in deciding the nature of the works undertaken and supported by the programme. However, MEGS provided an opportunity for women workers to mobilize in groups. Jain (ISST, 1979) also noted that there was greater participation by women who were already a part of some organized group.

Thus, while the rights laid down for women in the NREGA constitute a valid first step, the MEGS experience indicates that efforts at meeting both their 'practical' and 'strategic' needs are essential to realize these rights adequately. Participation by women that is 'empowering' would require attention to several issues. Participation in itself cannot always be seen as positive: it would also be essential to consider what work women do and on what terms, whether equal wages are paid, and the awareness levels of men and women about their dues and privileges as equal. Critical attention would need to be focused on the prevailing conditions of work – the availability of water, toilet facilities and child care, or the suitability of work timings – which would increase the time and energy available to women for paid work. Further, if the programme is to be more than just a dole, the programme must seek to strengthen existing skills or help women acquire new skills. There must be corruption-free implementation, without which it will be difficult to acquire trust, and older unfair patterns of work will continue to persist. If the objective is sustainable and gender-sensitive development outcomes, then prevailing systems and structures need to encourage substantive participation by women in planning projects that address their needs.

Some findings[1]

We can draw on some findings from the state of Rajasthan, often described as one of the more 'successful' of NREGA efforts,[2] to establish some preliminary findings. We briefly discuss the findings of a household survey on the participation in NREGA and examine the conditions of work on sites, nature of the assets currently supported through the programme and some of the emerging issues.

Sample

A quick study of selected villages in Abu Road was carried out by the Institute of Social Studies Trust (ISST) Household Survey in partnership with Doosra Dashak, in early 2006. The study was supported by the International Labour Organization (ILO), New Delhi. Village Mahikhera located in the plains and Nichlagarh located in the hills were part of this study. A year later, in early 2007, a household survey was carried out in a group of villages surrounding these two villages. The sample was distributed over 11 villages out of which 6 villages were located in the hilly area and 5 in the plains. The objective was to study the participation level of the rural households in National Rural Employment Guarantee Scheme (NREGS), with special attention to women's participation; the types of works completed during April 2006 to March 2007 under NREGS; the conditions of work on the sites and worker entitlements; and the current nature and level of migration. These studies provide a baseline from which the progress of the scheme can be assessed.

Participation in NREGS

Table 12.1 below shows the number of households reporting participation in the NREGS works as well as those that did not participate and the reasons why – which include migration, refusal of work, no job cards and those that had cards but did not want to access this work.

Approximately 1% of households in the sample did not participate and instead migrated away. Entire families go to places in Gujarat and work there as agricultural labourers for 6–8 months. Most of these families are given shelter to stay near the field and food to eat. Such migrants return home for 4 months during the monsoon. In some households we managed to collect information

Table 12.1 Number and types of surveyed households (hhs) reporting participation in the National Rural Employment Guarantee Scheme (NREGS) in India

	Bhakar (hilly area) (%)	Bhittrot (plain) (%)	Total (%)
Migrant hhs	1.0	1.2	1.1
Hhs refused work on job cards	0.4	0.3	0.4
Hhs with no job cards	2.2	3.1	2.6
Hhs where job cards not used	4.8	12.3	8.2
Hhs participated in NREGA	91.5	83.1	87.6
Total	672	579	1251

Source: ISST Household Survey (2007)

from their relatives/family members left behind. One of the reasons given for migration was that the wage offered under NREGA is too low therefore they continue the tradition of going out of the village for wage work.

Less than 1% of households reported that they were refused work on grounds that work was not available, or the muster roll already had the necessary number of workers required for the particular work site. A few households (2.6%) reported not having any job cards, usually because adult members of the household were away at the time that cards were being issued. Some households (over 8%) did not use their cards. However the survey found that an impressive 87.6% of the sampled households did participate in NREGA works.

Another aspect of livelihoods in the area is the fact that many people cannot find work within the village and therefore commute short distances on a regular basis. This is summarized in Table 12.2 below. The usual place of work for men in the hill villages requires commuting to places outside the village but within the block (55%) and similarly for 22% of men in the plains. Most others (35% in the hills, 70% in the plains) find work within the village. With women, however, the majority find work within the village (68% in the hills and 93% in the plains).

Table 12.2 Distance to place of work reported by surveyed households (by gender)

Place of work	Hilly Area		Plain Area		Total	
	Male (%)	Female (%)	Male (%)	Female (%)	Male (%)	Female (%)
Within 5km from the place of residence	35	68	70	93	52	81
Outside village within the block	55	28	22	3	39	15
Outside the block within the district	4	2	4	1	4	1
Outside the district within the state	–	–	–	–	–	–
Other	5	2	4	3	5	2
Total	381	244	279	243	690	487

Source: ISST Household Survey (2007)

Table 12.3 Households working in NREGS by number of days in hilly and plain areas

Number of days worked in NREGS	Number of households		Total
	Hilly Area	Plain Area	
Less than 15 days	20	58	78
16-31 days	35	55	90
32-47 days	46	55	101
48-63 days	114	73	187
64-79 days	123	52	175
80-95 days	156	63	219
96+	121	125	246
Total	615	481	1096

Source: ISST Household Survey (2007)

It is also found that over 50% of women report being workers and more than 50% of men and women seek casual wage work. Among the households participating in NREGA, 55% are from the hilly area as against 45% from the plain area. Percentage of male participation works out to be 44% as against 56% female participation. If we look at the ratio between households participated in NREGA and individuals, it works out to be an average of 1:5 persons per household.

Some further details of participation in the NREGS are given in Table 12.3 which shows that roughly a fifth of the households had been able to get over 96 days of work. In general women outnumbered the men in terms of number of days of participation in NREGA. Among those who have completed 100 days of work in NREGA, 70% are women as against 30% men.

Creation of durable assets

Works carried out under NREGA are expected to build up durable assets in the village in turn stimulating further development. The process of implementation is expected to involve local communities through representative institutions so that assets created will respond to felt deficiencies in the local economy. An analysis of the responses of the households on works completed in or near their village is presented below. Table 12.4 indicates that 53% of people reported that the nature of the works was 'gravel road construction', of which 22% were described as 'incomplete road' and another 27.4 % responses were for *nari kodai* (irrigation pits) (Table 12.4). Another 12% said 'nothing happened' i.e. no impact was felt of the works/purpose of works was not clear to the participants.

Road construction dominates the choice of works. Data from the Block Development Office confirms that during February 2006 and March 2007, priority has been given to gravel roads and digging of tanks. *Anicuts* and *Medband,*[3] effective in preventing soil erosion, especially in the hilly areas of the district, are practically missing.

Table 12.4 Number of works completed in/near the respondents' villages under NREGS

No.	Responses	Hilly Area	Plain Area	Total
1	Incomplete Gravel road	(55)	(45)	285 {21.8}
2	Gravel road construction	(88)	(12)	408 {31.2}
3	Nari Kodai	(62)	(38)	359 {27.4}
4	Anicuts are made	(100)	–	4 {0.3}
5	Canal cleaning/reconstruction	–	(100)	3 {0.2}
6	Nothing happened	(6)	(94)	153 {11.7}
7	No idea	(12)	(88)	93 {7.1}
8	Not Applicable	(100)	–	2 {0.1}
	Total			1307

Source: ISST Household Survey (2007)
Note: Figures in brackets indicate row percentage; Figures in { } indicate column percentage

The survey also tried to find out if households had observed any perceptible impact of participation in the NREGA and the responses are summarized in Table 12.5.

As the table shows, roughly 45% report an economic benefit through additional cash in hand, 7% of the responses suggest benefits from easier availability of water and 34% from easier access to roads. The balance 14% reported no benefits or negative benefits.

Table 12.5 Benefits accruing to the respondents from NREGS works

No.	Responses	Hilly Area	Plain Area	Total
	More cash in-hand			**45%**
1	Could buy food grains and clothes	(94)	(6)	34
2	Got wage work	(42)	(58)	468
3	Could spent on children's education	(100)	–	8
4	Save money on transportation	(80)	(20)	5
5	Earned extra money	(100)	–	1
	Roads and improved access			**34%**
6	Access to road	(81)	(19)	373
7	Benefited but road is far off	(78)	(22)	23
8	Sick people can be taken to the hospital	(100)		2
	Water related benefits			**7%**
9	Due to nari kodai animals are getting enough water	(38)	(62)	37
10	Availability of drinking water	(91)	(9)	11
11	Water can be stored	(89)	(11)	36
	No gain			**14%**
12	No gain	(39)	(61)	147
13	Due to monsoon the structure got washed away	(67)	(33)	9
14	Canal water leaked into the agricultural field	(100)	–	2
	Total			**1156**

Source: ISST Household Survey (2007)
Note: Figures in brackets indicate row percentage

Entitlements of workers

Entitlements of the workers at the worksite have also been an important dimension of NREGS implementation. A review of worksites around selected villages once a month between October 2006 and April 2007 showed that, for example:

- Crèche facilities have not been provided at the sites.
- Drinking water facilities have been provided at all the sites.
- Medical kits have not been available on the sites (only a few medicines were kept by the mates for emergencies and the medicines/gel/bandages needed to treat cuts/injuries were missing).
- Tents have been provided for shade but not at all sites.
- The measurements of tasks remain a puzzle for the mate/Panchayat/labour.

For example, it is hard to understand from the parameters who decides what and against what norms. However, the Junior Engineer[4] gave the measurement details which he follows to make the payment of wages to ISST researchers. For a person to get the state minimum wage of Rs73 per day, she/he has to dig up 1.67 cubic meter or 58.96 gun ft. A recent task revision has reduced the task for per person to 1.36 cubic meter/54 gun ft. It found that no one has received Rs73 as wage. But the rate has improved and in some places people have received as high as Rs63. But an earlier study recorded the receipt of wage could be as low as Rs25.[5]

Comparing the situation in early 2006 and early 2007, it seems there has been some improvement in the average wages earned, but this is still below the state minimum wage.

At a minimum, a crèche ensures that young children do not hurt themselves at the worksite and are provided with basic care. Failure to provide crèches may be restricting the participation of women. Alternatively, children may be left alone or unattended while the mother works, or in the care of an older sister who would then stay back from school.

Discussions at a workshop confirm that this often happens. As one woman put it, 'we will fill our stomach first, study comes later' ('*pet pehle bharenge, padhai baad me sochenge*'). Her own granddaughter had dropped out of school to look after the younger siblings at home while her mother was away at the worksite.

Summary

Considerable excitement has been generated, equally among rural people in poverty and civil society organizations, by the opportunities opened up by NREGA. The excitement is, however, tempered with caution and the awareness that many of the structural and systemic underpinnings for this brave new Act have not changed since previous employment guarantee schemes.

Traditionally, wage employment guarantee schemes in India have faced implementation problems, including corruption and leakages, poor targeting, inadequate accountability of public officials and inappropriate asset creation, often of indifferent quality. Ensuring that women's needs and priorities get a place in the choice of works, that they get their proper entitlements, and that such additional work does not lead to unanticipated adverse outcomes in the realm of reproductive work is a challenge for all those concerned with administering or monitoring the programme. Much more advocacy and effort is needed to ensure that resource allocations are responsive to these concerns.

Preliminary survey findings in Abu Road shows that a significant percentage of households have participated in the NREGA works including a high percentage of women. The wages earned however are below the State minimum and this is the first issue that needs to be recorded, i.e. the lack of awareness and information about the basis on which wages are to be paid and the level of earnings that are possible. Conditions of work on the sites do not meet the intentions, and in particular, reasons behind the failure to provide crèches need to be further explored as well as the inadequate training/information/awareness of the mates regarding the medical kits and medicines provided for use at the sites. Until wages improve and quality of assets improves there is unlikely to be any impact of NREGA on either migration or local development.

It is difficult to avoid the conclusion that so far the 'success' of NREGA has been some amount of cash transfer to the needy. The process of implementation involves articulation of priorities by villagers and choice of works to reflect these priorities and result in the creation of durable assets, in turn stimulating local development. However, in this area it was found that the majority of people especially the women in the village do not attend *gram sabha*. It seems that *gram sabha* is not yet capable of formulating projects and negotiating further. Until these systems become more responsive and better informed the choice of assets will continue to be determined at the convenience of local officials and will be restricted by the skills that are locally available.

Endnotes

1. Findings based on Bhattacharya and Sudarshan (2008).
2. Yamini Aiyar (*Indian Express*, 27 Decebmer 2007).
3. *Anicut* is a mole made from wood, stone or other materials and set in the course of a stream for the purpose of regulating the flow of irrigation; and *Medbandi* is a stone embankment built on the lower side of an agriculture field on a hill slope to conserve soil and moisture and create a level field for cultivation.
4. Researchers from ISST and Doosra Dashak met the junior engineer on 20 January 2007 at the Employment Officer's chamber to get some insight on the task measurement issue. Also we wanted to know if officials of Abu Road block follow any measurement rate list like the one used in Dungarpur district. We were informed that the measurement of task is done against the norms mentioned in the text. However there was no

official document as such kept on record in the office of the employment officer who co-ordinates NREGA programme in the entire block.
5.   ILO/ISST (2006).

References

Bhattacharya R. and Sudarshan, R. M. (2008) 'NREGA in Abu Road, Rajasthan', paper prepared for conference on *Employment Opportunities and Public Employment Policy In Globalising India*, Centre Of Development Studies, Tiruvananthapuram, 3–5 April 2008.
Dattar, C. (1987) *Maharashtra Employment Guarantee Scheme*, Institute of Social Studies Trust, New Delhi.
Government of India (2006) *The National Rural Employment Guarantee Act 2005 (NREGA): Operational Guidelines*, Ministry of Rural Development, New Delhi.
ILO/ISST (2006) *Women and the NREGA*, Institute of Social Studies Trust, New Delhi.
ISST (1979) *Impact on women workers: Maharashtra Employment Guarantee Scheme*, Institute of Social Studies Trust, New Delhi.
Kannan, K. P. (2005) 'Linking guarantee to human development', *Economic and Political Weekly*, 15 October 2005: 4518 – 4522.
Krishnaraj, M., and Pandey, D. (1990) 'Women assist change by not changing themselves', *Samya Shakti* [now *Indian Journal of Gender Studies*], IV and V, 1989–90: 143–155.
Krishnaraj, M., Pandey, D., and Kanchi, A. (2003) *Gender sensitive analysis of Employment Guarantee Scheme*, UNIFEM, New Delhi.
Krishnaraj, M., Pandey, D., and Kanchi, A. (2004) 'Does EGS require restructuring for poverty alleviation and gender equality?', Part II – Gender concerns and issues for restructuring, *Economic and Political Weekly*, 24 April 2004, 39(17): 1741–1747.
Scandizzo, P, Gaiha, R. and Imai K. (2009) 'Option values, switches, and wages: an analysis the employment guarantee scheme in India', *Review of Development Economics* 13(2): 248–263.

About the authors

Rina Bhattacharya is Research Fellow at the Institute of Social Studies Trust (ISST), New Delhi. Her research interest includes Poverty and Gender. She joined ISST in 1987. Before joining ISST she worked in NCERT and JNU. She has researched widely in the field of poverty and gender. She has a PhD in Psychology from Delhi University.

Meera Pillai is Senior Consultant at the Institute of Social Studies Trust in New Delhi.

Ratna M. Sudarshan is currently Director at the Institute of Social Studies Trust, New Delhi. Primary research areas include women in the informal economy and governance in the context of on going development processes in India.

CHAPTER 13

Strategies for promoting decent contract labour: Experiences from South African and UK agriculture

Stephanie Barrientos

Employment can play a central role in eradicating extreme poverty. However, much of the work being generated by contemporary processes of globalization may not be 'decent work'. This chapter explores the reasons for the intensification of labour contracting in contemporary food production and distribution through a comparison of South Africa and UK horticulture supplying fruit and vegetables to UK supermarkets. At the bottom of these food production chains lies an army of workers hired through third party labour contractors.

Workers hired through these labour contracting systems can experience high levels of exploitation and deprivation. They have no employment security, and rarely have access to legal employment entitlements (for ill-health, old-age and other contingencies). Often they are migrants and have little knowledge of their rights or the channels for accessing them. The case studies reveal that many workers hired by labour contractors are highly vulnerable to poverty. Often the critical point of exploitation is not within the work place itself, but in related arrangements (which could involve different agents) for activities such as the movement of workers between countries, accommodation or provision of documents. At the extreme, some workers find themselves in modern forms of 'economic slavery'. Yet these workers are employed at the bottom of a highly profitable modern food chain, dominated by some of the world's best known supermarkets.

There are significant challenges in addressing the rights and protection of contract workers. The main regulatory channels require open employment records, but these workers are often 'invisible'. The mobility of labour contractors between employers makes it extremely difficult for labour inspectors or social auditors to monitor their employment practices. Innovative ways of improving the conditions of casual labour are discussed and, for example, some supermarkets have promoted the extension of voluntary codes to contract labour in response to adverse publicity. If paid work is to provide an effective route out of poverty, it needs to ensure basic rights and protection for all workers and especially contract workers.

Introduction

As we saw in the previous chapter, the role of employment in eradicating extreme poverty is extremely important. In this chapter we focus on the experiences of workers hired through third party labour contractors, in relation to South Africa and the UK and global food production, and how the promotion of decent contract labour may come about.

The increasing dominance of supermarkets is leading to rapid changes in the way food is produced and has implications for waged labour in the food sector. At the bottom of this food chain lies an army of casual workers. Their employment is insecure, they have little or no protection and are vulnerable to poverty. Many are employed through third party labour contractors,[1] who coordinate the movement of a mobile labour force between growers to meet production schedules. They provide a cheap and flexible labour force that keeps production costs to a minimum and food prices down.

The use of labour contracting at the height of the season in agriculture is not new, but it appears to be intensifying as modern forms of food distribution and retailing advance. Workers hired through the system of labour contracting can experience high levels of exploitation and deprivation. They have no employment security, and rarely have access to legal employment entitlements. They are exposed to risk of extreme poverty if unable to find work, face ill-health or old age. Often they are migrant (internal or international), and have little knowledge of their rights or the channels for accessing them. Labour contracting does provide, however, a channel for accessing paid work, and making a living.

This chapter explores the reasons for the intensification of labour contracting in contemporary food production and distribution and highlights the global nature of this trend by drawing on a comparison of South Africa and UK horticulture in the supply of fruit and vegetables to UK supermarkets. The next two sections examine how the changing dynamics of food production, distribution and retailing are fuelling the use of contract labour, and considers the implications for workers, and the perpetuation of vulnerability to extreme poverty at the bottom of the modern food chain. In the penultimate section we explore how the rights and protection of workers could be addressed, before concluding.

Background: Global production and labour contracting

The conceptual analysis of employment relations within both the global value chain or production network literature has to date remained limited. The main focus has tended to be on the firm with labour treated primarily as an economic factor of production with a given unit price (wage or income). Analysis has primarily been on the changing international division of labour, global outsourcing and increasing labour flexibility as a means of reducing costs (Gereffi, 2006; Millberg, 2004). A broader socio-economic perspective draws on the analysis of the capabilities and entitlements of workers, and their functionings as people (Sen, 1999). This facilitates a multidimensional analysis not just of employment levels and wage income, but the wider well-being and empowerment of workers attained through their access to paid work. In the context of global production networks, an important factor is the employment environment. To what extent does the type of paid work generated allow access by workers to their rights and enhance their well-being, or compel workers to economic servitude and a future perpetually exposed to the risk of extreme poverty?

Global production networks have been increasingly characterized by a shift in manufacturing jobs away from developed to developing countries, where multinational corporations (MNCs) no longer own but outsource their production from a network of suppliers (Gereffi, 2006). Multinational buyers and retailers coordinate a system of production and distribution based on flexible and 'just in time' output that minimizes costs and stock holding, and maximizes quality and speed of delivery. The maintenance of standards requires a small core of workers that have the experience and skill to ensure consistency and quality. But it is complemented by an increased demand for flexible and mobile workers that can help to maintain flexible output.

Labour contractors play an increasingly important role in the supply of labour within global production networks. Labour contracting can take two forms: specialist or independent contractors who use discretion based on skill in how a task is undertaken, supplying their own materials; and 'labour-only contractors' who have no specialist skills, provide no materials and are paid by completed task or for the provision of labour (Theron and Godfrey, 2000). Here, we are only concerned with the latter form of labour contracting with a focus on the provision of low or unskilled workers. The mechanisms of recruitment and the employment relationship can be very variable, and differ between countries and sectors. Case studies suggest the use of labour contractors is common in many countries and sectors (Plant, 2007; Martin, 2005; Barrientos and Kritzinger, 2003; Frances et al., 2005). Labour contracting takes many different forms, as shown in the following typology:[2]

- Labour agency or contractor supplies workers to a producer for a fee, where the producer becomes the direct employer.
- Labour agency or contractor supplies workers to a producer. The agent pays the workers (taking a percentage), but the producer supervises the workers.
- Labour agency or contractor supplies workers to a producer on the basis of a contract for a specific task for which payment is made (e.g. clearing a field), where the agent or contractor pays the workers and supervises their work.
- Informal contractors – individuals (often workers) who recruit other workers for a farm or factory, may also be a worker or ex-worker, and receives a payment or unofficially takes a deduction from wages.

Labour contractors will often use a combination of labour sources, drawing on both migrant and local workers depending on labour market conditions. They have connections to different sources of labour (such as people smugglers), and have direct knowledge of the needs of producers in any given sector or location. They help to match supply with demand for labour, and play an important role in meeting sudden surges in demand. As orders or seasons peak and fall, labour contractors are able to provide sites with variable numbers of workers at short notice to meet supply requirements (Frances et al., 2005; du Toit and Ally, 2001). This helps to keep down labour costs through the more 'efficient' use of labour, and removes many of the obligations of employment from the producer themselves. The use of this type of labour also provides an important buffer for producers in global production networks, who are caught in a pincer movement where dominant agents and buyers extract value up the chain and drive risks down the chain (Barrientos and Kritzinger, 2004). Non-government organizations have highlighted this as a potential source of poor employment practice (ActionAid, 2005; Oxfam, 2003).

Labour contractors can provide an important route to employment for workers who lack information on the availability of jobs, and can help to maintain the continuity of employment in an insecure labour market. They also organize many of the logistics of moving between jobs, such as arranging transport, food, and accommodation. But workers employed through this route also face high levels of insecurity and risk, which make them vulnerable to abuse and extreme poverty. Workers rarely have any security of employment, written contracts, their employment is often very insecure (with no certainty from one day to the next) and these factors are often compounded by the fact they are already likely to be the most vulnerable and poorest in society. They rarely receive employment benefits such as social insurance, and have no coverage if sick, injured or pregnant. They rarely have access to information or unions, and are often unaware of their rights. Such workers usually suffer regular periods of unemployment, when they have no income or support, and face extreme hardship. Desperation for paid work can trap them into a mouth to mouth existence, where they are dependent on contractors for survival.

Ultimately, in global production networks where powerful economic agents and buyers strive to maximize the value gained at the upper end and pass risks downwards, contract workers are the final stop in the risk chain, in turn affecting the well-being of those at the bottom of the food chain. We will now explore this in more depth drawing on the specific example of the UK and South Africa.

Contract labour in UK and South Africa horticulture

In the UK, women traditionally provided an important source of local casual seasonal labour. The introduction of new forms of centralized food supply demanded by supermarkets led to more intensified working practices, extended hours and uncertainty of work availability. As more women entered regular employment they found better jobs elsewhere in the labour force, their availability in agriculture declined in the late 1980s. Initially they were replaced by unemployed male workers displaced from industries such as coal mining. But producers increasingly needed a pool of workers which was low cost, and would accept new labour practices required to meet changing supermarket demands. The use of foreign nationals working temporarily in British horticulture became widespread in the 1990s, largely recruited through labour contractors or 'gangmasters' as they are known colloquially. Initial studies into the nature of employment relations with migrant workers in UK horticulture suggest that foreign nationals are sought not just because it may be possible to pay them less, but also because they provide reliability, flexibility and compliance, and above all a 'hunger' which is not found among nationals of the 15 EU member countries.[3]

Changes within the food chain have impacted on the demand and deployment of temporary workers with an increased use of third party labour contractors. One study examined labour use in 21,603 enterprises in the horticulture sector, of which 6,594 sold to supermarkets (Frances et al., 2005). Enterprises with supermarket customers employed 26% of directly recruited temporary workers, and 54% of temporary workers recruited through labour contractors (including the Seasonal Agricultural Workers Scheme). The 15,000 farm enterprises that did not have supermarkets as a customer were responsible for 74% of direct recruitment of temporary workers and 46% of recruitment through labour contractors. Yet enterprises supplying supermarkets accounted for a larger amount of permanent employment than those without supermarkets as a customer.

There are a number of possible explanations for this finding. Labour contractors generate a more 'flexible' source of temporary worker provision than direct temporary recruitment. This helps to meet fluctuations within the ordering system and 'just in time' deliveries to supermarkets, particularly in response to promotions and sudden changes in consumer demand. To remain competitive, and in the face of declining prices, growers have had to reduce labour costs, which account for over 50% of production costs. The use of labour contractors helps to reduce the 'ongoing' costs of retaining directly employed temporary workers. Supermarkets tend to source from larger growers, who have less ability to find alternative work if they retain a large directly employed temporary labour force.

South Africa is an important supplier of fresh fruit (with some vegetables and flowers) to the UK during its 'window' from December through to March. Approximately 60% of fruit exports go to Europe, the majority to the UK. At the end of the 1990s there were approximately 2000 deciduous fruit farms in South Africa, employing an estimated 283,000 workers. Under apartheid, coloured workers had lived on-farm, supplemented by migrant black African workers from the 'homelands' at the height of the season. However, South African agriculture has undergone a rapid process of change since the early

1990s, with the introduction of a raft of labour regulation. This redressed the lack of protection and rights experienced by agricultural workers under apartheid. At the same time, South Africa has opened up to increasing competition from other Southern Hemisphere producers, and suppliers became more exposed to commercial pressures from supermarkets as described above. Many growers introduced a process of 'retrenchment', laying off on-farm workers and increasing employment of off-farm casual labour. With this there has been a steady increase in the use of labour contractors, or labour brokers as they are known in the country (du Toit and Ally, 2001). Studies suggest that approximately 50% of farms use contract labour in their operations (Barrientos and Kritzinger, 2003, and WIETA, personal communication).

Evidence from case studies in the UK and South Africa has revealed significant differences in the employment conditions of contract workers compared to non-contract workers. Contract workers are often not in receipt of legal employment benefits, such as a formal contract of employment, social insurance or pension (except in the UK following the introduction of the Gangmasters Licensing Act, discussed below). However, relations between workers and contractors can vary. Whilst some labour contractors at the bottom end of the spectrum are highly exploitative, others have a paternalistic relationship with migrant workers they recruit, creating a sense of belonging, even though these workers usually lack access to formal employment rights (Kritzinger et al., 2004; Frances et al., 2005). Some labour contractors thus provide informal benefits to their workers, such as food and medicine if they are ill, and teams of contract workers can provide mutual support to each other to offset risks.

Data on wages for contract workers in global production are difficult to obtain, and are unreliable. Employers and labour contractors are usually reluctant to divulge this information, or massage the figures. Many workers are paid on a piece rate basis and are unsure of their weekly or monthly wages. The labour contractor often takes deductions from their wages, with no proper documentation, and they are not paid for days they do not work (even if they turn up but are prevented, for example, by bad weather). Irregular payment and wage deductions can leave those with access to waged work in poverty, and worse in debt servitude to their contractor. The following examples provide an indication of wage data from the case studies:[4]

South Africa: A 2002 case study of 14 fruit export farms involving semi-structured interviews with 16 contract workers found that wages were quite variable. Individual wages for male contract workers ranged between SAR 150 and R400, with an average of R261.25 (US$43) per week. Female contract workers had individual weekly incomes ranging from R125 to R180, and an average weekly income of R152.75 ($25). For men the average was above the minimum wage of R187.50. But women were particularly vulnerable, with none earning above the minimum wage. Men worked on average for 10.5 months per year, whilst women worked on average for 9.3 months, yet their earnings had to cover them for the whole year (Barrientos and Kritzinger, 2003).

UK: A study carried out in 2003 of 36 workers, the majority recruited through 'gangmasters', highlighted the difficulty of calculating wage incomes. Formally all workers were meant to be paid the prevailing minimum wage at the time of GPB £4.20 per hour and £200 a week without overtime pay. Payment methods vary, with fieldworkers more likely to be paid a flat rate and pack house workers piece rates. However, wide variability in wages was found. Workers on piece rates on one site reported they could earn between £6 per day and £50 per day from piece rate depending on production conditions and productivity. Many workers had deductions made for accommodation, transport and undocumented migrant workers were also likely to have deductions made for their 'papers' (Frances et al., 2005).

Even where workers are recruited through formal legal channels, and have regular employment, they can be open to abuse through unscrupulous contractors or 'gangmasters'. Often this involves payments and forms of indenture away from the place of work. One example of abusive practices was highlighted following an audit of a UK gangmaster in 2004. He employed South African workers who had come to the UK as part of the Commonwealth Working Holidays Scheme and were, therefore, working legally. Their visas to the UK had been arranged by a travel company in Pretoria with whom their gangmaster had an arrangement. The travel agency provided travel loans, but with 100% interest charges and the workers had to sign an agreement that they would not leave the employment of the gangmaster until the loan was paid off. This agreement also said legal action would be taken against whoever had given a reference to the worker, usually their parents. Repayment of the loan would be taken from the workers' wages until the full amount was paid. Once they had arrived in the UK most of the workers were provided with overcrowded accommodation by the gangmaster. They were paid below the minimum wage, were discouraged from obtaining National Insurance numbers, and had deductions for transport, rent, loan repayments and sometimes other unspecified charges. They were often required to work long hours and continuous days. When these violations were put to the gangmaster, he claimed that he did not employ these workers as he had sub-contracted the work to another gangmaster and, therefore, was not committing any offence (*Guardian*, 29 March 2004).

In the UK media interest in the plight of gangmaster labour was most tragically bought to the fore by the death of 21 Chinese cockle pickers in Morecambe Bay in 2004. These were all undocumented migrant workers, controlled by unscrupulous gangmasters, who extracted long hours at low pay in hazardous and dangerous conditions. They had arrived in the UK via networks of people smugglers that channelled them to their gangmasters. They were committed to repayments for their 'passage' of sums around £5,000 to £10,000. These had been made with the assurance of their families, some of whom were forced to continue paying after their deaths (*Guardian*, 29 March 2004). Trade unions and NGOs have been particularly vocal in highlighting abuses of migrant and contract labour (Anderson and Rogaly 2005; Pollard 2006). The Ethical Trading

Initiative (ETI) Temporary Labour Working Group (TLWG) bought a number of different actors to address the problems associated with labour providers in UK agriculture. This contributed to the introduction of the Gangmaster Licensing Act, discussed below.

Contract workers can thus become entrapped in an informal system of debt servitude that exposes them to poverty whilst in work, and makes them highly vulnerable to extreme deprivation if they are unable to obtain work, become ill or infirm. Those working for unscrupulous contractors are often exposed to abusive labour practices. They are often 'invisible' because of the indirect nature of their employment. If they are undocumented migrants, their vulnerability is compounded by fear of exposure to the authorities and possible deportation. They may be caught in a circle of debt to their contractor and/or a related network of people smugglers, amounting to 'economic slavery'. Whilst the modern food system can provide many workers with good jobs, at its lowest depths in the twilight world of labour contracting, it also generates work that perpetuates extreme poverty and vulnerability.

Strategies to promote decent work for contract workers

There are a number of challenges addressing decent work for contract workers in global production networks, as examples above highlight. Firstly, their employment is inherently highly insecure. Labour contracting removes responsibility from the producer, and helps to keep labour abuses hidden from the normal mechanisms of labour regulation. Secondly, low levels of employer attachment mean the normal channels for accessing their legal rights and social protection are not available. Contract workers are also often unaware of their rights and face language barriers in obtaining information. Thirdly, job insecurity and lack of information undermine collective organization and voice amongst migrant and contract workers, who often fear they could loose access to already precarious employment if they speak out.

Labour contracting is likely to persist given the demand for flexible labour generated by the dynamics of supermarket retailing. Here we examine some approaches that have been developed at three levels: voluntary, multi-stakeholder and regulatory.

Trade Union initiatives

To access their rights, migrant workers need to have greater information, and the ability to access their rights. One challenge has been the difficulty for trade unions to organize contract or migrant workers. The mobility of workers, their lack of attachment to any one employer, poor language skills and fear of association with trade unions are all factors. Trade unions have traditionally focused on permanent or regular workers, and remained distant from contract or migrant workers. Some trade unions are recognizing the importance of developing innovative strategies to support and organize mobile workers, and have played an important role in campaigns to regulate labour contractors. A challenge for trade unions is whether they could begin to organize workers through labour contractors. This would depart from the production site as the point of organization, but would help them access workers irrespective of their mobility between sites.[5] A number of local and international NGOs have developed advocacy and provide support for migrant workers. NGOs and trade unions are increasingly collaborating to raise issues at country level, regionally and internationally. Collaborative approaches that link employment conditions, workers' rights and provision of social protection for migrant workers will help to generate greater social dialogue, and address the wider issues of decent work.

Voluntary company approaches

Under pressure from civil society organizations, some supermarkets and multinational food companies have introduced codes of labour practice for their suppliers, which are audited to ensure minimum employment conditions are met. Examples were found in the ETI impact assessment study where codes had had some positive effects in improving employment conditions for contract workers. In the UK two suppliers who had experienced problems in the use of 'gangmaster' labour had switched to the use of workers recruited under the Seasonal Agricultural Workers Scheme, or direct recruitment of workers from EU Accession Countries in Central Europe (Barrientos and Smith, 2006; Smith, 2006). However, codes appear to have been limited in their ability to address the situation for contract and migrant labour, and many suppliers keep such 'ghost workers' out of view when social auditors or large buyers visit their premises. Other studies also highlight limits of codes and social auditing as a means of addressing such embedded problems (Clean Clothes Campaign, 2005).

Multi-stakeholder initiatives: Relying on voluntary actions by individual suppliers is very unlikely to be sufficient. In South Africa and the UK there have been moves to rein in labour contractors, both through voluntary registration and monitoring through local multi-stakeholder initiatives and regulation. In the UK, the ETI set up the multi-stakeholder Temporary Labour Working Group (TLWG) in 2002 to establish minimum standards for labour contractors. The TLWG is composed of trade unions, NGOs and supermarket members. Its work was given impetus following the Morecambe Bay tragedy, and in 2004 it published a voluntary code and supported the registration of gangmasters. In South Africa, the Wine and Agriculture Ethical Trading Association (WIETA), was set up following the ETI wine pilot in the country, to provide independent monitoring of its own local code of labour practice. Its members include trade unions, NGOs, wine estates, agricultural producers, exporters, government and UK supermarkets. WIETA has also moved to include labour contractors in its membership, with the aim of monitoring their labour standards against its code of labour practice. Producers (wine estates and growers) who use registered labour brokers will then know that they are meeting accepted employment standards.

Regulation: Multi-stakeholder initiatives provide one form of independent monitoring of labour contractors, but will only ever cover those labour contractors who wish to opt into the system. They will always be under pressure from less scrupulous contractors who undercut them. Ultimately, therefore, regulation has to play a role if decent working conditions are to be ensured under a labour contracting system. Martin (2005) has argued that addressing labour contractors alone is insufficient, without also including the producers who hire them. In South Africa, the government amended the Basic Conditions of Employment Act (BCEA) to include labour contractors, and extend joint liability to the producer, even if they are not the direct employer, for all workers on their site. A big challenge, however, is enforcement given lack of resources for labour inspection. In the UK, following the Morecambe Bay tragedy, the TLWG played an important role in pressuring the government to support the Gangmasters (Licensing) Act (Pollard, 2006). Under this Act, all labour contractors have to be registered and monitored by the Gangmasters Licensing Authority, and producers have been made jointly liable if they do not use registered contractors. There are criticisms, however, that the Act is not extensive enough in its scope, as it only covers the agriculture sector.

Concluding remarks

This chapter has explored the changing dynamics of contract labour, using the example of seasonal agriculture in the UK and South Africa, and is particularly important in the context of extreme poverty given that this potentially effects the poorest and most vulnerable in society.

We have highlighted that the use of contract labour has facilitated a change in the type of employment relationship. Contractors are able to secure the 'right type of worker' whereby the intensity of work can be increased at peak times whilst maintaining quality of output. Labour contractors can provide large numbers of workers, often at short notice, with no long-term employment obligations, reducing the costs to the supplier but allowing them to meet tight production schedules. Many workers hired by labour contractors are thus highly vulnerable to poverty due to volatility of work, low wages, and lack of any benefits or protection. Often the critical point of exploitation is not within the work place itself, but in related arrangements (which could involve different agents) for activities such as the movement of workers between countries, accommodation or provision of documents. At the extreme, some workers find themselves in modern forms of 'economic slavery' that perpetuates their vulnerability to extreme poverty. Yet these workers are employed at the bottom of a highly profitable modern food chain, dominated by some of the world's largest supermarkets.

There are significant challenges in addressing the rights and protection of contract workers. Much labour regulation is premised on the assumption of stable employer attachment, which such workers rarely have. The main regulatory channels require open employment records, but these workers are often 'invisible'. The mobility of labour contractors between employers makes it extremely difficult for labour inspectors or social auditors to monitor their • employment practices. However, the positioning of such labour arrangements within wider social and institutional settings of global production networks does provide new points of leverage to promote decent work. Supermarkets keen to avoid adverse publicity promoted the extension of voluntary codes to contract labour.

However, much further empirical and conceptual analysis is needed to better understand the changing nature of labour contracting and its impact on the extreme poor, within global production or other sectors. In this case we have been restricted to analysing the role protective measures may take for contract labourers. However, if, as these case studies suggest, this type of labour arrangement is intensifying, it has important implications for addressing extreme poverty in the context of contemporary globalization, and to further understand this relationship at the micro level. There is increasing recognition that if paid work is to provide an effective route out of poverty, it needs to ensure basic rights and protection for workers. This commitment is reflected in the introduction in 2007 of decent work as a target under Goal One of the Millennium Development Goals. But if a significant proportion of the employment generated is through unregulated labour contractors, many more workers drawn into the system could find themselves trapped in a perpetual cycle of deprivation. It is essential that more innovative strategies are found to address abusive labour practices if this employment is to contribute to sustained poverty reduction.

Endnotes

1. In this chapter we use the generic term 'labour contractors' to describe different arrangements whereby third party agents recruit and employ workers. Many other terms are used in different countries including 'gangmasters' and 'labour providers' in the UK, and 'labour brokers' in South Africa.
2. This typology is based on investigation of labour contracting systems in South Africa, India and the UK. It can vary between countries, but this summary captures the main features.
3. For a more detailed discussion of the use of temporary and migrant labour see TUC (2003); Lawrence (2004); Anderson and Rogaly (2005); and Taylor and Rogaly (2004).
4. The data should be treated with caution given difficulties of accurate estimates of contract workers' wages. US$ equivalents were calculated using market exchange rates, not Purchasing Power Parity. The prevailing Rand exchange rate in 2001 was US$1 = R6.06.
5. Unions in the USA have begun to pursue this strategy.

References

ActionAid (2005) *Power Hungry: Six reasons to regulate global food companies*, ActionAid, London.

Anderson, B. and Rogaly, B. (2005) *Forced Labour and Migration to the UK*, Compass, Oxford and Trades Union Congress, London.

Barrientos, S. and Kritzinger, A. (2003) 'The poverty of work and social cohesion in global exports: the case of South African fruit', in D. Chidester, P. Dexter and J. Wilmot (eds), *What Holds Us Together: Social Cohesion in South Africa*, Cape Town, HSRC Press.

Barrientos, S. and Kritzinger, A. (2004) 'Squaring the circle – global production and the informalisation of work in South African fruit exports', *Journal of International Development*, 16(1): 81–92.

Barrientos, S. and Smith, S. (2006) *Ethical Trading Initiative Impact Assessment Summary Report*, ETI, London. Available from: www.ethicaltrade.org/d/impactreport [accessed 15 July 2009]

Clean Clothes Campaign (2005) *2005 Report – International Secretariat Clean Clothes Campaign: The Right to Organise – The Right to Know*. Available from: http://www.cleanclothes.org/documents/CCC_Activities_2005.pdf [accessed 22 July 2009]

Du Toit, A. and Ally, F. (2001) *The Externalisation and Casualisation of Farm Labour in Western Cape Horticulture*, Centre for Rural Legal Studies, Stellenbosch.

Frances, J., Barrientos, S. and Rogaly, B. (2005) *Temporary Workers in UK Agriculture and Horticulture*, report by Precision Prospecting for Department of Environment and Rural Affairs, London.

Gereffi, G. (2006) *The New Offshoring of Jobs and Global Development*, ILO Geneva.

Kritzinger, A., Barrientos, S. and Rossouw H. (2004) 'Global production and flexible employment in South African horticulture: experiences of contract workers in fruit exports', *Sociologia Ruralis*, 44 (1): 17–39.

Lawrence, F. (2004) *Not on the Label*, Harmondsworth: Penguin.

Martin, P. (2005) 'Merchants of labor: agents of the evolving migration infrastructure', International Institute for Labour Studies, DP/158/2005, ILO Geneva.

Martin, P. (2006) 'Regulating private recruiters: the core issues', in C. Kuptsch (ed.) *Merchants of Labour*, ILO, Geneva.

Milberg, W. (ed.) (2004) *Labor and the Globalization of Production: Causes and Consequences of Industrial Upgrading*, Palgrave, London.

Oxfam (2003) *Trading Away Our Rights*, Oxfam International, Oxford.

Plant, R. (2007) *Forced Labour, Slavery and Poverty Reduction: Challenges for development agencies*, mimeo, ILO, Geneva.

Pollard, D. (2006) 'The gangmaster system in the UK – the perspective of a trade unionist', in S. Barrientos and C. Dolan (eds) *Ethical Sourcing in the Global Food System*, Earthscan, London.

Sen, A. (1999) *Development As Freedom*, Oxford University Press, Oxford.

Smith, S. (2006) 'The ETI code of labour practice: Do workers really benefit?', report by the Institute of Development Studies, Brighton, UK.

Taylor, B. and Rogaly, B. (2004) 'Migrant working in west Norfolk', Norfolk County Council, Norwich.

Theron, J. and Godfrey, S. (2000) *Protecting Workers on the Periphery*, Institute of Development and Labour Law Monograph 1, Cape Town.

TUC (2003) 'Overworked, underpaid and over here: migrant workers in Britain', London, Trades Union Congress.

About the author

Stephanie Barrientos is a Senior Lecturer in the Institute of Development Policy and Management at The University of Manchester. She has researched and published widely on gender, global production, employment, decent work, trade and labour standards, corporate social responsibility, fair trade, and ethical trade.

CHAPTER 14

The role of health equity funds in meeting health-related needs of the poorest in urban areas of Cambodia

Chean Rithy Men and Maurits Van Pelt

In this chapter, we highlight the role of equity funds by using one Health Equity Fund (HEF) case study programme, operating in an urban area of Cambodia, a country that has the highest out of pocket health expenditure in the world. We firstly examine the role of HEFs in meeting the health-related needs of the poorest and review evidence regarding whether the schemes have any impact on the very poor, by analysing household data from the Urban Sector Group's (USG) database, and also by looking at hospitalization data to determine levels of hospitalization for the poor and the very poor in terms of length of stay in the hospital, cost of hospitalization, and benefits received from the HEF. In addition, we also examine whether the HEF has any impact on household health care expenditure, particularly debt related to health care costs among the poor and very poor living in urban slums in Phnom Penh city.

Introduction

There is a body of evidence showing that barriers to accessing public health care services can lead poor households into poverty and worsening health conditions (Whitehead et al., 2001; Wagstaff, 2002; Meessen et al., 2003). Among the many barriers, lack of financial means to pay for health care costs has been considered a major obstacle to the poorest people accessing care and treatment, as most health-related expenditure is made up of out-of-pocket payments. There is a growing literature showing that illness is in fact one of the main causes of impoverishment (Kassie, 2000; Kenjiro, 2005). It has been found that out-of-pocket spending by health service users is a major cause of indebtedness and impoverishment (Van Damme et al., 2004).

For this chapter we focus on Cambodia, a country that has the world's highest level of out-of-pocket payments as a proportion of total health care expenditure, at 70.6%. As a result, the poor spend more resources on health and suffer more poverty (Whitehead et al., 2001; Meessen et al., 2003). It has also been found that the poor population underutilizes public services; that is, fewer than 60% of the poor who are in need of health care use health services, as compared with 74% of better-off people (NIS, 2005a). Limited access to public health service leads poor patients to cope with their illness in various ways: reducing household consumption; borrowing money from others; selling land and assets to pay for health care costs; or forgoing treatment are some of the coping strategies often employed by the poor when they are confronted with illness (Meessen et al., 2003).

In many developing countries, governments have tried to find appropriate health financing strategies to improve health care access among the poor and very poor. Studies have shown that user fees at public health facilities have become one of the barriers to accessing health care for the poorest in many developing countries (Palmer et al., 2004). As a result, alternative strategies have been developed, such as fee exemption schemes, Health Equity Funds (HEF) and Community-Based Health Insurance (CBHI). This provides an excellent link between the 'programmes' and 'financing' sections of the book, by focusing on alternative health financing strategies, and specifically providing an example of the role health equity funds can play in this process.

The chapter is structured as follows. In the next section we provide further, Cambodia specific, background, and in particular focus on the role of HEF and CBHI's. The following section provides details on the samples used for the analysis before providing results in the penultimate section and summarizing the findings in the final section.

Background

Cambodia has a population of 13.6 million people, the majority of whom (more than 84%) are residing in rural areas, practicing traditional wet rice cultivation and other forms of agriculture and with poor access to basic services (NIS, 2005b). Cambodia is a low-income country (GDP per capita in 2005 was US$380), with few government resources to spend in the health sector. It is estimated that 35% of the population still lives below the national poverty line of less than $0.46–$0.63 per capita per day (NIS, 2005b). Rural poverty accounts for almost 91% of total poverty (World Bank, 2006). Poverty in Cambodia, as elsewhere, is caused by many factors. The two most salient health-related problems linked to poverty in Cambodia are malnutrition and access to health care (ibid.). The poor population underutilizes public services – that is, less than 60% of the poor who are in need of health care use health services, as compared with 74% of better-off patients (NIS, 2005b).

A study carried out by Hardeman et al. (2004) identified four barriers for those suffering from acute illness in Cambodia: financial, geographical, informational and intra-household. Another similar study was carried out on barriers related to accessing health care for acute illness among poor people in Cambodia; this identified various types of barriers, such as: physical access; ability to pay health care expenditures; knowledge and information about availability of assistance schemes; personal beliefs and perceptions of need and quality of health care; lack of trust in public health care facilities; and socio-cultural practices of health and treatment (Annear et al., 2006). However, these studies focused only on acute illness, not exploring the complexity and the dynamic nature of these barriers for patients with chronic conditions. The problem of access to health care for chronic non-communicable diseases (NCD), with the exception of HIV/AIDS, is much more significant than for acute illnesses, since the current health system in Cambodia is not set up to deal with chronic diseases. Very little effort is being put into addressing the burden of chronic diseases by either international or national actors. As a result, poor people suffering from chronic diseases, such as diabetes and hypertension, encounter complex and multiple barriers to access care and treatment, which often leads to a financial burden for households (Men, 2007).

Cambodia today has one of the highest proportions of out-of-pocket payments as a funding source for the health sector. Nationwide, out-of-pocket expenses and user fees represent 86% of total health expenditure per capita, or six times more than government expenditures on health.[1] Mean expenditure on health care has been pegged at $19.4 per household per month, 68% of which goes towards private medical or non-medical sectors. Only 18.5% is spent in the public sector (NIS, 2000). This owes primarily to payments to unregulated private practitioners, to unofficial payments in the public sector (Jacobs and Price, 2004; Van Damme et al., 2004) and to various participation costs, such as transportation costs (Hardeman et al., 2004).

The Cambodian government recognizes that health financing is one of the core functions of any health system, linking up with poverty reduction. As with all countries in the Asia-Pacific region, at different times there have been different financing arrangements in place to mobilize health resources. Cambodia is a poor developing country with an under-resourced health system. A number of health reform mechanisms have been tested or pioneered in the country, such as the user fee system; sub-contracting of government health service delivery to non-governmental providers (contracting); and CBHI and HEF schemes (Annear et al., 2006; MOH 2007).

Among these existing health financing schemes in Cambodia, HEFs have recently been marked as an important strategic part of the National Health Sector Strategy 2003–2007 (MoH, 2006). HEFs are considered an alternative strategy to help the poor and the poorest access public health services through a partnership between government and NGOs. HEF strategies attempt to improve access to health care services for the poorest by paying the provider on their behalf, acting as a third party payer. Thus the aims of HEFs are:

1. To increase the utilization of priority health services by the poor;
2. To reduce health related poverty (catastrophic health expenditures).

HEFs were pioneered in Cambodia in 2000 and spread rapidly across the country (Bitran et al., 2003; Hardeman et al., 2004; Jacobs and Price, 2006). During this time the number of HEFs has increased significantly, particularly in the past two years. For several years now, HEFs are no longer a private development initiative of NGO's: They have become part of official government policy. Government funding has been committed and disbursed to third party paying NGO's in order to be paid to public hospitals to reimburse them afterwards for having provided health services to the poor.

At the time of this study, there are 24 hospital-based HEF schemes in operation in Cambodia. These are mainly implemented by international and local NGOs, with funding from international donors. Of the 24 different HEF schemes operating as of January 2006, all but one (the Phnom Penh urban health project in squatter communities) operated in rural areas.

Several studies on HEF schemes have been conducted to measure their effectiveness in helping the poor access health care services. One of the earliest studies was carried out in Sotnikum operational district in Siem Reap province, where the scheme was first pioneered. This study indicated that the HEF had improved access to public health services for the poor and had increased community participation in health service improvement (Van Damme et al., 2001; Meessen et al., 2003; Hardeman et al., 2004; Jacobs and Price, 2006). A case study conducted in urban and rural areas pointed out that HEFs worked to increase access to health services for the poor at the referral hospital level in rural areas (Annear et al., 2006). However, the poor continue to face many constraints to timely access.

The studies mentioned above provide some evidence that HEFs to a large extent are effective in removing barriers to accessing public health care services for the poor. A recent paper by Noirhomme et al. (2007) comparing four HEF schemes in rural areas in Cambodia suggests that the schemes had a positive impact regarding utilization of hospital services by the poorest patients, which accounts for 75% to 52% of total hospital use. Although HEFs have been seen as improving access to hospital care for poor people, there is as yet no clear evidence to show whether HEF schemes are effective in helping to protect poor households from economic ruin by preventing them falling into debt owing to health care costs (Van Damme et al. 2004).

Objectives and methods

Objectives

In this section, we highlight the role of equity funds by using one HEF case study programme, operating in an urban area and coordinated by a local NGO known as the Urban Sector Group (USG). The first objective is to examine the role of HEFs in meeting the health-related needs of the poor and to review evidence regarding whether the schemes have any impact on the very poor, by analysing household data from USG's database, also looking at hospitalization data to determine levels of hospitalization for the poor and the very poor in terms of length of stay in the hospital, cost of hospitalization, and benefits received from the HEF. This section hypothesizes that both the poor and the very poor who are entitled to the scheme have equal access to health care services.

The second objective of the study is to examine whether the HEF has any impact on household health care expenditure, particularly debt related to health care costs among the poor and very poor living in urban slums in Phnom Penh city. This study hypothesizes that HEFs help to protect households from falling into the indebtedness that arises as a consequence of health care costs, and to reduce poverty through positive impacts on health care expenditure. In looking at this objective, we conducted qualitative research on health-related debts among poor households in two urban slums, one with the HEF and one without.

USG health equity fund

USG is a Cambodian NGO, established in 1993 and working in 48 poor communities in Phnom Penh. USG was originally established by a group of local and international NGOs working in Cambodia with the aim of helping squatter communities to address issues of poverty, including land, housing, basic infrastructure services, water, sanitation and solid waste disposal.

In 2002, USG took responsibility for implementing the equity fund of the Urban Health Programme (UHP), in partnership with the Municipal Health Department of Phnom Penh. Financial support to support the provision of the urban HEF for referral health services came from University Research Co Ltd, at least until March 2006. USG's HEF project covers six slums in the Phnom Penh vicinity, in Boeung Kak, Anlong Kagan, Anlong Kong, Samaki, Tonle Bassac and Borei Keila. These six slum areas were identified as having the most poor families.

USG uses pre-identification as its mechanism for identifying beneficiaries. The pre-identification process includes selecting poor families, first with the help of local authorities, and establishing a community-based network. Household pre-identification is carried out by user group members, who are volunteers who support the HEF programme in the communities where they live. They are recruited because they use public health services frequently, are engaged in many community activities, and are aware of and concerned about the well-being of the people in their community. They not only are involved in the pre-identification of poor families but also work to support people's health care access. User group members have three important capacities in the functioning of USG's HEF programme: *i)* they can find practical solutions towards helping poor people obtain access to health care; *ii)* they can hold the system accountable, all the way up the hierarchy; and *iii)* they are trusted by, close to and available for the people in their community.

In the pre-identification process, the user group members carry out interviews with poor families. They are trained on the theory of pre-identification and on how to conduct interviews, and use an interview form with questions relating to household composition, income and expenditure, assets and debts. Households are given different poverty scores and classified into different categories, 'non-poor', 'medium poor', 'poor' or 'very poor', based on the number of points that they score in interviews. Once all interviews are complete, the forms are sent to the USG office to be entered as records into a computer database, to be used for future analysis on household status. There are currently 10,358 households in the database in all 6 slums. Out of these, 711 are non-poor, 3,794 are medium poor, 5,970 poor and 378 very poor. Only the medium poor, poor and very poor qualify for support from the HEF. Households that qualify for such benefits receive their entitlements in the form of an HEF card, known locally as the USG book.

The distribution of the USG book is carried out in public places, such as temples or community centres. Families are thumb-printed on receiving their book(s). Everyone in the community has the right to participate in the procedure, so that other people in the community can observe who has received a USG book and who has not. This also allows people to make a complaint or demand a card if they feel they are poor also.

USG's HEF provides 100% benefits, which includes payment of user fees, medical costs, transportation and food for all beneficiaries, to cover both Minimum Package of Assistance at health centres and Complementary Package of Assistance at municipal hospitals in Phnom Penh. This is different from the HEF package in rural areas, which is divided into different packages: 50% (covers only hospital fees), 75% (covers transportation and hospital fees), and 100% (covers transportation, food and hospital fees). USG's HEF benefits package also covers chronic disease during a short in-patient stay at a municipal hospital. The situation for coverage for poor people with chronic diseases in the long term is not clear.

Site and sample selection

To measure the effectiveness of HEF schemes on hospital utilization among poor and very poor households in the study areas, we analysed USG's database on hospitalization. This contained information on length of hospitalization, total cost, and total payment from USG benefits. We took a total sample of 1,730 households which suffered from more than one day of hospitalization. These included: 45 non-poor, 769 medium poor, 835 poor and 81 very poor. The aim was to determine the median and mean length of hospital stay, total cost for hospitalization and total payments by the HEF to the municipal hospital. We then took a sub-sample of poor (835) and very poor (81) households, a total of 916 households, and correlated the poverty score (poor households have a poverty score between 10 and 14 points and very poor households have a poverty score between 15 and 16 points) with length of hospital stay, total cost and total payment by the HEF, using the Pearson correlation and 2-tailed testing.

For the analysis of the health care related debt, the sample for the study was taken from the USG database and included 1,704 poor and very poor households in the Boeung Kak squatter community, which had HEF coverage, and 1,505 poor households in the Tonle Bassac squatter community, where the HEF had not begun yet. Data were collected by USG user group members between October 2004 and April 2005 in the pre-identification process (see above), through yearly routine data collection. Data for analysis came from the households that are very poor, poor or medium poor. The non-poor are not included in the analysis. Respondents were asked if their household had borrowed any money over the past month and, if so, how much, the level of interest payments, the identity of the lender (friend, family member or money lender) and whether the debt was incurred to meet health care costs. The same questions were asked in relation to longer-term debt. To support the quantitative findings, 19 qualitative interviews were conducted with households in the Boeung Kak area and 24 in the Tonle Bassac area (a total of 43 interviews).

Findings

Hospital utilization by the poor and very poor

Table 14.1 indicates that only about 16% of all households in the USG database have received hospital care. The data also show that there is not much difference between the percentage of poor and very poor households receiving hospital care. Very poor households are gaining access to hospital care at the same rate as medium poor and poor groups.

If we look at length of hospital stay, we find that the very poor stay longer in the hospital than the other group, with a mean of 7.9 days (see Table 14.2). This means either that the illnesses of the very poor take longer to treat or that they can obtain more support from the HEF to stay longer in hospital. However, if we look at the total paid cost in Table 14.2, we see that there is not much difference between the poor and the very poor in terms of the benefits they receive from the HEF in terms of payment for hospitalization.

This means that the poor and very poor receive equal benefits from the HEF, despite their different poverty status. What seems troubling about this data is that non-poor households also appeared in the database as receiving hospital care, although they are not supposed to receive any benefits from the

Table 14.1 Hospitalization percentage in Cambodian sample

		Yes	No	Total
Number	Non-poor	47	664	711
	Medium poor	780	3,014	3,794
	Poor	853	5,117	5,970
	Very poor	81	297	378
	Total	1,761	9,092	10,853
%	Non-poor	6.6	93.4	100
	Medium poor	20.6	79.4	100
	Poor	14.3	85.7	100
	Very poor	21.4	78.6	100
	Total	16.2	83.8	100

Table 14.2 Length, cost and payment for hospitalization in Cambodian sample

		Cases	Median	Mean	SD*
Days in hospital	Non-poor	45	4	4.9	3.603029
	Medium poor	769	5	6.8	5.84072
	Poor	835	4	6.2	5.381415
	Very poor	81	5	7.9	7.284581
	Total	1,730	4	6.5	6.498844
		Cases	Median	Mean	SD
Total cost	Non-poor	45	60,000	85,011	83,291
	Medium poor	769	70,000	86,531	87,570
	Poor	835	54,500	78,891	87,716
	Very poor	81	50,000	88,054	92,299
	Total	1,730	60,250	82,876	82,876
		Cases	Median	Mean	SD
Total paid cost	Non-poor	45	60,000	84,744	83,549
	Medium poor	769	60,000	79,880	85,544
	Poor	835	47,000	79,097	188,145
	Very poor	81	45,000	80,468	90,965
	Total	1,730	51,000	79,656	144,522

*Note: SD = Standard Deviation

HEF scheme. Either there is a mistake with the data entry or there has been a mistake in record keeping by the HEF manager at the hospital. Or is there a leakage occurring to the non-poor?

In our sub-sample of the poor and very poor – when we carried out the Pearson correlation between poverty score and length of hospital stay, total cost and total payment by the HEF – we found that there was no significant difference between the poor and the very poor in terms of length of hospitalization and benefits received from the HEF scheme.

The evidence from the USG database indicates that there is no significant difference between the poor and very poor accessing health care services,

Table 14.3 Pearson correlation between poverty score and length of hospital stay, total cost and total payment by the Health Equity Fund in Cambodia

		Poverty score
Days in hospital	Pearson correlation	0.099
	Sig. (2-tailed)	0.003
	N	916
Total cost	Pearson correlation	0.008
	Sig. (2-tailed)	0.804
	N	916
Total paid cost	Pearson correlation	0.031
	Sig. (2-tailed)	0.355
	N	916

Note: Correlation is significant at the 0.01 level (2-tailed)

which suggests that benefits received from HEF schemes by these two different target groups in terms of accessing hospital care are effective. The very
poor are not under represented in the sample when compared with the poor.
This finding confirms early findings that HEF improved utilization of public
hospitals among poor people (Hardeman et al., 2004; Noirhomme et al., 2007;
Annear, 2006). However, there is no evidence at this stage to demonstrate
whether the HEF has any impact on household economic situation, in terms
of helping to prevent households from falling into poverty owing to health
care costs, or on health-seeking behaviour at the household level.

Evidence has shown that borrowing money is one of the coping mechanisms of poor households when confronting health care costs. Other mechanisms for coping with health care costs among poor households include
selling of assets, such as land, animals or equipment used for livelihoods activities. Oxfam GB (2005) found that 44% of people had sold land to pay for
health care. Catastrophically high health costs can easily represent 50% of
a household's annual non-food consumption (NIS, 2000). Cambodia Demographic and Health Survey (CDHS) data also shows that 45% of patients borrow money to meet the expenses of hospital treatment, which average $65 for
a serious illness. Thus, debt related to health care costs can lead households
into poverty.

In the next section, we examine how the HEF can help protect households
from falling into poverty owing to health care costs by providing evidence
on indebtedness related to health care expenditure among poor people living
in the two slum areas under study: Boeung Kak (with HEF) and Tonle Bassac
(without).

Impact of the HEF on debt for health care

We used data collected by USG user group members who carry out pre-identification through yearly data collection from households in slum areas in
Phnom Penh, using an interview form with questions relating to household
composition, income and expenditure, assets and debts. Households qualify
as 'non-poor', 'medium poor', 'poor' or 'very poor' (see above). Data were collected between October 2004 and April 2005 in the two areas under study.

In the pre-identification process, community user group members interview household members on their socio-economic status as a way to identify
the level of poverty of the household. One of the elements associated with
poverty is debt for health care. To obtain information on household debt,
user group members asked whether the household had borrowed any money
over the past month, if yes how much, whether the household paid interest,
whether the lender was a relative, a money lender or another, and whether the
reason for the debt was health care or not. The same questions were repeated
for older debts, except that the interest level was not asked for these. The resulting data give an idea of the level of indebtedness of the slum households.

Besides analysing data from the USG database, we conducted interviews with 43 households (19 in Boeung Kak and 24 in Tonle Bassac) in order to verify data reliability (whether households exaggerate about their debt because they want benefits) and to obtain a deeper understanding of the nature of debts and associated factors, particularly exploring the relationship between health care-related debts and types of ill health.

Table 14.4 below gives the numbers of households with debt for health care reasons and whether this debt is old or recent (more recent than a month).

A simple first analysis comparing the slum with the HEF and the slum without the HEF shows that the proportion of poor households with a debt for health care is much lower in that with the HEF. Table 14.4 shows households with debt for health care. Qualitative data from the 43 households in both slums indicated that data in the database were for the most part reliable: only one case of cheating occurred among the 43 and the amounts of the debts reported in the database were overall slightly lower than the levels of debt for health care found during the qualitative interviews. This suggests that the profile of the debt situation in the slums is not exaggerated.

Socio-demographics as risk factors in debt for health care

This study found that in the slum with the HEF, there are *overall* four times fewer people with a recent debt for health care reasons than in the slum without the HEF. The only exception is for 'other chronic diseases', where only three times fewer people are in debt for health care in the slum with the HEF, compared with the slum without. In other words, living in an urban slum without an HEF appears to increase the risk of having (recently) to take a loan to pay for health care by up to four times.

The level of indebtedness among poor households in both slums remain the same after adjusting other variable such as age, sex, years of schooling, chronic disease and old health care debt (using logistic regression; see Table 14.5). However, we observe that people in the slum area without the HEF are 3.4 (3.1–3.7) times more likely to have a recent health care debt.

Reported chronic disease as a risk factor in health care debt

People in the slum areas were also asked to report whether they had suffered from major illness (i.e. chronic disease) or not, and if they had, what it was. Interviewees were given 11 types of diseases considered to be major illnesses.

Table 14.4 Poor households (hhs) with debt for health care in Cambodia

P<0.001	Boeung Kak (with HEF)	Tonle Bassac (without HEF)
No. of hhs	1,704	1,505
Hhs with debt for health care	297	705
% of hhs with debt for health care	17	47

Table 14.5 Risk of being in debt for health care in Cambodia

Risk of health care debts in Tonle Bassac (no HEF) versus Boeung Kak (HEF)				
		Odds ratio	95% CI	P-value
Age		1.00	[1.00 – 1.00]	0.059
Sex				
	Men	1		
	Women	0.93	[0.87 – 1.00]	0.043
Years of schooling		0.95	[0.94 – 0.96]	<0.001
Income		1.00	[1.00 – 1.00]	<0.001
Chronic disease				
	No	1		
	Yes	1.07	[1.05 – 1.08]	<0.001
Old health debt				
	No	1		
	Yes	2.46	[2.22 – 2.73]	<0.001
New health debt				
	No	1		
	Yes	3.37	[3.09 – 3.68]	<0.001

The list is tailored to help the HEF connect patients to national disease programmes and to monitor how much people are spending on accessing services for their health problems. The list includes: no chronic disease; kidney disease; liver disease; mental disorder; other chronic disease; diabetes; HIV/AIDS; tuberculosis; hypertension; heart disease; and leprosy.

There is an important caveat to be made here. We cannot be certain that an individual who reports a major illness actually has it, nor can we assume that those who report not having a chronic disease are indeed free of it. Based on interviews, it was found that the most often reported disease was 'stomach disease', which people considered a chronic condition. Chronic stomach disease and many chronic symptoms of diseases mentioned by more than 800 residents of one of the slums were not included in the options on the list. This may be why there is such a huge proportion of 'other chronic disease' in both slum areas.

We have found that being in debt for health care was much higher for people reporting a particular chronic disease, such as diabetes, HIV/AIDS, heart disease and hypertension. In other words, people reporting these diseases are much more often in debt. For these patients, the HEF appears to reduce the problem of 'indebtedness for health' (because in the slum with the HEF the odds are lower), but because for people reported to have chronic diseases 'access to appropriate care' is so much more problematic, 'many more' people reporting these diseases have a recent debt for health care.

Meanwhile, given that this category dealt with 'reported' illness, one could wonder whether people reporting HIV/AIDS, for example, actually had the condition. For both HIV/AIDS and tuberculosis, it is unlikely that people report such conditions to community members without having been diagnosed by a competent health service provider. Reliability of data is likely to vary

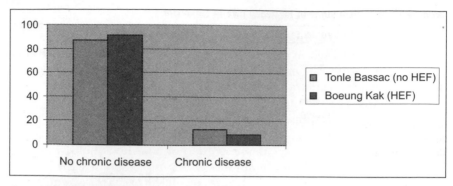

Figure 14.1 People reporting 'chronic diseases' (%) (P<0.001) in Cambodia

substantially according to reported chronic disease, thus *affecting data quality and comparability of the reported diseases* among themselves.

As such, reported chronic disease does not always mean that people have the reported chronic disease mentioned or selected during interview. However, we can note that the fact that proportionately more poor people report chronic disease in Tonle Bassac could simply be a symptom of less access to proper treatment there.

Lack of access to proper diagnosis in Tonle Bassac is illustrated by a higher number of 'other chronic diseases' in Tonle Bassac (8.89%) when compared with Boeung Kak (4.79%) (see Figure 14.2). This difference is found to be significant at (P<0.001).

Poor people living in Tonle Bassac (with no HEF) are 0.45 (0.3–0.7) times less likely to report having tuberculosis than the poor in Boeung Kak and 0.7 times less likely to report having hypertension than those in Boeung Kak. Together with the increased likeliness of 1.8 (1.6– 2.1) of people reporting 'other chronic disease', this could be seen as a sign of more problematic access to appropriate diagnosis in Tonle Bassac, where there is no HEF to facilitate this.

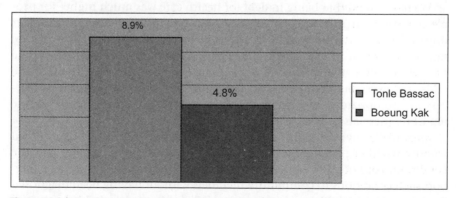

Figure 14.2 People reporting 'other chronic diseases' (%) (P<0.001) in Cambodia

Recent health care debt versus old health care debt

As mentioned above, the interviewer asks the household representative whether they had a recent debt (within the past 30 days) or not and, if so, if it was due to health care expenditures or not. The interviewer also asks who the money lender is and how much interest is being paid on this debt. Next, the interviewer asks the same questions about the existence of an old debt. Comparing the two slums, Table 14.6 below presents the total number of households with old and new debt due to health care expenditures.

As illustrated in Table 14.7 the proportion of poor households with debt for health care (long and short term) was significantly less where the HEF was implemented (17%) than where there was no HEF (47%). This was most pronounced for recent debt (incurred within the previous 30 days: 9% to 26%) but was true also for longer-term debt. Using a logistic regression analysis and controlling for age, sex, years of schooling and chronic disease, those living in the squatter community without the HEF were 3.4 times more likely to have a recent health care debt and 2.5 times more likely to have an old debt.

For a range of common chronic illnesses, poor households in the non-HEF area were on average four times more likely to incur debt for health costs than those in the area with the HEF. Using a logistic regression, these proportions remained almost the same after adjusting for age, sex, years of schooling, chronic disease and old health care debt, showing that those without HEF coverage were on average 3.4 times (3.1–3.7) more likely to have a recent health care debt.

Table 14.6 Numbers of households (hhs) with old debts vs. new debts for health care in Cambodia

	Boeung Kak (HEF) 1,704 poor hhs	Tonle Bassac (no HEF) 1,505 poor hhs
Recent debt, no old debt	160	394
Recent + old debt	37	113
Only old debt	100	198
Indebted hhs	297	705

Table 14.7 Percentage of households with old debt vs. new debt for health care in Cambodia

	Boeung Kak	Tonle Bassac
Recent debt, no old debt	9%	26%
Recent + old debt	2%	8%
Only old debt	6%	13%
In debt for health (P<0.001)	17%	47%

The availability of the HEF appeared especially to eliminate a large proportion of smaller debts for health care. In the HEF-supported area, there were few borrowers of small amounts (up to 50,000 Riel, or about $12); the majority borrowed larger amounts. In the non-HEF area, almost half of the households in debt had borrowed 50,000 Riel or less, whereas only some had borrowed more than 100,000 Riel. For debts above 500,000 Riel, the effect was the opposite: the proportion of borrowers with such debts was greater in the HEF supported area than in the non-HEF area. Consequently, the size of the average debt per household was slightly greater in the HEF supported area (277,558 Riel) than in the non-HEF area (248,593 Riel). Although the reasons for this outcome were not explained by the data, the trend may reflect behaviour related to prevailing interest rate conditions.

It appeared, however, that the HEF did not adequately cover the debt problem related to ongoing care for chronic diseases, and the likelihood of being in debt for health care was significantly greater for people reporting a particular chronic disease, such as diabetes, HIV/AIDS, heart disease or hypertension.[2] The study indicated that chronic disease patients were more vulnerable and more likely to slip through the safety net of financial support for the poor. Even so, the availability of the HEF still did appear to reduce the problem of indebtedness for health care for chronic diseases (indebtedness was lower in Boeung Kak than in Tonle Bassac).

The evidence from this study confirm that the availability of the HEF significantly reduces the need to borrow money to meet health care costs, strengthens the borrower's position in negotiating interest rates, and reduces the impact of health costs on impoverishment.

Conclusion

Previous studies have suggested that the HEF improves access to public health care among the poor population, particularly increasing hospitalization (Noirhomme et al., 2007, Hardeman et al., 2004; Annear, 2006). This study confirms these previous studies, showing that the HEF works to increase access to health services by the poor and to reduce out-of-pocket expenses for health care (including costs arising from transport, food and medication) for both the poor and very poor people despite one group being more disadvantaged in socio-economic terms than the other.

Further evidence from the USG database indicates that there is no significant difference between the poor and the very poor accessing health care services. The study also points out that, generally, beneficiaries greatly value their HEF entitlements and often feel empowered to demand better quality of service as a result. Prior studies only examined the evidence of HEF impact on hospital utilization, but not the economic impact of the scheme on the household. This study provides some evidence that the HEF schemes to some extent help to protect households from falling into indebtedness as a consequence of health care costs and to reduce poverty through impacts on health care expenditures. A recent study by Ir Por (2008) reported that HEF helped to protect households with a member suffering from HIV/AIDS from falling into debt due to healthcare costs, particularly at the diagnosis stage, as compared to HIV/AIDS affected households without HEF entitlement.[3] Mostly health care expenditure for HIV/AIDS patients occurred at the early stage of their disease but not at treatment stage as antiretroviral drug is free of charge according to the national policy (Men, 2007).

Currently, the success of the HEF in Cambodia has received wide attention, both from the national government and from international bodies. It has gained strong political support from the government, which sees it as a powerful mechanism to channel funds to the poor and as offering promising potential for direct service delivery to the most vulnerable of the Cambodian population.

The Ministry of Health, with support from donors and bilateral agencies and international NGOs, is implementing the scale-up of HEF schemes in the country. The attempt to scale-up national HEF has taken several years with several stakeholder meetings, expert consultations, national workshops and individual inputs. The first draft of the National HEF Implementation and Monitoring Framework was produced in 2003 and continued to be revised and finalized in 2008. The purpose of the national HEF implementation and monitoring framework is to provide guidelines and bring all the different HEFs that are operated by different NGOs under one umbrella overseen by the Ministry of Health.

However, up to now no study attempted to understand how the institutional arrangement works under which this framework operates or what lessons can be learnt and shared among such schemes. In addition there is still a lingering question about sustainability: to what extent will international donors and NGOs be willing to provide funding and what are their priorities? What are the responsibilities and commitments of the government in sustaining these schemes?

Recently, the Ministry of Health has been in the process of developing social health insurance (SHI)[4] as another alternative health financing strategy to reduce the impact of major health problems and to prevent people from falling into poverty. The government has recognized the potential of SHI as a major health care financing method for the future. Some broad policy guidelines and approaches have been formulated, but these have not yet been implemented.

As a popular, easy and effective poverty reduction instrument, donors have adopted the HEF more quickly to help reduce poverty than they have CBHI and SHI, which require particular technical expertise but which are, *per se*, more sustainable. Thus, to address the issues of sustainability and to find a way to support the very poor in the long term, one possibility would be to link HEFs with CBHI in such a way that the very poor can benefit. However, external donor money will be needed to pay the premiums so that very poor households can be enrolled in the programme. Coexistence and synergies with CBHI are the direction in which HEFs should be taken.

Endnotes

1. Out-of-pocket expenses are those paid directly by users and not covered by insurance or other provisions. The reference is from the World Bank report (2006).
2. Importantly, this data were not based on epidemiological records but on the perceptions of the patients themselves.
3. This information was presented at the EUROPEAID project workshop in Siem Reap, Phnom Penh, Cambodia on 19–20 December, 2007.
4. There are three approaches to SHI in Cambodia: *i)* compulsory social health insurance through a social security framework for public and private sector salaried workers and their dependants, through addition of health care to the Social Security Law passed in 2002 and administered by the National Social Security Fund; *ii)* voluntary insurance through the development of CBHI schemes sponsored by different development partners and national NGOs in the initial stages and health care providers for non-salaried workers' families that can contribute on a regular basis (SHI for this population sector should include all family members registered in the Cambodian Family Book); and *iii)* social assistance through the use of equity funds and later government funds to purchase health insurance for non-economically active and indigent populations.

References

Annear P. L., Wilkinson, D., Men, R. C. and Van Pelt, M. (2006) 'Increasing access to health services for the poor: health financing and equity in Cambodia', Working Paper, Phnom Penh, Cambodia.

Bitran, R., Turbat, V., Meessen, B. and Van Damme, W. (2003) 'Preserving equity in health in Cambodia: health equity funds and prospects for replication', online *Journal of the World Bank Institute*, World Bank, Washington, D.C.

Hardeman, W., Van Damme, W., Van Pelt, M., Ir, P., Heng, K. and Meessen, B. (2004) 'Access to health care for all? User fees plus a health equity fund in Sotnikum, Cambodia', *Health Policy and Planning* 19(1): 22–32.

Jacobs, B. and Price, N. (2004) 'The impact of the introduction of user fees at a district hospital in Cambodia', *Health Policy and Planning* 19(5): 310–21.

Jacobs, B. and Price, N. (2006) 'Improving access for the poorest to public sector health services: insights from Kirivong Operational Health District in Cambodia', *Health Policy and Planning* 21: 27–39.

Kassie, A. (2000) 'Credit and landlessness: impact of credit access on landlessness in Cheung Prey and Battambang districts, Cambodia', Centre for Advanced Studies, Phnom Penh, Cambodia.

Kenjiro, Y. (2005) 'Why illness causes more serious economic damage than crop failure in rural Cambodia', *Development and Change* 36(4): 759–83.

Meessen, B., Van Damme, W., Por, I., Van Leemput, L., and Harderman, W. (2003) 'The New Deal in Cambodia: the second year', Working Paper, Phnom Penh, Cambodia and Médecins Sans Frontieres, Belgium.

Men, Chean R. (2007) '"I wish I had AIDS": qualitative study on health care access among HIV/AIDS and diabetic patients in Cambodia', Research Report, Phnom Penh, Cambodia.

Ministry of Health (2006) 'Report of Health Equity Fund Forum', Phnom Penh, Cambodia.

National Institute of Statistics (NIS), Ministry of Planning (2000) *Cambodia Demographic and Health Survey 2000 (CDHS)*, NIS, Phnom Penh, Cambodia.

National Institute of Statistics (NIS), Ministry of Planning (2005a) *Cambodia Socio-Economic Survey 2004 (CSES)*, NIS, Phnom Penh, Cambodia.

National Institute of Statistics (NIS), Ministry of Planning (2005b) *Statistical Yearbook 2005*, NIS, Phnom Penh, Cambodia.

Noirhomme, M., Meessen, B., Griffiths, F., Por, I., Jacobs, B., Thor, R., Criel, B. and Van Damme, W. (2007) 'Improving access to hospital care for the poor: comparative analysis of four Health Equity Funds in Cambodia', *Health Policy and Planning* 22: 246–62.

Oxfam GB (2005) 'Briefing background: data analysis of patterns and trends in land dispute', Working Paper, Phnom Penh, Cambodia.

Palmer, N., Mueller, D. H., Gilson, L., Mills, A., Haines, A. (2004) 'Health financing to promote access in low income setting – how much do we know?', *The Lancet* 364: 1365–70.

Van Damme, W. and Van Leemput, L. (2004) 'Out-of-pocket health expenditure and debt in poor households: evidence from Cambodia', *Tropical Medicine International Health* 9(2): 273–80.

Van Damme, W., Meessen, B., and Von Schreeb, J. (2001) 'Sotnikum New Deal: the first year', report Phnom Penh, Cambodia, and Médecins Sans Frontieres, Belgium.

Wagstaff, A. (2002) 'Poverty and health sector inequalities', *Bulletin of the World Health Organization* 80: 97–105.

Whitehead, M., Dahlgren, G. and Evans, T. (2001) 'Equity and health sector reforms: can low-income countries escape the medical poverty trap?' *The Lancet* 358: 833–6.

World Bank (2006) *Cambodia: Halving Poverty by 2015? Poverty Assessment 2006*, World Bank, Phnom Penh.

About the authors

Chean Men is a Ph.D. candidate trained in the field of Medical Anthropology at University of Hawaii, Manoa, working specifically on therapeutic injection practices in Cambodia. Currently, Chean is a senior researcher at the Center for Advanced Study, managing two research projects related to poverty and illness and social protection, funded by the European Commission, and a board member of MoPoTsyo's Peer Education Programme on chronic diseases in Cambodia.

Maurits van Pelt is the Director of MoPoTsyo Patient Information Centre, (http://www.mopotsyo.org) a Cambodian NGO with Peer Educator networks on chronic diseases such as diabetes and high blood pressure. Maurits undertakes consultancies on health and poverty issues doing work that can strengthen the evidence base for innovative health interventions. The practical work described in the article continues and there is continuously a need to share the findings from analysing routine monitoring data.

PART IV

Making it Work: Finding the Money and Spreading the Knowledge

CHAPTER 15

Linking microfinance and safety net programmes: New pathways for the poorest

Syed Hashemi and Malika Anand

In this chapter we further bridge the link between specific programmes that have worked for the poorest and how to finance such schemes. The chapter considers the lack of provision of financial services to the poorest, within a social protection context. More specifically, we highlight that microfinance requires further innovation to reach down to ever-poorer people while safety net programmes need to link-up with financial service providers to empower the destitute to seek better and more sustainable livelihood opportunities. Microfinance, providing opportunities from the top, and safety nets, providing support from below, create the framework for the poorest to chart their way out of poverty. While some vulnerable people will always require state assistance, deliberate and carefully linking of microfinance and safety nets services can offer a new hope for achieving the Millennium Development Goal (MDG) of reducing poverty and graduating many of the poorest out of destitution. The graduation initiative of the Consultative Group to Assist the Poorest (CGAP) aims to develop new pathways of cooperation between social protection and microfinance experts. Too few people in microfinance truly comprehend its potential to open up opportunities for the poorest. Too few people in social protection realize how microfinance linkages can create tremendous potential for the destitute.

Introduction

Most governments and development agencies have committed to achieving the Millennium Development Goals (MDG) by the year 2015. A key goal is to halve the number of people living in absolute poverty or on less than a dollar a day. This commitment has motivated the development community to focus on economic growth that benefits the very poor. They seek to promote growth and reduce poverty through policies in sectors as diverse as infrastructure, social services, agriculture, industry, trade and macroeconomic policies.

Microfinance – or financial services for the poor – has proven to be a powerful tool to counter the exclusion of poor people from formal financial services. Access to financial services is so important because it underpins the ability of poor people to achieve the MDGs on their own terms in a sustainable way.

Microfinance allows poor people to benefit from reduced vulnerability, greater economic opportunities and increased income. Evidence shows that financial services also indirectly lead to improved schooling, better health conditions and greater empowerment of women (Littlefield et al., 2003).

But microfinance is not a panacea. With some notable exceptions, microfinance has had limited success in reaching the very poorest and the destitute. For the most part, microfinance providers select clients that are micro entrepreneurs – those who are already economically active and able to take advantage of market opportunities. Better delivery of financial products to the very poorest is needed. In this chapter, we further bridge the divide between micro-based studies of specific programmes that assist the poorest to consider some of the new pathways. This chapter furthers the previous chapter, by Men and van Pelt, that started to link between specific programmes that have worked for the poorest and how to finance such schemes. The chapter moves on from equity fund possibilities and considers the lack of provision of financial services to the poorest, within a social protection context. By providing a brief explanation of a microfinance graduation model, through the example of the Consultative Group to Assist the Poorest (CGAP), we provide alternative suggestions on how to reach the poorest through microfinance. The following section provides further background, from this perspective, before we review the 'graduation' model and present key lessons, and summarize in the final section.

Background: Social protection and providing financial services for the poor

The provision of financial services for the poor are essentially a matter of helping the poor turn their savings into sums large enough to satisfy a wide range of business, consumption, personal, social and asset-building needs (Matin et al., 2002) and the main product offered in microfinance has been a micro-credit designed for high-turnover microenterprises. The destitute – those without a sustainable livelihood, who are chronically food insecure, and who are so vulnerable that they require food aid or employment – have been largely excluded from most microfinance programmes. Recent efforts to increase the depth of outreach through effective targeting, a better understanding of client needs and more demand-responsive products (e.g. savings, insurance, money transfers, more flexible loans) are promising. Yet, it is also increasingly evident that many of the poorest may not be able to effectively use credit. Lending to poor people who cannot rapidly set up activities to generate immediate earnings for repayment will only result in over-indebtedness and lead to further impoverishment and increased vulnerability.

The poorest clients, those that microfinance has difficulty reaching, are precisely the focus of another fundamentally important development strategy – social protection. As we have seen (A. Barrientos, this volume) social protection policies aim to protect and promote the economic and social security of the poor.[1] Social protection encompasses a range of interventions, from safety net programmes to social insurance programmes. Safety net programmes such as food aid, free service provision, and guaranteed employment (Bhattacharya et al., this volume) serve those with immediate, desperate needs while social insurance programmes such as pensions, health insurance, unemployment benefits buttress those at risk of slipping down to the ranks of the destitute.

Though there is considerable overlap between the people microfinance and safety nets serve, the microfinance discourse has generally ignored safety nets and deliberately distanced itself from them. Microfinance practitioners often equate safety nets to grants and subsidies, which distort markets and hamper efforts to reach sustainable solutions. In turn, safety net experts commonly associate microfinance with credit services that create indebtedness and increase poor people's vulnerability.

However, after carefully studying different models (especially BRAC – see Hulme and Moore, this volume, for one such example) for serving the destitute, CGAP has recognized the potential for safety net programmes to work with microfinance services. Linking these two interventions can provide an important pathway for the destitute to 'graduate' out of extreme poverty (which we define as chronic food insecurity). CGAP is actively promoting this 'graduation' model by facilitating dialogue between social protection and microfinance experts and by conducting pilots to test the model in different countries.

The context of social protection

Considering the context of social protection further, the 1990 *World Development Report* called for state support for poor people, positing 'safety nets' as one of three components of a global poverty reduction strategy.[2] Throughout much of the 1990s, however, such safety nets were seen as a residual state responsibility to support those who fell below a minimum standard of living, rather than an integrated element of a broad based development strategy. Beneficiaries of safety nets were seen as passive recipients of aid rather than actors in a dynamic development programme.

The 1997 financial crisis in Asia and the ensuing crises in Latin America and the former Soviet Union sparked a renewed interest in social protection. During these crises, national governments and the donor community witnessed the extreme vulnerability of large segments of the population to macroeconomic shocks and realized their responsibility to provide a cushion to protect poor people in times of crisis. This realization broadened people's ideas about what social protection policies are meant to achieve. In the World Bank, this shift translated into an analytical framework that is evident in Conway and Norton's (2002) analogy of a safety net (that helps people at a certain level), a safety rope (that helps them only after they had fallen) and the trampoline which then helps them bounce back.

Social protection now includes two types of policy interventions. The first relates to *coping* policy actions aimed at people already living in absolute deprivation. These actions involve resource transfers and include famine relief, feeding programmes, public works programmes, and other traditional safety nets for the destitute. The second are *preventive* mechanisms intended to help plan for or counteract anticipated and unanticipated life events that can lead to sudden loss of livelihoods and reduction of income. Examples of these mechanisms include social insurance and pensions.

Strategies and thinking around coping policies, aimed at people living in absolute deprivation, has further progressed in recent years. These policies now go well beyond welfare and protection, to creating opportunities to enable the poorest to 'bounce back', by improving their economic conditions and participating in mainstream economic life. Safety net programmes are constructed to focus on both livelihood *protection* and livelihood *promotion*. While protection strategies seek to maintain and protect the assets already present in a household or community, promotion strategies seek to increase those assets. Livelihood promotion programmes have the goal of increasing income, building assets and otherwise strengthening the earning potential of participants (Norton et al., 2002).

Critical constraints to the success of social protection policies nonetheless persist. Foremost amongst these is the assumption that all households can be readied for the market and that, with adequate support, all households can independently pursue market driven economic activities. A more important problem is the absence of well-designed exit strategies. Most safety net programmes do not adequately prepare beneficiaries to enter the market. The economic activities of beneficiaries fail to provide them with an adequate stream of income to be sustainable once the programme ends. While they may be able to increase income in the short term, few programmes take into account the market viability of these income streams. Hence, in most situations, once the safety net support ends, beneficiaries' incomes decrease and they fall back into the ranks of the very poor and food insecure.

Financial services for the poor

Thinking about microfinance has also changed dramatically in the past few years. Microfinance has evolved from a niche market about one product (microenterprise credit) to a more diverse market with a wide range of financial services (Table 15.1). Market research has demonstrated that poor people – like all people – need diverse financial services to cope with risks, build assets, and plan for the future. Poor people need, and are willing to pay for, more services than just loans for businesses. For example, they need credit for emergency consumption, safe places to save, old age pensions, reliable remittance services, insurance, and other services to mitigate risk. Savings and insurance are particularly relevant for poor people because of their vital need to manage risk. Until recently, however, most microfinance providers only offered working capital

Table 15.1 Range of financial services available to the poor

Type of Service	Common Products	Uses
Deposits (pensions)	Fixed Flexible Long term contractual	Consumption smoothing Short-term emergencies Life cycle needs
Microinsurance	Life/accident Property Health Crop	Mitigating unanticipated risks
Credit	Emergency loans Consumption loans Small loans	Meeting sudden emergencies Start-ups for the very poor

loans. With increased competition and a greater emphasis on understanding client needs, microfinance institutions (MFIs) are now moving away from offering a 'mono-product' to offering more client-responsive products.

However, and as noted at the start of the chapter, there are limits to the outreach of microfinance. In spite of this pro-poor product development, microfinance has achieved limited outreach amongst the poorest. Even in Bangladesh, where almost all MFIs are focused on the poorest, less than a third (32%) of NGO clients live on less than a dollar a day (Zeller and Johannsen, 2006). Rigorous assessments of conventional MFIs indicate that between 15% and 30% of the entering clients of conventional MFIs (*Compartamos* in Mexico, ACODEP in Nicaragua and KWFT in Kenya) are in the bottom third of the economic spectrum (Figure 15.1).

Even among the most poverty-focused MFIs (Nirdhan in Nepal and SEF in South Africa), less than half of incoming clients are in the bottom third of the economic spectrum (Figure 15.2).

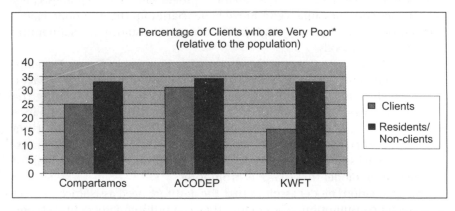

Figure 15.1 Percentage of MFI clients who are very poor (relative to the national population): Compartamos, ACODEP and KWFT
* Very poor people here are those in the bottom third of the economic spectrum.

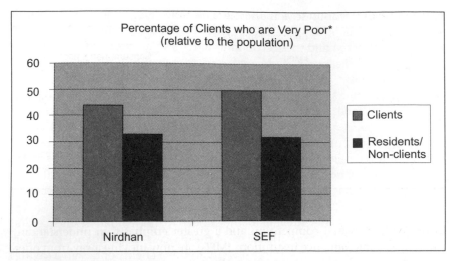

Figure 15.2 Percentage of MFI clients who are very poor (relative to the national population): Nirdhan and SEF
* Very poor people here are those in the bottom third of the economic spectrum.

The graduation model: Linking safety nets and microfinance

Hence, although large proportions of microfinance appears not to have reached the poorest, one example, provided by CGAP is slightly different – having been actively promoting pro-poor financial products and better targeting to identify the poorest. It has also been searching for excellent innovations in how to serve the poorest. The Bangladeshi Rural Advancement Committee (BRAC) has emerged as a powerful example of successfully serving the poorest. It has developed a 'graduation' programme that combines safety net services and microfinance to move beneficiaries up the economic ladder from chronic food insecurity and dependence on assistance, to maintaining sustainable livelihoods.

The BRAC IGVGD (Income Generation for Vulnerable Group Development) programme, which links food grain distribution to financial services, has reached 2 million destitute women. Even a year after completing the programme, two-thirds of the participants have remained in microfinance programmes (Hashemi and Rosenberg, 2006). BRAC's Targeting the Ultra Poor (TUP) Programme, which links consumption support and asset transfers to financial services, has served 150,000 beneficiaries and is the basis of the graduation model that CGAP is promoting.

The 'graduation' model assumes that the destitute need assistance to meet their urgent consumption needs before they can utilize microcredit. It therefore starts with safety net services, such as food aid or a subsistence allowance, to meet consumption gaps and provide beneficiaries with the 'breathing space' to build economic activities. Beneficiaries also receive a sequenced package of livelihood support services including business advice, training and an asset transfer to build these economic activities. At the end of this supportive process, beneficiaries can use a microfinance loan to further expand their economic activity.

The model starts with first addressing poor people's urgent consumption gaps through food aid or a living stipend (see Figure 15.3). An assessment of local economic opportunities and market linkages are conducted at the same time to determine a menu of livelihood options. Beneficiaries then receive business development advice and skills training on an economic activity of their choice (chosen with programme staff guidance). After the training is completed, a small grant (generally around US$100-$150) or a productive asset is provided to 'kick-start' the activity.

Savings services are integral to the model to both build resilience and financial discipline. At the early stages of this process, microfinance providers can either provide savings services directly to these clients or design a savings product that the safety net programme implements. While savings cannot kick-start the complex process to escape deep poverty, it plays an important role in mitigating sudden risks (emergency cash requirements) and in building up capital. Sometimes microfinance providers will also extend small loans to beneficiaries a year into the programme. This helps with the economic activities they have selected to pursue and also builds confidence and credit discipline.

After the economic activity grows for a period, beneficiaries are ready for credit services to build the activity further. At this point – once clients have

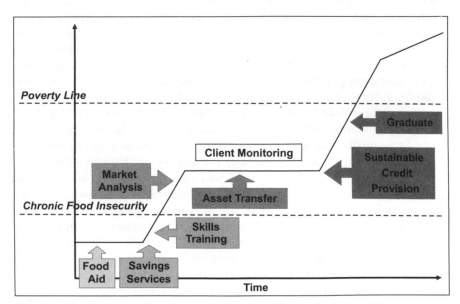

Figure 15.3 From chronic poverty to microfinance chart: The graduation model

met their consumption needs, accumulated savings, learned simple business skills, and ultimately, managed small loans – they are weaned off the consumption subsidy. As the grant programme phases out, most participants are prepared to pursue independent economic activities and graduate to becoming clients of regular microfinance programmes, and escape chronic food insecurity and material deprivation.

Key lessons

The first key to the 'graduation' model is appropriate sequencing – grants, followed by savings and livelihood support services, followed by small amounts of credit. The second key to the model is to ensure that safety net programmes and microfinance programmes concentrate on their own comparative advantages. Financial institutions need to focus on developing financial services that are appropriate for people towards the bottom of the spectrum. Safety net programmes need to focus on targeting and delivery of grants, transfers, or livelihoods and employment support. A sequenced linkage between these two development interventions will allow many of the poorest to start with safety nets, gradually move to savings services and small credit, before finally graduating into conventional microfinance programmes.

Demonstration pilots

CGAP and Ford Foundation are currently managing five pilots to demonstrate the graduation model – three in India, and one each in Haiti and Pakistan. Each pilot is expected to last two years. In India and in Haiti, microfinance institutions (SKS, Bandhan and Fonkoze) have been the lead partners, working mostly independently to provide grants, training and health-care services. The model has provided these otherwise commercially oriented MFIs a concrete way to serve the very poor. In Pakistan, the pilot is jointly managed by a large government poverty alleviation programme (PPAF) and the World Bank. In addition three other pilots are planned – one in Yemen with the government's Social Fund for Development, another in Ethiopia, with USAID's Food for Peace Programme and a third in Honduras, with Plan International.

An experimental impact assessment is in place for most pilots to assess the model's success in creating changes in the lives of participants. After selection, participants are randomly divided into a beneficiary group and a control group (in some cases control group members still receive safety net services, in some they receive no services at all). This method utilizes a randomized control group and is able to control for all selection biases. Information on economic, health, schooling, and other variables will be collected every six months from both groups. The assessment will seek to test if safety net clients who are gradually linked to financial services demonstrate greater economic and social well-being relative to excluded individuals.

Summary: Partnership between social protection and microfinance experts

In this chapter we bridge the link between specific programmes that have worked for the poorest and how to finance such schemes. The chapter considers the lack of provision of financial services to the poorest, within a social protection context. More specifically, we highlight that microfinance requires further innovation to reach down to ever-poorer people while safety net programmes need to link up with financial service providers to empower the destitute to seek better and more sustainable livelihood opportunities.

Microfinance, providing opportunities from the top, and safety nets, providing support from below, create the framework for the poorest to chart their way out of poverty. While some vulnerable people will always require state assistance, deliberate and careful linking of microfinance and safety nets services can offer a new hope for achieving the MDG goal of reducing poverty and graduating many of the poorest out of destitution. CGAP's graduation initiative aims to develop new pathways of cooperation between social protection and microfinance experts. Too few people in microfinance truly comprehend its potential to open up opportunities for the poorest. Too few people in social protection realize how microfinance linkages can create tremendous potential for the destitute.

Endnotes

1. The World Bank defines social protection as 'public interventions to *(i)* assist individuals, households and communities better manage risk and *(ii)* provide support to the critically poor' (Holzman and Jorgensen, 2000).
2. The other two components were human development and labour-intensive growth.

References

Conway, T. and Norton, A. (2002) 'Nets, ropes, ladders and trampolines: the place of social protection within current debates on poverty reduction', *Development Policy Review* 20(5): 533–40.

Hashemi, S. and Rosenberg, R. (2006) 'Graduating the poorest into microfinance: linking safety nets and financial services', *CGAP Focus Note* 34.

Holzman, R. and Jorgensen, S. (2000) 'Social risk management: a new conceptual framework for social protection and beyond', *Social Protection Discussion Paper 6*.

Littlefield, E., Morduch, J. and Hashemi, S. (2003) 'Is microfinance an effective strategy to reach the millennium development goals?', *CGAP Focus Note 24*.

Matin, I., Hulme, D. and Rutherford, S. (2002) 'Finance for the poor: from microcredit to microfinancial services', *Journal of International Development* 14(2): 273–94.

Norton, A., Conway, T. and Foster, M. (2002) 'Social Protection: defining the field of action and policy', *Development Policy Review* 20(5): 541–67.

Zeller, M. and Johannsen, J. (2006) 'Is there a difference in poverty outreach by type of microfinance institution? The case of Peru and Bangladesh', paper presented at the global conference on *Access to Finance: Building Inclusive Financial Systems*, organized as part of the annual conference series of The World Bank and the Brookings Institution in Washington, D.C., 30 and 31 May 2006.

About the authors

Syed Hashemi is the Director of Bangladesh Development Institute (BDI) at BRAC University. Before taking up this post he was senior fellow at the Consultative Group to Assist the Poorest (CGAP) in Washington, D.C. He specializes in microfinance and has a particular interest in enhancing the poverty reduction impacts of MFIs and designing 'graduation' programmes that permit the extreme poor to gain access to MFIs.

Malika Anand is Associate Microfinance Analyst, joining CGAP in 2006. Before joining CGAP she spent a year in the Dominican Republic on a Fulbright Fellowship. She has a bachelor's degree from the University of Chicago in Public Policy Studies with a minor in South Asian Languages and Civilizations. She speaks English, Spanish, and rudimentary Hindi.

CHAPTER 16

Revenue mobilization for poverty reduction: What we know, what we need to know

Tony Addison

Mobilizing more domestic revenues to increase public spending on poverty reduction and human development is crucial, since aid cannot fill the entire financing gap. Taxation is a key dimension of effective governance. While economic growth can generate a rising tax base, too often the increase in growth does not translate into much of a rise in public revenues, especially when tax institutions are weak. As a result, poor people often face high taxes with little in the way of compensating public services or public infrastructure. This chapter explores the means of raising funds for 'pro-poorest' programmes. It focuses on the fiscal dimension of growth and poverty and discusses the growth-revenue-poverty nexus. The chapter analyses the impacts of globalization, trade liberalization and climate change on public revenues. It also examines the tax reforms required for developing countries to deliver revenues needed for pro-poorest programme spending. The chapter concludes that trade liberalization and climate change can in fact undermine the efforts to raise funds for pro-poor programmes. Tax reform is therefore needed to strengthen tax institutions and promote revenue mobilization for poverty reduction programmes.

Introduction

Over the last few chapters we have focused on how programmes highlighted as potentially useful for the poorest might be financed. In this final 'financing' chapter we conclude with a macro viewpoint by considering how we might mobilize public revenue options for such poverty reduction programmes. We focus on public finance as this is inherent to effective state-building; states that cannot mobilize revenues, spend those revenues on pro-poor services and infrastructure, and raise additional resources from domestic and international public borrowing, will be states that fail to provide appropriate financing for the programmes that meet the needs of the poorest. They also tend to become failed states as grievances around who gets taxed – and who gets the public money – undermine their legitimacy.

Much attention is given to mobilizing more aid particularly in light of the ambitious Millennium Development Goals (MDGs) (Commission for Africa,

2005; UN Millennium Project, 2005). Although increased aid is certainly needed, aid cannot be fully effective without heavy investment in the institutions of public finance – tax collection, budgeting, auditing, and debt management (Addison, 2006; Brautigam et al. 2008). These institutions determine whether the resources added by aid are transmitted through the system of public expenditure management and then into pro-poor services and infrastructure. Domestic revenues are also necessary to complement aid, since aid-financed capital investments have large recurrent budget implications.

The expenditure side of the public finances receives much attention. This is understandable given the many problems that countries have in focusing public money on development priorities and managing its use. But the revenue side is equally important, for the reasons given above, and therefore is the focus of this chapter. The next section discusses growth's role in raising the tax base, with the resulting increase in revenue offering the potential to fund more pro-poor programme spending. The section places the growth-poverty debate in the context of World Trade Organization (WTO) trade liberalization and rising world commodity prices as well as long-term climate change, all of which affect the South's prospects for growth and therefore its revenue base. The following section assesses where we stand on tax reform, and its relationship to poverty reduction, while the final section concludes that there is much that we do not know in the area of revenue reform in the context of reaching the poorest, and that revenue mobilization is crucial for ensuring that the services, programmes and infrastructure needed by the poorest are properly funded.

The fiscal dimension of growth and poverty

Poverty's relationship to growth remains at the centre of the policy debate. The link from higher growth to chronic poverty reduction is direct if the extreme and chronically poor are smallholders achieving higher output or micro-entrepreneurs selling new manufactures and services, and indirect if rising labour demand provides more wage employment. Our evidence on how the chronic and extreme poor relate to growth is fragmentary. But what we do know indicates limited participation in many countries. In the worst cases, people are too sick or disabled to work at all, or elderly and infirm after a lifetime of back-breaking work. The healthy work hard but without much education their opportunities are limited, a disadvantage compounded by their few productive assets. And the extreme poor are often found in landlocked regions with the least agricultural potential and the worst transport and communications infrastructure – separating them from national growth processes (CPRC, 2008).

A country's tax base rises with the growth in national income, market activity and trade (both domestic and international) that accompanies growth. This provides greater scope for collecting more public revenue through indirect and direct taxes as well as customs duties. More revenues can finance more pro-poor public spending; cash transfer systems to poor families, of the type outlined by Chaudhry in this volume (often linked to incentives to send children to school); greater provision of basic health care as well as sanitation and water infrastructure; roads and communication systems that enhance existing livelihoods and generate new ones, and employment guarantee schemes (i.e. many of the programmes outlined in this volume). Many more items can be added to this list, but without higher public revenues, funding pro-poor spending will remain dependent on foreign aid (if it is available). And higher domestic revenues are essential to building the state itself, both at the centre and at regional and local levels, and therefore to the prospects of effective (and democratically accountable) service delivery. For these reasons it is vital to look to the revenue link between growth and chronic poverty reduction, not just to the direct (producer) and indirect (employment) links.

Discussion of the growth-revenue-poverty nexus is not just a matter of domestic policy. It must be placed in the context of the large forces now working their way through the global economy which affect the South's chances of growth and therefore its prospects for breaking out of poverty. Here I concentrate on just three areas that are of key importance in the global economy at the moment: trade liberalization under WTO auspices; the rise in world commodity prices; and long-term climate change (the consequence of global industrialization and urbanization).

Globalization promises to raise national income in the South, with the larger emerging economies benefiting the most. WTO trade liberalization promises a more efficient pattern of global production and exchange resulting in higher global growth. This has long been a matter of dispute (see the contrasting positions of Bhagwati, 2005, and Chang, 2002). But the South is heterogeneous and therefore the impact varies significantly across countries – there are losers as well as winners – and the impact for the South is not always as positive as it is made out to be. For example, world trade liberalization could be negative for those least developed countries (LDCs) losing preferential access to the protected European Union (EU) market – if the EU does reform its agricultural policy (Panagariya, 2005). West Africa's cotton farmers will gain from higher prices if the EU and the US reduce subsidies to domestic producers, but Bangladesh (a net cotton importer for its clothing and textile sector) will lose. And the impact on income distribution within countries is very uncertain and not necessarily pro-poor.[1] Much can therefore go wrong for the extreme poor, and a recent simulation of WTO trade liberalization for Bangladesh concludes that:

> Nominal income ... increases more for rural households, particularly landowners; consumer prices also increase more for rural households because of their high consumption of agricultural goods. More important, consumer prices increase more for the poorest household categories, for whom agricultural (food) consumption is proportionately higher. The net effect is greater welfare losses and poverty increases among the poorest households.

The greatest beneficiaries of the Doha agreement appear to be rural large farmers who capitalize on rising returns to agricultural capital (primarily land). (Annabi et al., 2006: 463)

The World Bank estimates that world poverty will fall by 95 million people if global agricultural and manufacturing trade are fully liberalized – an unlikely event it must be said, given the present impasse in the Doha 'Development' Round (Hertel and Winters, 2006).[2] But a scenario of lower global poverty is consistent with increased poverty in LDCs that lose favourable trade access. And within countries for which liberalization is economically favourable it is perfectly possible for gross domestic product (GDP) per capita to rise, for the 'least poor' to gain (e.g. smallholders producing export crops), and for the lot of the chronically poor to worsen (e.g. higher food prices for the unemployed and casual workers). We do not know exactly what the outcome will be, but many poor people could suffer very quickly. Nevertheless there is much complacency in policy circles on trade liberalization and its effects.

Promises of aid-for-trade (concessions) are made, but will this aid reach the poor when fiscal systems are weak, and how much will reach the chronic and extreme poor? We do not know. What will be the impact on domestic revenues and spending if GDP falls in LDCs that lose preferential market access, and can pro-poor spending be protected from the resulting revenue shortfalls? We do not know. Can poor countries successfully reform their tax systems to accommodate their reduced dependence on tariff revenues that accompanies liberalization of their own trade? We do not know.

Globalization, associated with strong growth in China and India, is also raising world commodity prices, after years of stagnation. Whatever the future holds, in this regard, it is clear that, for the moment at least, higher commodity earnings constitute a net external transfer to the South that far exceeds total aid flows.[3] Unlike aid, this transfer comes without any conditionality attached to its use, especially as regards to fiscal management (a point made by Collier, 2007).[4] Now that domestic agricultural marketing is less regulated, producers receive a larger share of higher 'soft' commodity prices and are capable of making good use of the windfall (although the benefits flow disproportionately to larger producers: Brazil's large estates, for instance).

Minerals and energy are different stories, and ones where fiscal management really counts. States share in these windfalls through taxation agreements with foreign investors in mining etc. or via direct ownership of producers. Botswana is one of the few examples of successful management of mineral revenues (Leith, 2005). Discouragingly, in many countries a great deal of this windfall never appears in the fiscal accounts; when it does its use is often opaque and, when information is available, it indicates that revenues are often spent unwisely – with little if any poverty impact. Angola and Equatorial Guinea are examples of deep poverty alongside enormous natural wealth that is not being used for the public good. Moreover, these valuable natural resources are often located in chronically deprived regions (e.g. the Niger Delta); the system of public finances does not share much, if anything, of the windfall with the people who live alongside the mines and oil wells.

In summary, the fiscal link between growth and poverty is especially important when growth itself is narrowly concentrated, and especially so in mineral-rich economies where the direct and indirect poverty effects of growth in the mineral enclave are very limited (the poorest generally participate in such enclave growth neither as producers nor as employees). We need to know more about how the revenue flows from natural resources are being used, how to get greater transparency around their use, and how to transmit them more effectively into pro-poor public spending.

The third aspect of globalization considered here is long-term climate change: globalization's downside is an adverse environmental impact via global warming. Some countries are disproportionately affected – the low-lying which are vulnerable to floods by rising sea-levels, for example – and the South is more vulnerable than the North because most developing countries are located in the tropics (where the effects will be most severe) and are more dependent on agriculture, the sector most vulnerable to changes in temperature and rainfall (H.M. Treasury, 2006). Crop yields in Africa could fall by 12% by 2080 according to some estimates (Pounds and Puschendorf, 2004). The retreat of the glaciers is of particular concern; increased flooding is already occurring in parts of the Andes, East Africa's highlands and the Himalayas.

What, the reader might ask, has all of this to do with public revenue, and thus the potential to finance poverty reducing programmes? A great deal is the answer. Climate change will cut Southern growth rates, leading to a loss in tax revenue that, if not offset by increased external transfers, will endanger efforts to increase pro-poor spending.[5] It therefore makes sense for developing countries to be given a share of the global tax base, especially the carbon taxes that could cut carbon emissions (Sandmo, 2004). For the low-income countries this would supplement their meagre domestic tax bases. However, one of the main stumbling blocks for poverty reduction is the quality of domestic fiscal systems and their ability to absorb and spend the additional resources from global taxes effectively in a pro-poor way. Of course a large proportion of the revenue from global taxes can be transferred to, and used by, the very best NGOs (Bangladesh's BRAC and Grameen for example) and this needs to be incorporated into the discussion of 'innovative finance' mechanisms now underway in the UN and elsewhere. But some measures can only be taken by governments: very large-scale public infrastructure projects and effective and impartial legal systems to protect the poor and their assets from violence and expropriation. These all require an effective (and honest) system of public finances. In summary, we need to know how to help poor countries reduce their fiscal vulnerability to climate change, and how to mobilize the global tax base for poverty reduction.

Tax reform

The previous section discussed the global dimension of the growth-revenue-poverty nexus, raised some of the macro-based issues that are central in governments being able to provide adequate programme funds in order that programmes for the poorest remain a possibility. We now turn to the national dimensions of the issue, to ask: how much scope is there for tax reforms to deliver the revenues needed for pro-poor programme spending?

Taxation is now at the forefront of the fiscal policy debate, more attention having been previously given to the expenditure side of public finance (Addison and Roe, 2004, Di John, 2006).[6] Many countries in sub-Saharan Africa (SSA), but also some in South Asia, taxed agriculture heavily until reform began in the mid-1980s. This taxation was 'implicit' (in the structure of policy) rather than 'explicit' (since agricultural income is difficult to tax). In many cases implicit taxation of this kind exacerbated the plight of the poor by undermining agricultural growth. Reform therefore began by reducing this implicit taxation of agriculture through sector reforms (ending the monopoly of state marketing boards) and macroeconomic reforms (devaluation in particular, where overvalued currencies acted as an implicit tax on agricultural export producers). This went alongside reform of the customs and excise services so that revenues actually reach the government rather than ending up in private hands. Dependence on trade taxes has been reduced by: reforming sales taxes (and introducing the more efficient Value Added Tax (VAT)); reforming income and capital gains taxes, including taxes collected by local governments; and generally broadening the tax base and making the administration of tax institutions more efficient (and honest).

These reforms have had mixed results so far. Most developing countries hope to mobilize tax revenues around 15–20% of GDP. But in practice very similar tax structures and tax rates appear to generate very different revenues across different countries, and many countries have still not reached the 15–20% target (Heady, 2004). Tanzania and Uganda have both struggled to raise revenues despite successful macroeconomic stabilization programmes (while Rwanda has been a success in revenue reform). The revenue base in low-income countries remains highly volatile (reflecting the high variance in output when economies are relatively undiversified). There is also a balance to be struck in mobilizing more revenue and doing so in ways that do not discourage growth itself (through punitive tax rates that undermine investment incentives or encourage low-return investments). This includes investment by the poor themselves.

Despite these reforms, raising tax revenue-GDP ratios remains a tough task in poor countries where economic activity is predominantly rural, much urban economic activity is informal, and therefore the resulting incomes are difficult to tax (Heady, 2004). Tax administrations often have limited capacity to assess tax liabilities, and wealthier taxpayers are often adept at evasion. Improvements are generally patchy, and corruption has proven resilient to successive institutional reforms in many SSA countries (e.g. Tanzania and Uganda). Consequently, there is a wide gap between statutory tax rates and what people actually pay (the effective rate).

Simplifying the tax regime to make it institutionally straightforward is important to raising revenue, although this may sometimes reduce its progressivity (thus a 'flat tax' is simple but regressive). Much of the reform agenda has focused on central government taxes. But lower levels of taxation are important as well, especially for the poor. Again these are often complex and sometimes unfair in their burden. Local government taxes can be arbitrary and in some cases are harshly enforced. Unfairness arises when the resulting revenues are not spent on improving those local services that benefit the majority, including the poor. This increases the public's reluctance to pay, which is prevalent in Africa where the incidence of local taxes is often regressive (Addison and Levin, forthcoming). Just as bad taxation at the national level undermines the authority of the state, so bad taxation at the local level undermines the legitimacy of local government. Getting local taxation right is a big agenda, and we need to know more.

VAT is now in place across many countries in the developing world. If it is reasonably sure that this is funding pro-poor expenditures then there is less of a case for exempting items that the poorest consume: otherwise a careful analysis should be undertaken to determine whether there are any possibilities for exemptions that can benefit the poor. Excise duties can be used to dampen some of the regressivity of VAT on the overall indirect tax structure (Addison and Levin, forthcoming). Excise duties can potentially raise large amounts of revenue, and countries such as Mozambique have made progress on this in recent years.

Indirect taxes have been at the centre of the reform agenda for years, partly because they are the easiest to collect. But direct taxes also offer scope for mobilizing more revenue. An increased role for direct taxation has been a pro-poor strategy in Ghana (Colatei and Round, 2000; Younger, 1996). More revenue can be mobilized by simplifying the structure of direct taxes since this facilitates compliance. In Kenya, only 30% of those who should pay income taxes do so (Karingi, 2004). A single rate of income tax with a high exemption level is usually feasible and not too demanding of the capacities of tax institutions (Heady, 2004). The income tax threshold should be high in order to protect poor households; in Kenya, the personal income tax threshold is four times the per capita income and has been regularly raised relative to per capita income to avoid over taxing low-income earners (Addison and Levin, forthcoming). Ultimately, countries must create comprehensive income tax systems if they are to fund inclusive comprehensive pro-poor programmes, and welfare states in the manner of European countries, that target the poorest households (CPRC, 2008).

Finally, we must improve national capacities to understand the incidence of the tax system, and to simulate the distributional impact of alternative revenue structures. This is especially urgent now that WTO liberalization is reducing tariff rates and new tax structures need to be implemented to compensate for the lower share of trade taxes in government revenues. Micro-simulation models of tax reform are common in developed countries and do much to inform public debate and policy-making. Shortly after the UK's annual budget is presented the Institute of Fiscal Studies releases an analysis of what this means for key household groups (the single mother with two children, for example). Micro-simulation remains a rare tool in developing countries; one exception is a UNU-WIDER project, which has built micro-simulation models for five SSA countries. This has a user-friendly software interface through which policymakers can try out different types of tax reform – without technical knowledge of the models themselves.[7] Such tools generate a more informed political debate on tax reform and by reducing uncertainty regarding the distributional effects may improve the chance of building political coalitions in support of pro-poor reform. We need to know more.

Conclusions

This chapter has provided a macro perspective on raising funds for programmes for the poorest, discussing the relationship between growth and poverty through a fiscal lens. In the section on the 'fiscal dimension of growth and poverty', we placed the growth-poverty debate in the context of globalization's impact on the South's prospects for growth, namely WTO trade liberalization, rising world commodity prices, and global climate change. Each of these has revenue implications. Trade liberalization will not necessarily be positive for all the world's poor, especially the chronic and extreme poor, and revenues need to be mobilized to maintain poverty reduction programmes. Trade liberalization could cut the revenue base in some countries, and global climate change could undermine efforts to increase pro-poor public spending by reducing national output. We conclude that there is too much complacency among policymakers in this area, and too little is known about the impact on the poorest.

In the following section we assessed where we stand in tax reform and how much progress countries have made in building the tax systems needed to meet the poverty challenges set out in previously. But major differences remain between statutory and effective tax rates due to weak tax administration, ad hoc exemptions, and corruption. Local taxes are problematic for the poor – their share of local public spending is low – and taxing the informal sector remains difficult to justify until the net fiscal incidence (the incidence of taxes and spending taken together) is pro-poor. This chapter has certainly not covered all issues. For example the gender dimensions of revenue mobilization are noticeably absent. There is much that we do not know about the role of revenue mobilization in poverty reduction, and this remains a fertile area for research and policy-making.

Endnotes

1. Nissanke and Thorbecke (2006) discuss the methodological difficulties in understanding globalization's impact on the poor.
2. See Stiglitz and Charlton (2006) on the Doha Round.
3. This is in aggregate; the commodity windfall is distributed unevenly across poor countries and for those without large endowments of minerals or energy, or large agricultural exportables, aid flows remain the largest external inflow.
4. This is not to imply that *all* aid-conditionality is bad.
5. Heller (2003) discusses the fiscal impact of climate change.
6. This section draws upon ongoing work with Jörgen Levin (Addison and Levin, forthcoming).
7. Available at: http://models.wider.unu.edu/africa_web/ [accessed 16 July 2009]

References

Addison, T. (2006) 'Debt relief: the development and poverty impact', *Swedish Economic Policy Review* 13: 11–36.

Addison, T. and Levin, J. (Forthcoming) 'Tax policy reform in developing countries, UNU-WIDER, Helsinki.

Addison, T. and Roe, R. (eds) (2004) *Fiscal Policy for Development: Poverty, Reconstruction and Growth*, Palgrave Macmillan, London and New York.

Annabi, N., Khondker, B., Raihan, S., Cockburn, J. and Decaluwé, B. (2006) 'Implications of WTO agreements and unilateral trade policy reforms for poverty in Bangladesh: short- versus long-run impacts', in T. W. Hertel and L. A. Winters (eds), *Poverty and the WTO: Impacts of the Doha Development Agenda*, pp. 429–466, World Bank., Washington, D.C.

Bhagwati, J. (2005) *In Defense of Globalization*, Oxford: Oxford University Press.

Brautigam, D. Fjeldstad, O-H. and Moore, M. (eds) (2008) *Taxation and State-Building in Developing Countries: Capacity and Consent*, Cambridge University Press, Cambridge.

Chang, H-J. (2002) *Kicking Away the Ladder. Development Strategy in Historical Perspective*, Anthem Press, London.

Colatei, D., and Round, J. I. (2000) 'Poverty and policy: experiments with a SAM-based CGE model for Ghana', paper presented at the XIII International Conference on Input-Output Techniques, 21–25 August, Macerato, Italy.

Collier, P. (2007) *The Bottom Billion*, Oxford University Press, Oxford.

Commission for Africa (2005) *Our Common Interest: Report of the Commission for Africa*, Commission for Africa, London.

CPRC (2004) *The Chronic Poverty Report 2004–05*, Chronic Poverty Research Centre, Manchester. Available from: http://www.chronicpoverty.org/cpra-report-0405.php [accessed 23 July 2009]

CPRC (2008) *The Chronic Poverty Report 2008–09*, Chronic Poverty Research Centre, Manchester. Available from: http://www.chronicpoverty.org/cpra-report-0809.php [accessed 23 July 2009]

Di John, J. (2006) 'The political economy of taxation and tax reform in developing countries', *UNU-WIDER Working Paper* 2006/74.

Heady, C. (2004) 'Taxation policy in low-income countries', in T. Addison and A. Roe (eds), *Fiscal Policy for Development: Poverty, Reconstruction and Growth*, Palgrave Macmillan, London and New York.

Heller, P. S. (2003) *Who Will Pay? Coping with Aging Societies, Climate Change, and Other Long-Term Fiscal Challenges*, International Monetary Fund, Washington, D.C.

Hertel, T. W. and Winters, L. A. (eds) (2006) *Poverty and the WTO: Impacts of the Doha Development Agenda*, World Bank, Washington, D.C.

H.M. Treasury (2006) *Stern Review on the Economics of Climate Change*, H.M. Treasury, London.

Karingi, S. N. (2004) 'Tax reform experience in Kenya: a country case study', paper prepared for the tax project, UNU-WIDER, Mimeo, Helsinki.

Leith, C. (2005) *Why Botswana Prospered*, McGill-Queen's University Press, Montreal.

Nissanke, M. and Thorbecke, E. (eds) (2006) *The Impact of Globalization on the World's Poor: Transmission Mechanisms*, Palgrave Macmillan for UNU-WIDER, London and New York.

Panagariya, A. (2005) 'Agricultural liberalisation and least developed countries: six fallacies', *World Economy*: 1277–1299.

Pounds, J. A. and Puschendorf, R. (2004) 'Clouded Futures', *Nature* 427: 37–42.

Sandmo, A. (2004) 'Environmental taxation and development', in A. B. Atkinson (ed.), *New Sources for Development Finance*, Oxford University Press for UNU-WIDER, Oxford.

Stiglitz, J. and Charlton, A. (2006) *Free Trade for All: How Trade can Promote Development*, Oxford University Press, New York.

UN Millennium Project (2005) *Investing in Development: A Practical Plan to Achieve the Millennium Development Goals*, United Nations, New York.

Younger, S. (1996) 'Estimating tax incidence in Ghana using household data', in D. E. Sahn (ed.), *Economic Reforms and the Poor in Africa*, Clarendon Press, Oxford.

About the author

Tony Addison is Professor of Development Studies at the University of Manchester, Associate Director of the Brooks World Poverty Institute (BWPI) and Associate Director of the Chronic Poverty Research Centre (CPRC), University of Manchester. His publications include *From Conflict to Recovery in Africa* (Oxford University Press), *Debt Relief for Poor Countries* (Palgrave Macmillan), *Fiscal Policy for Development* (Palgrave Macmillan) and *Poverty Dynamics: Inter-disciplinary Perspectives* (Oxford University Press with D. Hulme and R. Kanbur). He is currently working on chronic poverty, post-conflict reconstruction and development finance.

CHAPTER 17

Making poverty reduction work for the poorest

David Hulme and David Lawson

Introduction

This book has argued that tackling extreme poverty is the global priority for our generation. In the volume we have sought to raise awareness of the problems faced by the poorest and provide practical examples of the types of knowledge, programmes and policies that can help the extreme poor improve their lives and the prospects of their children. We hope that these examples help to inspire policymakers and programme planners and managers to work more effectively with the poorest people and communities.

This focus on extreme poor people is founded on robust ethical grounds – that the poorest people merit the greatest international, national and personal attention and effort if our world is to achieve a minimally acceptable level of social justice. Beyond these, there are strong pragmatic grounds. Addressing issues of extreme poverty sooner rather than later will achieve much greater results at a dramatically lower cost. The demographic window of opportunity (lower household dependency ratios) open for the next 20 years will never be available again. More broadly, reducing extreme poverty can provide global public benefits in terms of political and economic stability, public health and more manageable patterns of international migration.

As the book has shown, the poorest are not a homogeneous group. Most of them are 'working poor' but a minority are unable to engage with the labour market and take advantage of any benefits that may arise through the processes of globalization. The poorest include those who are discriminated against; socially marginalized, ethnic, religious, indigenous, nomadic and caste groups; migrants and bonded labourers; refugees and internally displaced people; disabled people, those with ill-health and the young and the old (see, for example, Bandyopadhyay et al., this volume). In many contexts poor women and girls are the most likely to experience lifelong poverty (see Bhattacharya et al., this volume). Despite this heterogeneity it is possible to identify five main traps that underpin extreme poverty. These are discussed in detail in the Chronic Poverty Report (CPRC) 2008–2009.

The first of these are *insecurity traps* – people who live in insecure environments (conflict and violence, natural hazards, economic shocks) and who are susceptible to individual shocks (especially ill-health – see Men and van Pelt, this volume) or household shocks and who have few assets or entitlements have little capacity to cope with these shocks and stresses. Often the only coping strategies available to them involve trading off short-term survival (by selling assets as a coping mechanism – see Lawson, this volume) with long-term goals (such as asset accumulation or children's education).

Social discrimination forms the basis of the second trap. The poorest people also often have social relations – of power, patronage, competition, collaboration and support – that trap them in exploitative relationships or deny them access to public and private goods and services. These are based on class and caste systems (see Bandyopadhyay et al. in this volume on the Siddi community of India), gender, religious and ethnic identity, age and other factors.

Poor work opportunities are also a major trap that undermines the efforts of the poorest. Where there is limited economic growth or growth is concentrated in enclaves, work opportunities are very limited or of a short term and casual nature (see Bhattacharya et al., this volume). Workers might also be exploited, through poor working conditions or poor work standards and ineffective labour laws (see S. Barrientos, this volume). Such work permits day-to-day survival, for the poorest, but does not enable a family to accumulate assets, educate its children or plan long-term work strategies.

Two further traps are *limited citizenship*, where the ultra poor have no meaningful political voice and lack effective political representation, and *spatial disadvantage* – living in remote areas, certain types of natural resource base, political exclusion and weak economic integration can all contribute to the creation of intra-country spatial poverty traps.

The chapters in this book have identified several key policy responses to the aforementioned traps. Of particular attention is the focus on a few policy areas, such as *social protection* (see the chapters in this volume by A. Barrientos, Hulme and Moore, and Chaudhry) with policies ranging from 'giving the cash' to the poorest to 'traditional' microfinance type programmes. Alongside this are issues of *anti-discrimination* and *gender empowerment* (see chapters by Bandyopadhyay et al. and Pillai and Sudarshan) and ensuring that the ultra poor are able to access *public services* such as health care (see Men and van Pelt) and are able to take advantage of microfinance-based programmes (see Hashemi and Anand, and this chapter), which can underpin long-term efforts to eradicate extreme poverty. Such programmes help to generate political and social institutions that ensure a distribution of public goods and services that contribute to justice and fairness within a society. However it is not just the programmes that are of importance, but also how to finance these from a macro level (Addison, this volume) down to the unique facets of programmes that are then able to target the ultra poor.

What we know

While some chapters have revealed that relatively little is known about the conditions and causes of extreme poverty, and even less about how to reduce extreme poverty, the knowledge base is strengthening. At the macro-level, it is evident that economic growth can reduce poverty and extreme poverty in some cases and for some parts of a national population. However, as revealed by the case of Bangladesh (Serajuddin et al. in chapter 2) economic growth by itself is not enough to eradicate extreme poverty. Other policies – providing social protection (see A. Barrientos and Chaudhry in this volume), making the delivery of public services (especially health and education) pro-poorest (see Men and van Pelt, this volume), tackling social discrimination (see Bandyopadhyay et al. and Bhattacharya et al., this volume), connecting rural areas to the national economy, and more – are needed if the poorest are to improve their prospects and the vicious circle of intergenerational poverty is to be broken. These policies need to be full-blooded social policies, such as the 'social protection systems' that Ravi Kanbur is arguing for (see Foreword to this volume) and not the short-term and token responses – social funds and social safety nets – that the World Bank has envisaged. The argument that such social policies 'cannot be afforded' must be tackled directly and indirectly. Basic social policies can be afforded in most countries (see Addison, this volume) if domestic resources and foreign aid are used more effectively and if domestic taxation is gradually raised. Indirectly, it is essential that the costs of 'not affording' social policy are spelled out – increased child and maternal mortality, the intergenerational transmission of poverty, reduced social cohesion and increased prospects for social and political breakdown. A lack of economic growth may keep people in poverty, but so does a lack of basic human security.

At the micro-level, our knowledge base is also strengthening. It is clear that microfinance can rarely reach the poorest and make a significant different to their life chances. The world's leading microfinance institutions in Bangladesh (ASA and BRAC) and elsewhere now publicly acknowledge this. Although Professor Yunus of the Grameen Bank, who has contributed so much to assisting the poor, still claims that microcredit helps 'the poorest of the poor', the portfolio of the Grameen Bank reveals that this is not the case (see Hulme, 2008). As is revealed by BRAC's Targeting the Ultra Poor (TUP) Programme (see Hulme and Moore, this volume) and Chile Solidario (see A. Barrientos in this volume) the extreme poor will often need much more than a microenterprise loan to escape poverty. Combinations of social assistance, improved access to services, confidence building, training and even asset transfers may be needed.

While knowledge about such programmes can be transferred from organization to organization and from country to country such knowledge needs to be carefully adapted to different contexts and systematic experimentation and social learning are required. Several microfinance institutions have begun to ask how they can reach down to people who are 'too poor' to be their clients and how to design 'graduation programmes' (see Hashemi and Anand in this volume). One of the hopes for the future must be that some of the social entrepreneurs who have helped make 'the poor bankable' will move on to the task of making 'the very poor less vulnerable'. Interestingly, the training and attitudes of field-level staff who work with the poorest may need to be distinct from those who work with the poor on microfinance, microenterprise development and agriculture. The vulnerability and social exclusion of the poorest may mean that they respond best to field staff with counselling and social work skills rather than the more discipline-oriented and rules-based approaches of microfinance and other development workers.

Beyond the issues of 'what' types of policy and programme can assist the poorest, this book has also pointed out the opportunities that now exist to increase knowledge about why some people are very poor and remain very poor. There are now an increasing number of panel datasets available so that the analysis of how the poor and poorest are faring during periods of growth and/or periods of recession, can be examined. This has been done for Bangladesh (Serajuddin et al., this volume) but could be done in many more countries. Economists and econometricians could deepen their findings by adopting Q-squared (quantitative and qualitative) methods (Lawson and Kabeer, this volume). And, collaboration between researchers and practitioners can identify simple but robust criteria for identifying the poorest and targeting programmes on their needs and rights (see Sen and Begum and Alviar et al. in this volume). In the past researchers may not have had the data or methods to find out about the lives of the extreme poor but that is no longer the case. This is also the situation for practitioners: if knowledge seems to be lacking then organizations can ask fieldworkers to have conversations with non-clients (i.e. people who are too poor, too excluded, too sick, too old to be clients of that organization). They can ask them questions such as: 'Why haven't our organizations reached you?', 'Is what we do irrelevant to what you need?', 'What could we do that could make our services useful for you?', and many other simple but useful questions that could reveal the obstacles that hinder the targeting and assisting of the poorest. You do not need to be an academic to make useful knowledge.

Ways forward: Learning from experience and advancing policy to the poorest

There are huge *Policy and Political Challenges* that must be faced if the needs and rights of the extreme poor are to be advanced. They need two related but distinct forms of assistance (CPRC, 2008). In the short term, to survive and improve the immediate prospects for themselves and their children, the poorest need practical actions that meet their most pressing needs and create a platform for future improvements. This entails policy change, the allocation of additional resources and finding effective ways of delivering services to them. In the longer term, to promote social and political institutions that give the extreme poor voice (directly or through representatives or enlightened elites) and support their demands, they need strategic guidance that helps them organize and develop political linkages.

Poverty Reduction Strategies (PRSs) are a vehicle that could do this. They have made some progress in shifting the style of policy-making towards a more evidence-based approach and on raising the attention paid to poverty analysis. However, a detailed analysis of the most recent PRSs (CPRC, 2008) indicates that the extreme poor are generally invisible to those who make and implement national policies. While some of the policies identified in PRSs would be beneficial for the poorest there is little evidence of specific analyses being made, or policy choices selected, that focus on the problems of the extreme poor. While social protection is on the agenda in several PRSs how it will reach and benefit extreme poor people is unclear. Issues of justice and citizenship are not themes for PRSs, anti-discrimination and gender empowerment are marginal and, surprisingly, urbanization and migration rarely feature in PRSs.

While policy choices are important it is the allocation of resources and the quality of implementation that determines their poverty reduction impact. This depends on the political processes that underpin public policy and management. PRSs could have been a device to mobilize political constituencies in support of the poor and extreme poor and to build fairer social compacts. To date this opportunity has not been seized. Both first and second generation PRSs are widely regarded as donor-owned products in most countries. The third generation PRSs must be seen as a national political project that opens up formal political processes (parliamentary debates, party manifestos, electioneering) and informal spaces and networks for the voices of poor and extreme poor people and their representatives and for the growing body of evidence that is available.

The volume confirms and extends the findings of the Chronic Poverty Reports (2004 and 2008) that *social protection, and particularly social assistance, has a crucial role to play in reducing extreme and chronic poverty*. It directly tackles the insecurity trap by protecting poor people from shocks and reducing their extreme vulnerability; it helps them conserve and accumulate assets so they can improve their livelihoods and productivity; and, it contributes to transforming economic and social relations in ways that strengthen the longer-term livelihood prospects of the poorest.

There is now a growing body of evidence that shows social protection is a cost-effective means of reducing extreme poverty, that it is affordable and that it can be scaled-up even in relatively poor countries. However, effective social protection policies require a supportive domestic political environment to agree to their initiation, expansion and financing. In many countries social protection has been introduced by dominant political parties, and often by 'executive champions', rather than being the result of civil-society lobbying. Programmes have often been seen as a component of nation building rather than the donor's 'poverty reduction' perspective. Providing sound technical advice to political parties and executive champions is thus a key activity – and this needs to be linked to domestic debates about ideology and national goals. Often, it is claimed that economic elites and the middle class will oppose social protection because they fear it will lead to dependency and tax increases.

Transformative social change is also required to assist the poorest. Social orders, such as class, caste or gender relationships, have a profound influence on the lives, well-being and aspirations of extreme poor people. Such orders are not fixed but they evolve over time. At present, under the pressures of globalization, they are changing more rapidly than ever but the convergence hypothesis (that at some stage in the future all societies will be relatively similar) has been discredited. Existing social orders underpin at least three of the poverty traps that keep poor people poor – social discrimination, limited citizenship and poor work opportunities.

Promoting progressive social change is an issue that is barely mentioned in PRSs and poverty reduction policy documents, but it is central to tackling extreme and chronic poverty. Extreme poor people do not just need 'good policies' they need societies that will help them achieve their rights and voice their issues. The present volume has provided further evidence of three priority social goals – gender equality, social inclusion and increased agency (options to exit from oppressive relationships and to articulate voice).

Finally, poverty reduction and development efforts to assist the poorest should not be classified as social expenditures that will not yield an economic return. While some programmes (disability grants, humanitarian aid) may not give a clear return, many programmes aimed at the poorest (child support grants, conditional cash transfers) are both poverty reducing and raise the prospects for improved productivity and grassroots economic growth in the future.

We hope that the materials in this book will help to inspire researchers to be more innovative in their work, to work with practitioners, and to listen more closely to what the world's poorest people say about the problems they face and the support they would like. Those who seek to assist the poorest must not let their commitment mask the fact that the extreme poor themselves are the leading actors in overcoming their poverty. To date, when their existence is recognized at all, the poorest are perceived both by policymakers and in the popular imagination as dependent and passive. Nothing could be further from the truth. Most people in extreme poverty are striving and working to improve their livelihoods and the prospects for their children, in very difficult circumstances they have not chosen. They need real commitment, matched by actions and resources, to support their efforts and overcome the obstacles that trap them in poverty and deny them citizenship.

References

CPRC (2004) *The Chronic Poverty Report 2004–05*, Chronic Poverty Research Centre, Manchester, UK. Available from: http://www.chronicpoverty.org/cpra-report-0405.php [accessed 16 July 2009]

CPRC (2008) *The Chronic Poverty Report 2008–09*, Chronic Poverty Research Centre, Manchester, UK. Available from: http://www.chronicpoverty.org/cpra-report-0809.php [accessed 16 July 2009]

Hulme, D. (2008) 'The story of the Grameen Bank: from subsidised microcredit to market-based microfinance', *BWPI Working Paper no. 60*. Available from: http://www.bwpi.manchester.ac.uk/resources/Working-Papers/bwpi-wp-6008.pdf [accessed 22 July 2009]

About the authors

David Hulme is Professor of Development Studies at the University of Manchester and Executive Director of the Brooks World Poverty Institute and the Chronic Poverty Research Centre. His recent publications include *Poverty Dynamics: Inter-disciplinary Perspectives* (2009, Oxford University Press with T. Addison and R. Kanbur), *Social Protection for the Poor and Poorest: Risks, Needs and Rights* (2008, Palgrave with A. Barrientos), *The Challenge of Global Inequality* (2006, Palgrave with A. Greig and M. Turner) a Special Issue of the *Journal of Development Studies* (2006) on 'Cross-disciplinary research on poverty and inequality' and many articles in leading journals. His research interests include rural development; poverty analysis and poverty reduction strategies; finance for the poor and sociology of development.

David Lawson is Lecturer in Development Economics and Public Policy at the Institute for Development Policy and Management and Faculty Associate of Brooks World Poverty Institute, University of Manchester. He specializes in the analysis of poverty dynamics, particularly in relation to health and gender in Africa. He has published in leading journals with his work focused on the econometric analysis of panel datasets. More recently he has been utilizing Q-Squared methodologies (quantitative and qualitative) to further understandings of poverty.

Index

abuse 126, 176, 212, 215
acceptance 97, 111, 191–2
access 31, 67, 74, 79, 93–4, 140
    to education 80, 143
    to finance 37–8, 41, 125, 173–6,
      181–7, 243
    to health services 4, 7, 15, 69,
      124–5, 224–36
    to land 7, 71, 155
    to programmes 104, 107, 141–2
    to public services 6, 31, 205,
      264–5
    to water 71, 86, 143
    to work 180, 200, 202, 209–17
accident 68–70, 247
accommodation 14, 209, 212, 215,
  218
action 1, 3, 10, 17, 120, 215
    see also development; models, for
adaptation 11, 130
administrative costs 10, 99–105
advocacy 126, 176, 207, 217
afforestation 184, 199
Afghanistan 2, 151
Africa 1–2, 105, 179, 253, 257–9
age 31–5, 73–4, 103–4, 117, 200–1,
  232–5
    of household head 32, 45, 65–6,
      107–10
    see also old age; school
agency 9, 112, 139, 141, 146, 198
    see also aid
agricultural 17–8, 33, 36–9, 120,
  170, 205
    export *or* trade 217, 254–8
    labour/ers 88–9, 91, 93, 181,
      197, 202
    wage 71, 83, 85, 88, 214
agriculture 35–6, 83, 150, 181–4,
  224, 266
    sector 25, 243, 257–8
    see also non-agriculture; UK
aid 80, 162–3, 169, 245, 253–6. 265
    agencies 6, 12, 155
    see also food; medical

AKRSP (Aga Khan Rural Support
  Programme) 180–92
alcohol 47, 180
allowances 109–11, 199
anti poverty 12, 85, 97, 104–5,
  138–9, 144–6
apartheid 213–4
appeals 100, 108, 110
applicants 99–103, 198–9
aspirations 14, 179, 184, 191–2,
  268
asset 17, 30–1, 55–6, 84, 249, 207
    accumulation 155, 264
    building 244
    creation 183, 199
    pentagon 156
    smoothing 9, 56
    transfer 12, 152–5, 160, 249
    see also durable assets
audits 15, 199, 209, 215–9, 254
authorities 170–2, 176, 179, 216,
  227
availability 60, 111, 187, 197, 212–3,
  224
    of food 158
    of the HEF 236
    of water 202, 205
awareness raising 1, 3, 152, 185,
  263

Bangladesh Institute of Development Studies (BIDS) 82–3, 88–91
basic
    infrastructure 179, 191, 227
    needs 26, 63–6, 73, 104, 111
begging 7, 18–9, 67–8, 71–4, 154,
  163
beneficiary households 98, 106,
  108–9, 144, 173–4
best practice 85, 130
borrowing 18–9, 154, 224, 231, 253
    see also money
Botswana 2, 256
BPL (below poverty line) 25–7, 40,
  105, 123, 197, 224